I WANT YOU

TO SHUT THE F#CK UP

I WANT YOU

TO SHUT THE F#CK UP

HOW THE AUDACITY OF DOPES
IS RUINING AMERICA

D. L. HUGHLEY

WITH MICHAEL MALICE

CROWN
ARCHETYPE
NEW YORK

CROWN ARCHETYPE with colophon is a trademark of Random House, Inc.

Library of Congress Cataloging-in-Publication Data
Hughley, D. L. (Darryl L.), 1963–
I want you to shut the f#ck up : how the audacity of dopes is ruining America /
by D. L. Hughley.—1st ed.
p. cm.
1. American wit and humor. I. Title.

PN6165.H84 2012
818'.602—dc23

2012010342

ISBN: 978-0-307-98623-8
eISBN: 978-0-307-98626-9

PRINTED IN THE UNITED STATES OF AMERICA

Jacket design by Michael Nagin
Jacket photography © Deborah Feingold
Photograph on page 201 © Laurin Rinder, www.rinderart.com

1 3 5 7 9 10 8 6 4 2

First Edition

DEDICATED TO MY AUNT NITA HUGHLEY,
WHO MADE SURE THAT I KNEW THAT I WAS LOVED

I WANT YOU

TO SHUT THE F#CK UP

## CHAPTER 1

LET US BEGIN BY COMMITTING OURSELVES TO THE TRUTH TO SEE IT LIKE IT IS, AND TELL IT LIKE IT IS.

—RICHARD NIXON

IF only Uncle Sam could see us now.

He'd roll up his sleeves, ball his hands into fists, and knock some sense into this nation of ours. But he's not around, so someone else has to take the mantle. Some other proud American has to tell this country what it needs to hear. Everyone else is telling it what it *wants* to hear—and that's not the path to progress.

When I was growing up, there used to be simple rules that we've now forgotten. The rules served us well, and they were easy to understand and follow. You do this, and you get that. You *don't* do this, and you *don't* get that. It was just a matter of quid pro quo.

My mother constantly used to tell us, "Don't nobody owe you

shit. You think the world revolve around you? It don't," or, "If you don't work, you don't eat." When's the last time an American missed a meal? When did he doubt that he was the center of the universe? If *I* came home and told my mother that I was hungry, she'd inevitably ask me what I did that day.

"Nothing," I'd admit.

"Well strangely, that's what's for dinner!" To hell with pork; *nothing* was the other white meat for me.

Back then, it was experience that was the best teacher. Parents used to say, "I can show you better than I can tell you." When we were growing up and went by the stairs, all you would hear is *Bump, bump, boom!* And your mother would go, "Uh-huh. A hard head makes a soft ass." Meaning: Being a stubborn troublemaker leads to many a spanking—paternal or gravitational. But these days, parents spend a lot of time babyproofing their homes. They put foam on corners, a gate by the stairs, and plastic over the outlets. The kids don't learn what it means to fall down and hurt themselves.

Every black adult I know has a scar from doing some shit they weren't supposed to be doing or from fucking with something they weren't supposed to be fucking with. I was jumping up and down on the bed when I was about five years old. Sure enough, I fell and split my eyebrow open. My mother came into the room and saw me wounded. All she said was, "You know now, don't you?"

"Mama, I'm bleeding!"

"Blood lets you know when you fucked up." There was no wringing of hands, no "Oh, my poor baby!" No, my mother was *mad.* "Now I gotta take your silly ass to the hospital. If you had just listened to me and settled the fuck down, I could have been making us dinner!" I was hurt, but I learned. Our communities are *hurting*, but they sure as fuck ain't *learning.* From an early age, we're not even being taught *how* to learn.

I only stumbled upon *how* to learn when I was in fifth grade. That's when I had a hippie teacher named Mr. Boston. He had long hair, a beard, and drove a Volkswagen. Mr. Boston loved listening to fucking hippie music, and he told us *all* about it. He loved karate, which he taught to us kids. I don't know how effective karate was supposed to be in a neighborhood where everyone is coming heavy, but it sure gave him peace of mind. Whether it was the martial arts or the shitty songs, he wasn't scared of our neighborhood.

Mr. Boston was one of those teachers that always went the extra mile. Unfortunately, that was often *actually* the case. He would drive out of his way to kids' parents' houses and tell on all the shit that was going down at Avalon Gardens Elementary. Every time I'd get in trouble, he'd be over. My father would have his van parked, and then Mr. Boston would park his little Volkswagen as far up as he could get it on the driveway. Whenever I saw the edge of that Volkswagen sticking out of the driveway, I knew shit was going to get fucked with. He would tell on me *all the time*.

One day I couldn't follow what Mr. Boston was talking about during the lesson. I raised my hand to ask him what he meant. As soon as my arm was up in the air, I remembered how my mother yelled at me when she grew sick of my pestering her. "Oh, I'm not supposed to ask you why," I said, under my breath. The comment was meant more for myself than anybody else, but Mr. Boston heard me.

"*Always* ask why," he told me and the entire class. "You can *always* ask why. Any time you don't know something, you're *supposed* to ask why. *Always question what somebody tells you.*"

It was the most empowering thing I had ever heard in my life up until that point. My mother may have given me life, but Mr. Boston gave me thought—or rather, he gave me *permission* to think. He taught me the *basis* of learning, and it sure as fuck ain't opening your mouth before you know the facts. From that day and even until now, it was like a switch was flicked in my mind. I knew that I *had* something. I didn't know *what* and I couldn't tell what would happen as a consequence, but I knew that *something* had gotten unlocked.

So when I hear someone spouting nonsense, I don't just disagree—I ask *why* they're doing that. When I witness Americans choosing self-destruction, I ask why. *Why* is this country on the wrong track? *Why* are we repeating the same mistakes over and over? *Why* are we so oblivious? It was my MO my entire life. That in itself was enough—until I became a father myself.

# # #

I was working sales at the *Los Angeles Times* in 1986 when my wife, LaDonna, got pregnant. My $4.75 an hour wasn't going to cut it, so I needed a raise. Getting a promotion to sales manager required a college degree. Having just gotten my GED, a college degree was not an option. I did the next best thing: I hustled. A dude I knew had connections in the dean's office at Long Beach State. I paid him $200, and he got me a sterling letter on official letterhead claiming that I was just a few credits away from getting my diploma.

My supervisor, a cat by the name of Ron Wolf, knew that I was full of shit and that the letter was a lie. But he took a chance on me and made me an assistant sales manager anyway, earning $30,000 a year. That was as much as a *cop*. I excelled so much at my gig that nine months later, they made me a full-fledged manager. A year and a half after *that*, they put me down in Ventura as the sales manager. I was in charge of the telephone managers, the assistant managers, and the detail clerks. In total I had eight managers and a sales staff of three hundred overseeing Ventura, Santa Barbara, Lompoc, and Santa Maria. In other words: white, ivory, vanilla, and snow white.

My region was known as the "goal post," since it had never made goal when it came to sales. I was the youngest sales manager in the history of the *Times*, and the first one to be black. I guess they thought I could do something different. But apparently some of the staff didn't *want* to do something different. When I walked into my office on my very first day, there was one of those black mannequin heads for displaying wigs. In case I didn't get the message, the note attached said, GO HOME NIGGER. I wasn't shocked. Hell, I'd been called a nigger all my life. What shocks me is when people think we're a post-racial society. Obama's election was fueled by his race. The opposition to him is fueled by race—and the deference to him by his own people is also fueled by race.

I stepped out of my office and called out to the entire sales floor. "I don't know who you all think you're scaring," I said, "but I'm not leaving. I'm not scared. I'm going to step out. When I come back, I want this wig head off my desk."

I did just like I said, and when I came back, the wig head was off my desk. The *Times* sent its security force down from L.A. to investigate. "I got it," I told them. "I'm fine." And I *was* fine. I had a kid to take care of, and a new house. I just had to hustle that much harder. Three months after I started, the area made goal for the first time. For the next year straight, we kept making goal. As a reward, the paper sent me on free trips—with all these old white *Times* dudes who hated me. It was a gas.

I was psyched that I could come through after Ron took a chance on promoting me. But he never got excited. "Don't get drunk on the numbers," he told me. "Don't ever believe it. You're never as good as you think you are, or as bad as people say you are." Ron always had these little sayings. It was like Yoda and Confucius had a kid who happened to be a middle-aged white dude.

This is around the time when I started doing stand-up. I would do my job in Ventura, then drive to host comedy shows in the suit and tie I wore for work—and I never stopped wearing them to this day. The thing is, these comedy clubs were not in white Ventura or in ivory Lompoc. I had to drive about three hours each way to get there. Obviously it was going to catch up to me at some point—which is why I passed out onstage one night, between Jamie Foxx and a bunch of other young comedians.

Immediately they took me to the doctor. "You didn't pass out," the doctor told me. "You fell asleep. You're not getting any REM sleep, and you're exhausted. You need to take some time off of work to rest."

I was a manager so I still got my salary—and still did my shows. I came back to the doctor after a while, still out of it. "You *still* haven't gotten your sleep," he told me. "I'm going to take you off another couple of weeks."

I got put on long-term disability at work, which meant that I'd be able to collect my salary for six months as long as I checked in with the doctor. That gave me time to focus on my stand-up career. Even though I was still getting a check from the *Times*, LaDonna and I now had a new kid to feed. Buying a house had taken all of our money. The only place that was regularly hiring black comics at the time was not-so-white Atlanta.

One day, Ron called my wife to check up on me when I was across the country performing. LaDonna is the worst fucking liar ever. She tried to make excuses, but Ron saw right through it. Hell, he saw through my college-letter bullshit, so LaDonna didn't really stand a chance. "Darryl's not there, is he?"

"No!" LaDonna blurted out—and hung up the phone.

When I came back to work to report what was happening with my disability, Ron took me aside. He knew that I had been doing stand-up, and that I was just trying to do what I could to launch my career while taking care of my family at the same time. He knew all this, and he understood. "I'm going to keep your benefits alive for a year," he told me, "and I'm going to keep your salary alive for a year." He did all that and more. My bonus should have $20,000, but Ron upped it to $30,000 for making goal. If there were any issues at work, Ron ran interference for me while I was gone pursuing my dreams. That window of time was what I needed to make it as a successful stand-up comedian, and the rest was history—or so I thought.

In 2005, I was playing a gig in Canyon Country. Ron came with his new wife. I hadn't seen him in years, so it was really cool to catch up after all that time had passed. When he went to get us a round of drinks, his wife could not help but gush. "He is so *proud* of you," she told me.

I admit it, that made me smile. "Man, that is so nice."

"You know, he lost his job because he gave you that bonus."

I could not believe what she was telling me. "*What?* He did?"

"Yeah. He got fired because he gave you that discretionary bonus and because he kept your benefits alive for that long. Then he got divorced. He totally hit rock bottom. It was a while before he got back on his feet."

I was in shock. When Ron came back to the table with our drinks, I had to find out what happened. "Ron, my man, did you lose your gig because of *me?*"

"Forget all that. Let's talk about something else." And that was that.

From then on, Ron and I stayed in touch and would talk on the phone from time to time. Eventually, though, I had to find out the truth. "Man," I said, "I gotta ask you why you did that."

"Why I did what?"

"Why did you jeopardize your career, your marriage, your *everything* for me?"

"Well, first off," he said, "if I had known that was going to happen, I wouldn't have done it. But I just knew you had something. I *knew* you did."

"Man, I can't thank you enough. I was grateful then and I am grateful now."

Then Ron, the middle-aged white dude who happened to be the son of Yoda and Confucius, dropped another one of his sayings. "Every time you're onstage," he told me, "you have the obligation to tell the truth. Be truthful, be straightforward. Never be afraid for people not to like you."

Even though Ron had gotten hired back at the *Times* and had found a new wife, for a while the dude had lost it all because he believed in me. That's why I take what I do so seriously and say what I mean and mean what I say. That's why it's not enough for me to *ask* why. It may sound funny, but to me this shit ain't no joke. When I'm onstage, when I'm on the radio, when I'm doing an interview, I have to call it like I see it.

# # #

Somehow our communities have gotten fixated on this idea that things have actually gotten better. It's to the point where they act like it's a completely different world. We so want to live in the future and not the present that it has warped our coping mechanisms. I would argue that those old rules would often still serve us well. I try to pass on those same lessons to *my* kids, but I've got someone fighting me at every turn: my wife. She lets them do whatever the fuck they want, even though whatever I've said has been validated time and time again.

When my son, Kyle, was about nineteen years old, he got into the habit of wearing his pants hanging off his ass. *He* thought he was so cool. But *I* knew he was sending out the wrong kind of message. "Boy," I told him, "you better stop dressing like that!"

"Aw, Dad!" he said. "I voted for Obama!" He genuinely felt that now that Obama was president, we had reached the promised land. I even have friends who say Obama is the best president in history. The only standard where *that's* true is on the color scale.

I knew that my son would find out the hard way that that wasn't true. "All right," I said. "You'll see."

So of course one day Kyle *did* see. There's an exclusive jewelry store in Los Angeles that I have a very good relationship with. The owner has been over to my house, and we eat together and we drink together all the time. Our families have known each other for over fifteen years.

I sold them a watch, so I told my son to go pick up the receipt and the money. He walked up to that fancy jewelry store, dressed *exactly* like I'd been telling him not to dress. When the security guard saw him, he immediately pulled a gun on Kyle and put him on the ground. The store had had two armed robberies in the preceding couple of months, and the guard was sure this was going to be the third. Why else would a young black kid be in there, dressed like that?

When things finally got sorted out, my jeweler friend called me. The man was in tears. He felt *horrible*. He could not apologize enough. I wasn't particularly happy about it, but I couldn't get mad at the guy, either. My wife, on the other hand, got all worked up. "I can't believe they would do that to my son!" she yelled.

Well, I could. I not only believed it, but I'd predicted it. Maybe I didn't predict the exact *circumstance*, but I knew some shit was going to go down at some point for my boy. It was inevitable.

When Kyle got home, his mother took time to cry with him and tell him how insulted and hurt she was. After they were done with that spectacle, I called him up to my room. "It's a shame," I told my son, "that you got a gun pulled on you. But *most* motherfuckers I know have had guns pulled on them. *You* lived through it. I feel bad that it happened to you, but now you know that *I don't just tell you shit for my health.*"

"I'm a good kid!" Kyle insisted.

"The world don't know that. The only people that know you're a good kid is *me* and your mother. That's it! That's all you've got. When you look back on this day, realize that you should *listen* to your dad. I'm not trying to stop you from living. I'm trying to *get you* to live. I *want* you to be where you want to be. It's my gig to help you get there in spite of how fucking stupid you are!"

I want to raise my son to face the world as it is, not the world he wants it to be. My son didn't fall off a bed or hurt himself *physically*. But I'm sure he'll remember that lesson just like I remember why I got that scar above my eye. My son actually learned from it, and that felt great to me. There is nothing that makes a parent angrier than when your kids make the wrong choices, after you told them it's a mistake. And there's nothing that makes a parent *prouder* than those extremely rare occurrences when your children do actually listen to you.

I'd always told my son that if he got pulled over by the police and asked questions, to be as respectful as possible. I reminded him about what every black man knows, to keep his hands at 10 and 2 on the steering wheel. That way, the cops know immediately that you're housebroken. You get the rules and know how things are supposed to be. "But if the police ask you anything that you think is beyond your capacity," I explained to Kyle, "you say two things.

First, 'Sir, I know you've got a job to do and I respect you.' Second, 'I'm not going to say one other thing. Call my father.' I don't care what they say to you after that, you don't say one other thing. I don't give a fuck if you're forty years old when this happens. I don't care. Because boy, you didn't have these experiences. You don't know this shit. You live in a world where you think everything is great. But that world doesn't exist. It's cute, it's a great notion. The brochure is a motherfucker—but I ain't ever been there."

Sure enough, at one a.m. one night Kyle got pulled over coming home from a club. "Have you been drinking?" the policeman said.

"No," my son told him. "I don't drink."

"Where are you coming from?"

"The club."

"Well, where have you been tonight? Because we had this report . . ." That's what the cops always say. There's *always* some mysterious motherfucking report.

To his great credit, my son said, "Sir, I know you've got a job to do and I respect you. I answered every question I could. I'm not going to answer another question. I want you to call my father."

Society will tell you that the more you talk to the police, the better shit will be. *That's not true.* That's the kind of shit they tell you on *Ironside*: "If you don't have anything to hide, why hide anything?" That ain't real. Motherfuckers get in legal trouble for talking too much, not talking too *little*. Don't most people *in life* get in trouble for talking too much? When has shutting the fuck up and minding your own business not worked for *anyone*? In marriage, in school, in church, in the library, at the restaurant: *Shut the fuck up!* Your dumb ass might even learn something.

"I don't feel comfortable," my son repeated. "You can call my father."

After twenty minutes of this, the police let him go. They didn't even bother calling me. My son raced to our house at precisely the speed limit. When he found me, he told me how elated he was that what I said worked.

"See?" I said. "I'm not telling you shit that's going to fuck you up."

That doesn't just apply to my son. It applies to everything I say. When I go through life, I ask, "Why?" just like Mr. Boston taught me to. When I see something that's fucked up, I can't remain silent because of the sacrifices that Ron Wolf made for me. I've worn a lot of hats in my life. I've been wealthy and I've been poor. I've been a King of Comedy, playing to an all-black crowd, and I've been a pariah for daring to defend Don Imus. I've been a comedian, a commentator, and an actor. I've been a "nigger," an "African-American," and an "Uncle Tom." As a stand-up I've traveled this country for decades, seeing it at its best and at its worst. And what I'm seeing is terrifying to me. Our culture is at a point where we can ignore one another, where people don't ever have to engage with others who don't think the same way that they do. The *tools* for us to come together are themselves falling apart—and the biggest tool for people to come together is *communication*.

We are failing to communicate in this nation on a fundamental level. It's not even political correctness. I am obviously not a PC person, but it's much worse than being extra-careful about how you say things. We are at a point where people can say things that are *nakedly* untrue, and everyone around them will smile and nod—and then repeat it, and on, and on. Well, just because a song is *popular* don't make it *factual*.

Communication is a relationship between two parties—and half of communication is *listening*. I can't remember the last time I watched a news program or interview show where one party stopped and considered what someone else is saying. It almost never happens. Everyone comes in with their talking points, waits patiently for their turn to spout their perspective, and then the people watching at home parrot what they have just seen. That's not communication. That's *repetition*.

One of the harshest criticisms of old-fashioned education was that it only got students to memorize and repeat names, dates, and numbers. They didn't get the perspective to know what these things meant. Well, our culture doesn't even get that far. We're not repeating names, dates, and numbers, which are *facts*. We're repeating talking points, aspersions, and allegations, which are *opinions*—and dubious ones at that. Shut the fuck up!

We live in the information age, but we're less informed than ever. The Internet is the most powerful repository of human knowledge that has ever existed, yet we're too fucking self-absorbed and stupid to actually go out and learn things for *free*. Why learn something when you can just look it up, right? That lazy mindset is pervasive. People genuinely believe America is the greatest, smartest, and strongest country in the world—and that *they* are therefore great, smart, and strong. Let me tell you something: Intelligence is not contagious. *Shut the fuck up!*

It used to be that people would grieve when one of their loved ones passed. I'm not *that* old to remember that this was the universal reaction. When you got that phone call, your heart skipped a bit and you paused. You remembered, and you reflected. Maybe you cried a little bit. Now people's *immediate* reaction is to Tweet or update their status. A human being has *died* and people run to express as publicly as possible how *they* feel. The right to bear arms doesn't mean you need to go out and shoot guns; the right to free speech doesn't mean you need to go out and shoot your motherfucking mouth. *SHUT THE FUCK UP!*

I hope this book will make people reflect, and possibly learn something. I'd be very glad if it makes people laugh. But if readers are to take one thing away from it, *just one thing*, it's this: If you're ever at a point where you're not sure what to do, stop for a minute and *think*. Examine the issue from the opposite point of view, no matter how uncomfortable it makes you feel. And if you're ever tempted to repeat one of the absurdities I discuss, *I want you to shut the fuck up.*

## CHAPTER 2

I BELIEVE AMERICA IS THE SOLUTION TO THE WORLD'S PROBLEMS.

—RUSH LIMBAUGH

THE American dream is in dire need of a wake-up call.

The *only* national consensus that exists is that *we are fucked*. We're fucked today, and we're going to be fucked in the future. No one seems to know the way out of this mess, and I can see why. That's because the first step to getting better is doing something no one is willing to do: identify the nature of the problem.

Healing and getting better works the same way with people as it does with countries. If you are in denial, if you think everything is fine, then things are simply going to keep getting worse and worse until you hit bottom. When it's a person that hits bottom, it's somewhat of a positive: He can turn his life around. He can get the help he needs. But when it's a nation that hits bottom, there might not be any going back. That means a country breaking up, or political repression, or economic collapse. No matter what form it takes, it means a great deal of suffering on a huge scale.

But our leaders don't tell us that we have a problem. They encourage us to maintain our delusions. They flatter us so we can stay fat, ignorant, and lazy. Every political leader anywhere on the political spectrum proclaims loudly and openly that America is the greatest country in the world. They're lying—*and they know it.* It's Chicken Little, but in reverse. The sky is falling, but we're supposed to act like everything's fine.

It may sound alarmist, but that's only because the *facts* are alarming. *There is no standard of living by which America is the best country in the world.* In terms of life expectancy, we're 36th—tied with Cuba, and behind Israel. We trail *every* Western European country in terms of life expectancy, with one exception. In terms of literacy, we're 20th—behind Poland and Kazakhstan. We sit here making Polish jokes and laughing at Borat while the Kazakhs sit in their homes *reading.* In terms of murders per capita, we're worse than such allegedly violent nations as Iran and Libya. We boast about being the world's one superpower and winning the Cold War. Yet our national debt is at a record $14 trillion, and the creditors are the Chinese. Russia's national debt, on the other hand, is $150 *billion* (dollars). We laughed when the Russians invaded Afghanistan and failed to remake the country—and now are repeating their mistakes.

Things are bad now and they're only going to get worse. Half of U.S. students who begin college never finish. Whether that's due to financial reasons or they just can't handle it, that remains a terrifying statistic for our future as a nation. Let's add to that high school dropout rates and kids who don't go to college to begin with.

There *is* a standard by which we're #1 in the world. We have more of our citizens locked up in prison than every other country. *Every* other nation, from dictatorship to democracy, has fewer of its people locked up. How is that the Land of the Free? How can we claim any moral high ground when we have so many of our own people behind bars? You can look at that as a gross misapplication of justice, which is evil, or you can look at it as a consequence of a nation rife with criminals. But how can a nation rife with criminals be considered moral?

I am not claiming for a second that telling people hard truths is an easy thing to do. It's *very* difficult. A person can't hear you if they refuse to even listen. I'm as guilty of this as anyone, and the person I lied to is *myself*. Five days a week, I go for a five-mile run. I used to pride myself on being able to jump on a treadmill and start going with no warm-up necessary. Today I have Achilles tendinitis and it's *very* painful. I've got to stretch, coax, and pray that my tendinitis won't flare up if I go for a run. I've been running for a very long time, since before I ran from the Crips in high school. It took a lot of physical pain and many bullshit explanations before I could admit to myself that *that's not me no more*. I'm *not* that young dude I liked to think of myself as.

When I looked up the causes for Achilles tendinitis, I found that one of them was being a middle-aged athlete. As athletes get older, they can't run as fast or as far as they used to. It's understandable why a record-breaking athlete believes that the rules don't apply to him. He made his career by overcoming insurmountable obstacles. After his glory days are behind him, he's too respected to have someone sit him down and tell him that his time has passed. The athlete goes on believing that he can keep running forever, that he's the one guy who can beat time. *That's what America is like.* We're that fat, middle-aged athlete who thinks he can do what he used to do.

Our recent history is full of examples of us thinking that the rules don't apply to America. We're the one guy that can cut taxes in a time of war. We're the one country that can beat Afghanistan— even though nobody else has. We're the one nation that can gut school spending and somehow produce an educated workforce. That's what I see when I see appeals to blind patriotism. It's saying that we are somehow so *inherently* different as a nation that we can violate socioeconomic principles without any consequences.

There's no country in the world that can sit America the middle-aged athlete down and tell him, "You're too old for this. Why do you keep embarrassing yourself? At a certain point, you've got to hang up the cleats. Stop! That's why people play golf! It's not disrespectful and it's not embarrassing. Golfers live longer, anyway."

We've all heard the expression "Put your money where your mouth is." Our money is in our mouth, and that's the military. Besides prison population per capita, the other standard we lead the world in is military strength. But are the most militaristic nations the best societies to live in? Nations that spend a lot of money on their militaries are not exactly happy utopias where the general population thrives. At the rate we're going, what's going to be left for the military to protect? Burger King?

# # #

Every empire that has ever existed has been brought down by circumstances similar to the ones we are experiencing now: overreaching, doing more than they should, and ignoring the signs of their own demise. *Everyone* thought it wouldn't happen to them. But when it did, it wasn't some twist ending. It was *inevitable*. We need to remember that we're not the only power in the world. There are seven other countries in the G8 summit, and by and large they're doing just fine. They're doing better than fine, because they don't have to carry around the burden of being the "world's only superpower." Being a superpower simply means we can kick everybody's ass—but that's *all* it means. It's not like being a *supercomputer,* solving problems with finesse, ease, and efficiency. It simply speaks to our great strength. And who relies on their great strength to solve problems? *Assholes.* That's what *makes* them such assholes!

What does that look like to all the other countries? No one ever dares to raise *that* question. When you're a teenager, being able to kick everybody's ass made you the baddest dude in the neighborhood. But as you outgrow that juvenile mentality, being able to whup everybody doesn't make you any cooler. The baddest dude in the neighborhood generally becomes the brokest, and it's the nerds that eventually run shit. That bad asshole never gets it. He thinks his skill set, being able to outfight everyone, is the most redeeming one. Well, it's *not. No one* thinks it is, except for him.

To most people around the world, America is a bully that throws its weight around. We're the dude who gets drunk all the time and starts bar fights, knowing he'll win. *No one* wants to be friends with that guy, yet they pretend to like him because they fear him. The instant that motherfucker gets it, they're all happy that it happened.

"Did you see what happened to Earl? Earl got his ass *whupped.*"

"Well, it's about time!"

The vast majority of the world is *happy* to see us get it. *We're the asshole who finally got what he deserved.* We don't get that, but that's just how it works. We would rather be feared than respected. We can't brag about being the world's superpower—and then complain about having our nose in everyone's business. We're the muscle, not the brains. We've declared it explicitly and implicitly, constantly and repeatedly. Barack Obama wasn't regarded as a strong leader until he killed a man, namely Osama bin Laden—a man "on the run" who still managed to have a better housing situation than most Americans. Every American leader is determined to show that we're strong and that we're going to whup some ass. In the Middle East, for example, it's always, "We have to show our strength."

But if you keep looking for a fight, eventually you're going to get one.

Other countries have been down this road before, and we can learn from their mistakes. At different points, Germany and Japan were the nations who wanted to be the baddest people in the world. The Germans were so certain that they could beat the world that they tried it *twice*. The Japanese genuinely thought that they were a superior race. They believed America was soft and that we could be taken. They hit *us* first.

But now Germany and Japan are part of the G8, aren't they? They let go of the idea of having to be a military power, and instead they became economic and intellectual powers. They do a lot of things we don't, like having universal health care and investing heavily in education. I don't need to explain how well that's worked out for them. We all know where Japan lies on the curve. Germany outranks us in virtually every reliable skill except for the military. Those nations own a great deal of America. As does Russia. As does China. All these nations that are supposedly "worse" than us are doing all right. Would it be so bad to take a page from their book? Let's be Europe for a while. Let's act like Japan.

Damn, I think I'm turning Japanese. I really think so.

It will be very hard for us to change our ways for the better. The only way we can change is if we admit that what has worked for us in the *past* isn't working for us in the *present*. The last vestige, the last thing to die, is the idea people have of themselves. It's true when it comes to athletes, and it's true when it comes to nations. As hard as checking ourselves may sound, the alternative is much harder.

Germany and Japan didn't wake up one day and decide to stop their military ambitions and educate their people. Far from it! A country couldn't have been more violent than Japan and Germany. Japan is a nation only about the size of California. How bad do you have to be to come from a country that small and then try to run the world? They were not big dudes, but they had some big ideas. Yet they weren't beaten by bigger *ideas*. What fixed Germany and Japan's perspectives was some good old-fashioned ass-whuppings. A bunch of people died, they were humiliated, and they said, "You know what? Fuck this shit! It ain't working for us!" Violence ain't so great when it's being done to you. When you get your ass whupped, you start to change your perspective. So do *we* have to go to that level before *we* get it? I sure hope not.

The other countries in the G8 got their asses whupped already. They had the idea of who they were beaten out of them. They *know* what it's like to not win. They had to either perish or become something else. They evolved into more genteel, humane, sophisticated, cohesive societies—even bloodred China is quietly making reforms in that direction. But let's look at the example of Japan again. The denim we wear, the most American of fabrics, is Japanese. We don't even own the mills anymore; they do. They exert major control over our banking system. They buy all the jazz albums, all the hip-hop albums. American musicians can't *wait* to tour Japan, because that's where they make the most money. The Japanese are the same people they used to be—only they went up the chain *mentally*.

Americans are also the same people we used to be—only we went the other way. All this time we messed around building up our muscle while our minds got duller and duller. We were the first nation to put men on the moon. We remain the *only* nation to put men on the moon. Now we don't even want to go into space. We canceled the program and said we'd rather hitch a ride with the Russians. I'm not going to ride with a Russian to Brooklyn, and NASA is going to go into outer space with them? Are they crazy? Ronald Reagan must be spinning in his sarcophagus.

Our delusional self-image prevents us from even considering certain solutions to our issues because they're "beneath" us, as if there's anything below rock bottom. I know a little something about hustling. Two years ago, I discovered that my credit rating had dropped. I had no idea why. I knew that I'd always kept up with my bills. When I called Ma Bell, they told me that I had an outstanding phone bill in the amount of $972. "I've *never* been late on my phone bill," I told the service rep. "I don't know what you're talking about."

"Do you live at 539 Lysander Street?" she asked me.

Right away I knew what had happened. 539 Lysander was my mother's address, the house I had grown up in. My mother had put the phone in my name when I was six years old. For the last couple of months, she hadn't paid—and it went into collections. The phone company had looked at the records. They *knew* that I was only six when I got that phone in my name. Decades later, they could pin it on me without any qualms whatsoever.

I doubt my mother had even asked me, as if a six-year-old would have insight anyway. But we needed a phone in the house, and that was that. In times of economic crisis, people tend to look to the powerful to figure out what to do. After all, they're used to handling large amounts of money. But the elites aren't the ones who have to figure out where to get their next meal from. They're not the ones who are struggling with surviving day to day. So who is *really* smart when it comes to handling economic adversity? Is it the wealthy—or is it the poor?

No one is coming to bail out Bushwick, Compton, or Newark. When you grow up in a place like that, you do what you need to do to survive. You know the safety net is very frayed—if it exists at all. There's nothing proud about starving, and there's no shame in gaming the system if you aren't hurting anybody.

I was watching the news recently, and the percentage of Americans who are collecting unemployment insurance was almost 16 percent. But if you combine that with the people who have stopped looking for work, the actual number of unemployed people was over 30 percent. Those people haven't stopped eating. They haven't stopped getting shoes and buying gas. So they sell weed. They turn a trick or two. They hook this dude up with that dude, and they take a cut. Instead of working, they hustle. They stop messing around in the streets and they get down to business.

America needs to do more shit like that. Let's put our phone bills in Mexico's name. We can open an unregistered day-care center, babysit some kids, and keep it off the books. Got a job? Make them pay you in cash. You can get an EBT card and sell it, like some dope dealers I know. ODB managed to be on welfare until he was dumb enough to show it off on MTV. If any man has to choose between some Chinese bankers he has never seen and feeding his family, his family will win every single time. Our politicians argue that we have to pay off the national debt immediately—when people are broke. But that debt is like the small print on the loan application. Would you rather Bank of America be mad at you, or your kids starve? I hear conservatives use these credit-card analogies for rednecks who don't understand that the national debt is not the same as personal debt. How the fuck are you worried about the Fed owing money when you live in a trailer park?

America *has* hustled in the past when things got tough. For years and years, gambling was a complete taboo. Liquor was regarded as such a vice that the Constitution itself was amended to prohibit its sale. These positions weren't reversed because people thought that drinking and gambling were now *good* things. Those weren't benevolent moves. People were broke and they needed jobs! We let go of our idea that we were a sober country that doesn't play cards. What must have seemed like a shocking legalization of sin at the time is met with shrugs today. It all reconciled pretty well with who we are.

Corporations hustle *all the time*. Lobbying is straight hustling. When GE or whoever gets their people to write the tax code with loopholes big enough to drive a Buick through, that's a hustle. It might be perpetrated by Harvard-educated lawyers in expensive suits and perfect ties, but the mentality of gaming the system is exactly the same.

The easiest hustle we can pull nowadays is the legalization of marijuana. Legalizing pot would mean *instant* revenue. It's not like pot farms don't already exist. It's called weed because the stuff is so goddamn easy to grow! We grow *a lot* of it. It's the biggest cash crop in America today. We grow *$35 billion* worth of the stuff every year. That's more than corn, more than beans, more than anything else. If it's not fair that huge corporations pay zero dollars in taxes, how absurd is it that we're not taxing the biggest crop in America?

That's just on the revenue side. Savings would also come from a decrease in spending. In Orange County alone, they spend a billion dollars in legal fees, prosecution, and containment simply on marijuana cases. That's just the court. That's not counting police man-hours, and that's not counting the investigations. The prisoners cost money too. They get housing, they get food, and they get $1,800 worth of medical care every year. Imagine how much more effective the police would be if they weren't worried about some dude selling weed.

# # #

But no one wants to think in these terms, because of our self-image. The biggest idea we have to give up is that we're a hardworking people. That reputation hasn't been warranted for a very long time—but it *was* warranted decades ago. We only became a hardworking nation because we came from immigrants. At the end of the nineteenth century and the beginning of the twentieth, America completely reinvented itself after beating the shit out of ourselves in the Civil War. The slaves had just been freed and the Great Migration began. People came from all over the world with their ideas about what they wanted to do. They came from Ireland and they came from China and they came from Eastern Europe. They all arrived with their ideas to make this country great and turned away from the bullshit that they had seen back home. "Fuck this," they said. "There's got to be a better way."

It was a certain kind of person who came here. If you were rich, you weren't going to get on a boat and cross an ocean to a country that had *nothing*. Whether you were a domestic slave who had been freed or you were from the slums of Europe, everybody that came here was a "nigger" where they were from. They left *everything* they had before and appreciated what they had here. The American experience *had to* work for them. We were plan B—*and there was no plan C*. This was it! *That's* why America was so tough. They came here, to Irishtown and Chinatown and Little Italy, and they got their first taste of freedom.

We became a *great* country with this huge influx of immigrants. The American character had to get cut with something instead of being that unadulterated colonial Puritan *bullshit*. Before the immigrants, we were just racist rednecks and white landowners. After the immigrants came, we were amazing. We became hybrids! You can see the same phenomenon happen even today, if you ever see someone who is racially mixed. They're just *prettier*, because they're the best of two things.

The two world wars came when all those immigrants had just about had enough. Before the world wars, people weren't scared of us. It wasn't until the many became one that America turned into a global force to be reckoned with. Take one of the many examples out of the conflict: World War II was the first time that black people were allowed to fly. At first, white people hated them. The Tuskegee Airmen had no support—but they had a lot to prove. That's why the whole time they were commissioned, they never lost a plane. Their record of protection was so great that the white pilots started going, "Gimme the coloreds." During this whole era, the one thing that held this nation together was that we were broke motherfuckers who weren't taking any shit. Back any dude who has just tasted freedom into a corner and see what happens next. Spoiler alert: It will not end well for you.

All those immigrants had *pride* in what they did. Wearing a uniform and putting in a hard day's work at the factory meant something to them. Even when the Great Depression hit, many men were too proud to accept "handouts" in an economy collapsing through no fault of their own. Everyone likes to think that America is as proud as ever. But is it? Or is pride the exception? Take a look at photographs of people shopping at Woolworth's back in the day. Now compare them to people at Walmart. Are they from the same country? Are they even from the same *species*? Our leaders are only as good as our people.

# # #

I've seen how businesses handle pride from both sides. One recent Saturday night, I had a performance in San Francisco. The showtime was technically 8:00, but since I had an opening act I didn't have to get there until 8:45. I went with a couple of my friends to a restaurant called Farallon. We arrived at 6:45, which would give us plenty of time to enjoy our meal before I had to go on stage.

They served us the bread, and they served us the salad. I got my Dungeness crab appetizer, and I had my roasted tomato soup. They were spectacular. But by 8:20, we hadn't gotten our meals yet. I called over our waiter, knowing I had to leave. "Box up our orders," I told him. "We're getting ready to go."

Immediately, the manager came over. "Was everything to your liking?"

It's not like I was irritated and had been complaining. "Everything was *excellent*," I told the dude. "I just have a show, and I gotta go."

"I'm not going to ask you to pay for this," he said to me.

"I can't do that," I said. Between the food and wine, I knew that the bill had to be over five hundred dollars.

"No," he insisted, "we didn't get your food to you. We don't want you walking out with bags of our food when you didn't get a chance to enjoy your meal."

Next, the *chef* came out of the kitchen and apologized.

Even the owner of the restaurant, who was having dinner in a booth by us, came over and apologized. Then they gave me the box of food to take with me for *free*.

The next night, I went back to Farallon—and this time I paid. Every time I go to San Francisco, I go back there because they had such pride in their product and their service. American service used to be head and shoulders above everybody else's, and the customer was always right. Even motherfucking Domino's Pizza used to promise they could get you their "food" in thirty minutes or less.

I told my friend this story and he just rolled his eyes. "Yeah, but you're a celebrity. Of course they treated you well." He exactly proved my point: It was such an aberration that a person gets exemplary service, even at a top-class restaurant, that there must be some other explanation. That kind of thing might happen to you if you're known, but the Average Joe is SOL.

My friend was right in one sense: Nowadays, nobody promises you *shit*. A month after I was in San Francisco, I took a Delta Airlines flight to Chattanooga. It was a small commuter plane, with gateside bag check. I gave my bag to the guy at the base of the plane just like I was supposed to. When they gave it back to me, I saw that my wheel had been bent off. I went to complain about the damage to the customer-service desk.

The lady listened to what had happened, glanced at my bag, and then waved her hand at me to dismiss me. "We don't fix wheels," she said.

"Can you find someplace that'll fix my bag and have it fixed for me, so I don't have to buy another one?"

"We don't do that."

There was no apology. There was no sense of guilt or embarrassment that they had damaged someone else's property. She could have said, "We normally don't do this, but we're going to just accommodate you." Instead, she treated me like I was annoying her about some trifling nonsense that didn't matter.

I gave the woman my frequent-flyer number so she could look up how often I flew Delta. "Let me tell you something," I said. "I've flown three million miles with this airline. Three *million*. Do you know why I am going to *stop* flying this airline? Because of that wheel that you broke."

Now it became about the principle. Not only was the customer not always *right*, they were acting like the corporation was never *wrong*. I spent an hour and a half arguing at that desk. They broke it, but they sure as hell weren't going to buy it.

Finally, the customer-service lady buckled. "We'll give you a three-hundred-dollar voucher to fly on this airline in the future."

"Why would I take a ticket?" I asked her. "Your reward to me is to fly on the very airlines that I fucking hate?"

She'd had enough. She went and got her supervisor—which she could have done ninety minutes earlier. The supervisor came out with a big checkbook. "We don't normally do this," he told me, "but here's a check for your trouble."

I guarantee, getting that bag fixed themselves would have cost them less than three hundred dollars. I also guarantee that taking five minutes to take care of a problem would have felt a lot better and been a lot less stressful than spending an hour and a half arguing with a pissed-off D. L. Hughley. But people don't think like that anymore. They just shrug their shoulders and say that it's not their problem.

When was the last time customer service felt like actual *service*, instead of an imposition? Half the time when you call for help, you literally have to sit through an automated message and press the right buttons. What kind of "servant" won't even take your calls? A person won't take your calls if they're more important than you, not if they're trying to help you! The computerized voice will do everything in its power to keep you from speaking to an actual person. That robot on the other end of the line doesn't want to help you. It doesn't actually *want* anything!

When was the last time an American corporation bragged about the quality of its product? No, the commercials always talk about how it's cheap, it's fun, and you can have a lot of it. That sounds a lot like taking a big shit, don't it? Ford had ads that said, "Quality Is Job 1." But that was over twenty-five years ago. It's gone from being an American motto to being the answer to a trivia question.

They always say that pride goeth before a fall. Well, America's already had its fall. Maybe it's time for some of that pride to come back. That would require men and women of leadership and courage to come forward and turn this fucker around. But *there are no incentives for extraordinary men to come forward*. Bill Gates is an extraordinary man. Steve Jobs was an amazing person. Traditionally, those are the types of men who would be up there with the Rockefellers. They would be running the country, whether politically or socially. They would have a sense of civic duty to not only make money but to make this country better and to give it the benefit of all they know. You don't have to deny Andrew Carnegie's evils when you recognize the good he did in his later years. The founding fathers stepped into their roles because they were the outstanding citizens of their time, not because they were politicians. Our leaders are just not extraordinary today, and that extrapolates out to *everything*.

What would happen to an extraordinary man who stepped forward to lead America? Would he be treated with respect and dignity? Would people come together to forge a way forward? We don't need to argue these issues as hypotheticals. It's playing out right now in full public view. All we need to do is look at Barack Obama—the man who embodied the American dream—and the reaction to his presidency.

## CHAPTER 3

IF THERE IS ANYONE OUT THERE WHO STILL DOUBTS THAT AMERICA IS A PLACE WHERE ALL THINGS ARE POSSIBLE, TONIGHT IS YOUR ANSWER.

—BARACK OBAMA

THERE'S a profound difference between *disagreement* and *disrespect*. I respect a lot of people I disagree with, and I have no respect for many people who happen to share my views. Not everyone who cares about the environment, for example, cares about humans as passionately—and sometimes they're just dicks.

Let me refresh everyone's memory about how Senator Obama became President Obama. To even get the Democratic nomination, he had to take down the Clinton political machine. The Clintons had been working behind the scenes for over a *decade* to get Hillary into the White House. No one can claim that Obama got the nomination through chicanery or playing dirty. He beat her fair and square. In doing so, he achieved a goal that the Republicans were desperately trying to achieve for sixteen years: *He got Hillary Clinton to shut the fuck up.*

After he got the nomination, Obama didn't get elected by scaring the country. He didn't claim that a vote for McCain is a vote for another 9/11, and he didn't attack McCain personally or attack his character. Every time Obama would say something or answer a question, people would go look at his books or go to his website. He created a perception that he could actually do things. This dude talked the country into voting for him based on the fact that he was going to go to Washington and change shit. He really told the country that although he may not have had any experience, he had this hope and this magic, and the country believed him. Did the Republicans regard him as a breath of fresh air, an opportunity to put partisanship in the past and to work together? Did they take it as an opportunity to disavow the wildly unpopular Bush years—or did the GOP immediately start plotting how to take the motherfucker down?

I don't need to catalog what a shambles President Bush left this country in, both domestically and abroad. Let me point out the abysmal level of *sophistication* that Barack Obama was replacing. Like every other frat-boy drunk, President Bush loved his fart jokes. What he especially loved was to meet idealistic young aides, then fart like mad and stink up the place. Bush found it hysterical to watch their faces, trying to maintain composure and give the presidency the respect it deserved. Bush's staff even had a name for it: the Austin greeting. *That's* who Obama should be measured against.

White people thought Obama was going to be charming. *I* thought he was going to be hard-core, that he was going to get in there, grab his nuts, and go, "Shit just got real." In the Bible it talks about "the last shall be first, and the first last." It was supposed to be that kind of thing. But it sure didn't work out that way.

When Obama was first elected, the right were crapping their pants. "How can we criticize him? He's the chosen one." They didn't know what to say or how to engage with him. But when Obama didn't respond when Joe Wilson said, "You lie!" in front of Congress, all bets were off. Let a motherfucker take your lunch once, and he'll be eating it for the rest of his life.

The right just got increasingly emboldened—and President Obama never really fought back, and definitely not in the manner that he should have. I think Obama believes that he's occupying some kind of intellectual and moral high ground. He definitely wasn't prepared for the level of animus that he got. It irritates me that a black man doesn't get how harsh things are and didn't get how hard it would be. On some level he really thought it would be cool for him, that he could just forget all the bullshit that's out there.

Then the dog whistles started, subliminal racist cues that your ear doesn't hear but that your mind registers. Michele Bachmann said he "stole" money. She said he *stole*. Rick Perry brought up the fact that Texas can secede. Was *that* an accident? Every time in America when race comes up, there's that same acrimony. It happened during the Civil War; it happened with the civil rights debate; it's happening with President Obama. These are the stretch marks, the last bit of fat that America needs to lose before we can really see ourselves as post-racial. That's why it's the hardest—and if people aren't interested in doing that, it's downright impossible.

On some level, John Boehner and Eric Cantor really feel as though they're superior to the president. They *must* feel that way, because that's how they act. President Obama was going to deliver a jobs speech before both houses of Congress. John Boehner refused to let the president speak on the date he wanted, citing security risks. If John Boehner felt that unsafe on the floor of the House of Representatives, John Boehner would not be setting foot on the motherfucking House floor himself! But the kicker is, President Obama rescheduled for the next day. The *speaker* got the *president* to reschedule. What the *hell* is that? President Obama is the leader of the United States! He had to ask for *permission*? That's like me asking my butler, "Can I come in?" John Boehner is *third* in line for the presidency, not first. Since when is the bronze medalist on the Wheaties box? Is that not a gratuitous slap at Obama to know his place?

The Republicans claim that our nation cannot survive another Obama term. So we can survive 9/11, two world wars, and the Great Depression, but we can't hack another four years of this decent, well-intentioned American success story? Black dick fucks up a lot, but surely it ain't powerful enough to fuck up a nation. This is coming from the party that alleges we are the greatest nation the world has ever seen! How strong were we to begin with, if one man can destroy us? How effective are these checks and balances, if one man can single-handedly overthrow all of them?

They treat this president as if he was a fucking affirmative action hire. Nobody marched for him to get that job. He overwhelmingly beat out an old white dude, something that had never happened before. This isn't *Trading Places*, where you dress some homeless guy up and stick him in the White House. That really is the fucking president. He's in charge! This ain't a dream, motherfucker. It's real! Americans loved the idea of voting for a black dude and endorsing him. But listening to what he has to say? Then it became, "I didn't sign up for *that*." Some parts of this country hate the fact that we have a black president so much, they can't even be honest about it to themselves. It would be a much easier conversation if they were.

For the first time in modern history, older white people took to the streets. The only thing different was that we had a black man in the White House. They didn't march when Bush increased spending enormously, or when he took us to war. They didn't march when Clinton tried to fix our health care system. They didn't march under the progressivism of Jimmy Carter, the record unemployment of Ronald Reagan, or the price controls of Richard Nixon.

We are watching our president get bullied—and he's letting it happen. I have never met Barack Obama, but I can state with absolute certainty that he was never bullied growing up. I know that this is true because of how he reacts to the way the Republicans and the Tea Party treat him. Being bullied as a kid changes your perspective forever.

# # #

In seventh grade, *I* was bullied by a half-black, half-white dude in my neighborhood named Bubba Rankin. Bubba was four years older than me, and he would pick on me all the time. He would always push me or kick me while I was walking, just all kinds of bullshit. If a group of us was hanging out, he'd slap the shit out of me. It was completely unprovoked. One second everyone is talking and having a good time, and the next this motherfucker would just feel like it and start slapping me. It got to where I couldn't even go to the store by myself. I wasn't bringing a motherfucker with me to the grocery so that he could help me fight. It couldn't even get to *that* level. I was bringing a motherfucker to pull Bubba *off* me, so I could get away from the store and run home.

One time I came upon Bubba fucking with this girl at school. Maybe it was to impress her, who the hell knows, but he ran, caught me, and then he tackled me. I felt my shoulder bone hit me in the chin. "You broke my fucking shoulder!" I yelled at him.

He just shrugged and walked away. It was just dislocated and not broken, but in either case it didn't matter to him. Bubba went back to his girl and did his thing. There was no way a small seventh grader is going to take on an eleventh grader and win, not even with some Mr. Miyagi Kung Fu Panda–type shit. I was genuinely afraid of him.

So one day my buddy Willie Brown, who I love to this day, took me aside. "We standing with you," he told me, "but you've got to fight. Fuck whether you win or not, man. You've got to let this motherfucker know it ain't going to be easy every time he wants to do something to you. He don't fuck with none of *us*, man. You know why? Because it ain't going to be easy."

I was still afraid, but now I wasn't going to roll over for him. The next time Bubba messed with me, I fought back. He hit me so fucking hard in the mouth that he split my lip wide open. I was drinking out of a straw all week, it was so bad. He left me a scar that is there to this day.

I kept fighting him, but I never beat him. What I *could* do was to get him to stop seeing me as an easy target, and that meant not slapping me whenever the mood struck him. That much I did accomplish. I wasn't scared of him anymore. He just meant nothing to me. I knew that if I fought hard, after a while there would be a certain amount of respect that was afforded. After all that, I could go to the store by myself. Which, when you're living in fear, is a big, concrete step and proof that you're doing the right thing. I learned what Obama never had to: You need to fight even though you know you ain't going to win. You can't keep letting some dude do whatever the fuck he wants to you.

# # #

Of course race is playing a part in both how Barack Obama is perceived and how he's dealt with. But my criticism isn't really with the Tea Party on this one. They'd oppose him if he came out for God, Mom, and apple pie. They'd tell him with a straight face that he must mean the Muslim God, that he's arguing for single mothers and the destruction of the nuclear family, and that he wants to make us all fat. The reason Obama's having these kind of problems is because *the people who love him aren't forcing him to do what he needs to.* Conservatives have no problem: If you don't do what they want, they will do something to you. It's quid pro quo. It's no secret and there's no trick; they treat him harshly because he's black. Conversely, liberals treat him with kid gloves for that very same reason.

Even as his approval ratings dropped, America kept up a personal affinity for Obama. It's hard to say you dislike him. The man has integrity. He seems forthright and honest and earnest and loves his family. He does *all* these things. A racist can like a black person who knows his place. But when it comes to having a black man being in charge of this country? People can't take it.

The national unemployment rate for black people during this recession was as high as 17 percent. In some cities, it reached 40 to 50 percent. If a white president had these kind of numbers, black people would be up in fucking arms—and they'd be blaming everything on the president! If it were a white president, he would feel guilty or shamed enough to do something about it (or at least give a speech to acknowledge it, even if there was no follow-up). Look at what the first President Bush did after Rodney King. Even his son spent more time touring the destruction in post-Katrina New Orleans than Barack Obama has spent in the slums of Detroit, Baltimore, and St. Louis.

It took *three years* for the Congressional Black Caucus to start speaking out against Obama. After a while, it starts to hurt so much, you've *got* to yell uncle. Obama has not been forced to deal with black people. The Democratic Party typically takes black people for granted—and President Obama is no different. Imagine a man making all these promises to a woman (particularly a black woman!): "I'm going to do this, and I'm going to do that, and I'm going to change everything, and it's all going to be great." If by *three years* into a relationship none of that has happened, that woman would be out the door.

Greatness is not coddled. It's *snatched*. When someone's a great athlete, there was a guy along the way who he thought hated him. It is only years later, after the athlete reaps the benefits, that he sees what the guy did. That guy drove him—or *her*—crazy. Look at the Williams sisters. They were trained since they were walking, and now they dominate their sport like no one dominated it before. Obama has got way too many cheerleaders and not enough coaches. It's easy to pooh-pooh people who don't like you, because you can never please them. To get *great*, the people who love you are going to have to be hard on you.

But the Democrats refuse to do it.

Barack Obama is the president of the United States of America, the most powerful man in the world. *He can take the criticism.* Because of stereotypes, people expected a certain thing from President Obama. The right were afraid they were going to get a nigger, and the left hoped they were going to get one: That angry, I-don't-give-a-fuck, I'm-going-to-set-shit-to-right attitude. But all they got is

Carlton Banks. Obama needs to *fight*. His political struggles would go a lot better if he just acknowledged that race played a huge part in the Tea Party and in the acrimony that he receives. I think that would be kind of a relief for everybody, to get the elephant (no pun intended) out of the room.

Obama doesn't have the luxury of being genteel about the situation. America needs him to step up for the sake of our country. We are not what we were from a manufacturing standpoint; we're not what we were from a banking standpoint. *But we can kick ass.* You can leave all the learning to India and China. But when you want some asses whupped, that's us. There has to be a guy who embodies that, in the same way that the queen is supposed to embody England. We are still cleaning up the mess that Reagan left us, but, boy, did America ever feel good about itself when he was in charge.

It's *not* the economy, stupid. We've had recessions before. Even during the Great Depression, we knew FDR was going to carry us through. What America is primarily suffering from is a *lack of confidence*. We don't have our swagger. Obama doesn't have it. Look at the other side of the aisle. Rick Perry has swagger. He's a fucking *idiot*, but he has swagger. What makes men have swagger is knowing their strengths—and not being afraid to use them. People have to be afraid of you. Republicans were *terrified* of Bill Clinton. They knew that politically, there would be repercussions. People may not have been afraid of George Bush, but they were definitely afraid of Dick Cheney. Now the Republicans fear the Tea Party more than they fear the president—again, *the most powerful man in the world.*

To some degree, President Obama allows this to happen. This dude is being disrespected *constantly*. That served him well in the electoral process, but it doesn't serve him in the governing process. When you're governing a country, you have to look like you're the leader. When you know that somebody's called you a liar and a thief the night before, *somebody* has to respond. Every president has hatchet men to do his dirty work for him. Dick Cheney did it for W; Clinton had James Carville and Paul Begala; Reagan had Nancy. Obama has many, many people who want to go on the attack, but he's the one telling them to shut the fuck up. He's *got* to be, or else they'd be going nuts.

Jimmy Hoffa Jr. begged the president publicly and explicitly for permission to take off the kid gloves. His exact words were, "President Obama, this is your army. We are ready to march. Everybody here's got a vote. Let's take these sons of bitches out and give America back to an America where we belong." What happened is that Fox News and their allies made Hoffa out to be a terrorist calling for assassinations, and President Obama said nothing. It's *irritating* as all hell.

# # #

Besides my bully, there's another half-white, half-black Bubba that President Obama can learn from: Bill Clinton. In the 2008 Democratic debates, there was a big laugh when Barack Obama was asked if he agreed with Toni Morrison's characterization of Bill Clinton as America's first black president. "Blacker," Morrison had said, "than any actual black person who could ever be elected in our children's lifetime."

Although the premise of the question was humorous, there really was truth to her statement. Obviously, in a strictly skin-color sense, Obama is black (or at least, mixed) and Bill Clinton is not. But in terms of which one of them is more a product of a black upbringing, I would argue that Clinton has the leg up on Obama.

Obama's upbringing wasn't just white—it was the American

dream! He was raised by a white family from Kansas. That's how *Superman* was raised. That's how Dorothy from *The Wizard of Oz* was raised, and that movie was so fucking white that they had to make *The Wiz* so that black people could relate to it. Obama worked hard and made his way through top colleges due to hard work and intelligence. It was a record of achievement and pulling himself up by his bootstraps.

Bill Clinton had more experiences that were common to black people than Barack Obama did. He grew up in a rural home in the Deep South and he had to hustle all his life. He was raised by a single mother who was a nurse. He constantly interacted with and had a lot of experiences with black people. From playing the saxophone and wearing the sunglasses to all the consequences of his slick talking, in many ways he acted like a black man—both good *and* bad. The dude used to be chubby and endangered his marriage for a big-assed shawty. Clinton loved his fried food and would jog with a fucking Big Mac in his hand. All that stuff is things that blacks could relate to, and it was really *him*.

This motherfucker got impeached, almost fired from his job, and he still went back to work like shit didn't happen. Only a black dude is going to do that. He could just slick-talk his way out of anything, like, "That depends on what your definition of 'is' is," and, "I did not have sexual relations with that woman." All those iconic statements that we now remember are the speakings of a hustler. Bill Clinton stole the Republicans' ideas and sold those very same ideas back to them as his own. That is straight hustling.

I definitely am not using the word *hustling* in a negative sense. The basic characteristic of a hustler, in my estimation, is *someone who gets shit done.* You might not like *what* he gets done, and you might want to avoid hearing about his methods, but that cat will deliver for you. That's what a hustler does, and that's what Bill Clinton did. He was one nickel-slick motherfucker.

President Obama is probably a more *principled* man, but in terms of political tactics, there is just no contest. A true politician doesn't keep getting his ass whupped like Obama does—and then do nothing about it. Bill Clinton got his own "shellacking" in 1994. But he learned that first lesson and then ran the table against the Republicans. If Bill Clinton talked as much as Obama talks, he'd get everything he asked for. When Bill Clinton took his case to the people, there has not been a more effective speaker. And by "effective," I mean *it had an actual effect.* His words caused people to take action. Famously, Bill Clinton's teleprompter went down when he was giving a State of the Union address. He didn't look at it again and delivered a rousing speech on no notes.

Barack Obama is an eloquent speaker, but you get the sense that he's detached from what he's saying. When Clinton said, "I feel your pain," people thought that this motherfucker really did feel our pain. I sometimes get the impression that Barack Obama doesn't feel *anything*. He is very intellectual, but I don't think he loves people the way Bill Clinton *loves* people. When Barack Obama is finished with the presidency, he'll go away and do lectures and be well regarded. But when it comes to Bill Clinton, politics is what he *is*.

Sixteen years after Clinton's government shutdown, the Republicans were about to try the same thing with Obama. "Don't call my bluff," Obama told Eric Cantor. Cantor did—and Obama folded immediately. The Republicans got everything they asked for and made no significant concessions. If that was Bill Clinton, the Republicans would have feared telling him no. They might have still done it, but they'd be waiting for the other shoe to drop at any minute. Obama needs to learn from Bubba. What the president doesn't seem to get is that you can be loved *and* feared. He is loved and *well regarded*, but Bill Clinton was loved and *feared*.

The ultimate test of blackness is not taking no bullshit. Who would be the fastest to slap the hell out of someone in an argument: Bill Clinton or Barack Obama? That's the answer to Toni Morrison's question, and it's an answer you don't need an Ivy League degree to know.

It's not too late for President Obama to change, and maybe he just doesn't have it in him. But the principle here is bigger than one man, even if that man is the president of the United States. Bubba Rankin taught me a lesson as a kid, and then I taught him one when we got older. After Bubba dislocated my shoulder and generally made a fool out of me, he moved out of our neighborhood. When I was eighteen or nineteen, he came back to visit. But things had changed in the intervening years. I had dudes around me who I got high with. They were *my* people.

So five of us young dudes were hanging out, and Bubba came walking down the block. He was now a grown man, reminiscing about the old days and glad to be in the neighborhood. Of course *his* memories were positive. He wasn't getting his ass whupped. No one remembered Bubba's and my history.

But I sure as fuck did.

When Bubba came up to us, I started saying something smart in response to whatever he said. Then he'd say something else and I'd say something *else* smart. I was like some sort of sarcastic parrot, and no one likes a back-talking bird.

"Hey man, how you doing?" he said.

"Motherfucker, how *you* doing?" I repeated.

Even though he came up to us all friendly, eventually I started to get on Bubba's nerves. "Hey, motherfucker," he yelled at me. "Who you talking to like that?"

Soon after that, we all jumped him. Now it was *my* street and *my* neighborhood. I *still* couldn't whup him—but six of us could. Man, oh, man, that was the best shit ever. My mother even saw what was happening, and she let it go for a while. Eventually she came out of the house and had to put a stop to it because it was getting so bad. I stood up, looked Bubba square in the face, and I said, "You can't never come on my street no more. It's my street." He never bothered me or my friends again. Now *he* feared me.

So Mr. President, I understand how you want to remain above the fray and not fight these people. But Mr. President, we're standing with you. Fuck whether you win or not. You've got to let these motherfuckers know it ain't going to be easy. If you're going to be treated like an angry black man, then maybe you should start acting like one. My entire street is behind you, and many, many other streets like mine. All we need is for you to give us the word.

What we need more than anything, Mr. President, is for you to lead. Because we sure as fuck aren't getting that from the other side of the aisle.

I THOUGHT BECOMING RICH AND FAMOUS WOULD MAKE ME HAPPY. BOY, WAS I RIGHT!

—MITT ROMNEY

PART of the reason our nation is so divided is because we have become a multicultural nation. We have two dueling cultures in America, the red states and the blue states, and they perceive things completely differently. You can watch a story on a network news show and get the facts—and then you can turn to cable news and see the same story interpreted and reinvented in a completely different way. We don't have a national dialogue anymore. Instead we have two national monologues.

We used to have national discussions and disagreements. There was a standard of truth and objectivity. Now, thanks to our mass media, people can believe whatever they want and never have their views questioned—and these views are simply based on who people surround themselves with. You live in the South, you're a conservative Christian. You live in San Francisco, you're a progressive Democrat. Our philosophies are not randomly distributed across the nation but instead lie in enclaves. People put themselves, or *try* to put themselves, in positions where they are constantly around others who edify their beliefs. Who would question their own views if everyone around them felt the same way?

But I don't like that mentality, and that hasn't been my approach. I have been around more conservatives than people on the other side of the aisle have been around liberals. I've traveled this country and know many people from various political perspectives. I've personally met prominent Republican politicians and interviewed them one-on-one. I've sat with them backstage in green rooms and had meaningful discussions—not elevator talk, but real conversations about the issues.

When I condemn specific politicians, it's only *after* I've listened to them. I think there are a lot of evil conservatives—but there is evil on both sides of the aisle. Robert Byrd, for example, was a fairly evil Democrat. There are things you can't square with me, like being in the Klan.

People on the left think that everyone on the right is stupid. But a politician can only get elected if he gets votes, so the Republican leaders have no choice but to kowtow to their crazy base. Mitt Romney is not a good actor. It's obvious he doesn't believe half of the shit he's being driven to say. But any deviation from the party line is like heresy. It's really like a religion for these people, and they're constantly searching for heretics. They even have a term for it: RINO, as in Republican in Name Only. This term has been applied to Rudy Giuliani, and it's been applied to Mitt Romney. But how far to the right do you have to be to consider Mr. Law and Order and a multimillionaire investment banker to be *Democrats*? From their perspective, there's no room for a *minority* opinion in the party. Isn't that *telling*? And isn't it a piss-poor strategy in a democracy?

The Republican Party has gotten so crazy that people are trying to forget just how nuts the process was for choosing their presidential nominee. A bunch of nobodies thought, "If this black dude could get elected president, surely *I* have a chance." Politicians like to sweep unpleasant things under the rug if it doesn't suit their interest. Well, I think I need to lift that rug up and remind everyone of just how demented things were this past election cycle.

The Minnesota Twins

People who are serious candidates and could do the job of president are finding it *impossible* to get through the gauntlet of crazies. There is no better example of this than Tim Pawlenty, the first man to drop out of the race for the Republican presidential nomination. When Tim Pawlenty started out, I thought he seemed like a bright and reasonable guy. Just like everyone else, I found him bland. He bored me to tears. He was kind of young to be *that* bland. It's hard to be *that* young and white and boring as fuck. You've got to be around for a long time to be that fucking boring. Mitt Romney is that boring, but he's had years to have all of his personality drained out of him. But boring is hardly a disqualification from the presidency. If that's the worst thing you can say about a man, then he'd probably be one of the greatest presidents ever.

The two-term Minnesota governor was knocked out by a batshit harpy from his own state, a congresswoman with no legislative achievements to speak of whatsoever. Michele Bachmann *went there.* She appealed to the crazies who hate gay marriage, and the crazies who only care about abortion. I'm not speaking about people who happen to be socially conservative or pro-life. I mean the *crazies.* Michele Bachmann went for the lowest common denominator— and those are precisely the people who vote in straw polls, whether they're left or right.

Let me quote Bachmann, because she once said something so telling that it really speaks to the heart of many in the GOP: "Those who are coming into France, which had a beautiful culture, the French culture is actually diminished. It's going away. And just with the population in France, they are losing Western Europeans, and it's being taken over by a Muslim ethic." She often brings up the specter of Sharia, or Islamic law, being imposed in Europe by the burgeoning Muslim population.

Bachmann and people like her know perfectly well that the possibility of Sharia being voted in in the United States is zero. Muslims constitute less than 1 percent of the American population. What she's playing on are fears of dark-skinned people "infiltrating" our society and imposing their perspective. So what is it that the Mexicans are bringing into the United States that's so bad? When the Irish came, they brought Saint Patrick's Day. *Every* politician walks in those parades. Italians brought pasta. Are Cinco de Mayo and tacos that much worse? She doesn't have a problem with foreign people and their cultures. She has a problem with foreign *brown* people and their cultures. In her vision of America, Reagan's "city on a hill" has become a gated community designed to keep out "undesirable" elements.

Newt Gingrich

Conservatives bitch that progressives think they're all fucking stupid. That's not true in the slightest. No Democrat would deny that a George Will or even a Dick Cheney is *bright*. Newt Gingrich certainly fits that bill. Gingrich is technically a very bright guy. He should probably be a professor somewhere teaching political science.

In 1994, Gingrich had a lot to do with the Republicans taking control of the House of Representatives for the first time in forty years. But he also had a lot to do with Bill Clinton looking so successful and earning a second term. Bill Clinton took that cat to the woodshed, and it cost Gingrich his speakership. *If you can't win when you're ahead, then you can't win.* That's snatching defeat from the jaws of victory!

For a while, people forgot what a nasty dude Newt Gingrich really is. He may not have originated the principle of making political fights personal, but he sure as fuck mastered it. He did everything he could to take down Speaker Jim Wright, and he eventually succeeded. If it ain't broke, don't fix it, so he tried to pull the same political dirty tricks with Bill Clinton. He even said that there wouldn't be an interview where he wouldn't bring up the Monica Lewinsky scandal. Meanwhile, dude's fucking his mistress in his office. I don't get how you can be that intellectually bright and still have a little bit of Lil Wayne in you. It doesn't make sense to me.

But politics is based on building coalitions in the population and alliances in the seats of power, and Newt Gingrich alienated even his closest allies. During his speakership, he was giving the Republican Party a very bad name. The House majority leader and the majority whip and several other major Republican congressmen all got together. Their plan was to oust Gingrich from power in the name of helping the party. Then Dick Armey got cold feet and turned snitch, and it all fell apart. If your entire team is plotting against you, that doesn't speak well of you as a person. Even Nixon had Republicans backing him until the very end.

Gingrich likes to talk about how President Obama is a dictator and how the presidency is becoming imperious. At the same time, he himself scored points with the Republican Party by lecturing reporters when they asked him questions. He even wagged his finger at them during debates, when he knew perfectly well that he signed up to be asked questions he might not like. What the fuck is he expecting them to do, throw him flowers and sing "Hosanna"?

In a technical debate, he probably is as bright a politician as we have on the scene. *But no one likes him.* He's the smart dude who thinks people hate him because they're intimidated by his intellect. But sometimes people hate you simply because you're a nasty asshole who doesn't know how to talk to others.

I don't blame the Republicans for hating Newt Gingrich. Forgetting their political positions, who's a worse person: Newt Gingrich or Mitt Romney? Mitt Romney is tapioca, but Newt Gingrich is *evil*. He bragged about his role in imposing supply-side economics on this country, the very philosophy that is the reason we're in trouble now. But even that is not the worst of his evil. I don't call him evil for marrying his side piece, taking on her religion, and publicly parading her around in Tiffany's jewelry. I've always thought the First Lady should be a *lady*, but maybe I'm old-fashioned that way. I don't know what the fuck *that* whole thing is about. Because Gingrich thinks of himself as a man of science, he saw the dangers of climate change, an issue that is much bigger than any party or even any country. Trying to do the right thing, he cut an ad with

Nancy Pelosi, and in a bipartisan, apolitical way tried to do something about the crisis. As a presidential candidate, and in an act of blatant political hypocrisy, he said that ad was the dumbest thing he'd done in recent years. But even *that* isn't why I call him evil.

I call him evil because of how the man ran his life.

I don't consider it anyone's business how a politician acts in the bedroom. If Bill Clinton wants to shove a cigar into a fat intern like it's some kind of bizarre Cuban tampon, that's his business. I like cigars myself, but I prefer to *smoke* them. But unless President Clinton's actions affected how he treated the tobacco industry, his kinky ways were his affair (literally and figuratively).

One of the most overlooked stories about Newt on the long list of horrors on his résumé is this one. A neighbor on Newt's block was babysitting Gingrich's young daughters. As the neighbor was walking down the street with the two of them, he spotted Gingrich sitting in a parked car on the street. As the neighbor walked by, kids in tow, he saw a woman's head going up and down in Gingrich's lap. Mr. Speaker was getting a hummer in front of his own house in broad daylight. The neighbor was just glad that the girls weren't tall enough to see what was going on. When you are getting a blowjob in front of your house as your children walk by, you are a depraved dude. But even *that* is not the worst of it.

Newt Gingrich told his wife that he was leaving her for his mistress while she was in the hospital facing a life-threatening illness. If he can't have compassion for his woman, how can he have compassion for his country? How the fuck can he care about somebody he's never seen, who's brown or black? If he can leave a woman that is suffering and in crisis, he can fuck this country up. That speaks to a person's *humanity*. A president has to be thirty-five years of age, and he has to have been born in the United States, and he has to be *a human being.* This is the problem I have with Newt Gingrich and political leaders like him (John Edwards is certainly on that list). They seem to have temporary morals—and that's why they must *never* become president.

Our system was actually working really well to keep men like Newt Gingrich from the presidency. If not for the *Citizens United* ruling by the Supreme Court, Gingrich would have had to shut down his campaign much earlier simply due to a lack of funds. That ruling allowed unlimited political contributions and led to the creation of SuperPACs, which can spend anything they want on behalf of their candidate. The only reason Newt Gingrich remained in the race is because he knew a billionaire, Sheldon Adelson, who was willing to write $5 million checks. That's not *democracy.* That's rich people's chess, and anyone can see how dangerous that is. This country is *nakedly* only for rich people, and the SuperPACs are doing everything they can to make sure it stays that way.

If this country weren't for rich people, how else can you explain a major presidential candidate saying that poor minority children should be made into janitors? You would have to go back a hundred years to find such brazen anti-poor sentiment. Gingrich *specifically* said this was for minority children so that they could learn the value of hard work, which they weren't learning at home.

Gingrich wants to take these jobs away from janitors and give the money to, by his math, thirty or so kids. I know a little bit about this, because my father was a maintenance man—in other words, a *janitor.* My childhood street was *full* of janitors. Mr. Tarver, Mr. Price, Mr. Ivy, Mr. Hamilton: Maybe fifteen out of the twenty houses on my street had their bills paid by janitors. Every lesson that the Republicans now talk about, my father the janitor taught me.

I'll work on a comedy special; I'll have an interview; I'll go do the radio thing; that is my janitorial service. It's my mop and broom, and my suits are my uniform. My father didn't wear a suit, but his uniform was always fucking neat. My father wasn't on the radio, but he busted his ass every day and didn't complain or make excuses.

My father didn't *like* sweeping the floors at the steel mill. He did it because it needed to be done. He worked the same job every day and came home at the same time *every day*. He got a watch from them for *never* being late. He never wore it and never took it out of its case. But the one time I borrowed it, he got so mad. "You can't be taking my shit!" he yelled. "That's my watch!" I shared *underwear* with this man. My mom would wash all the men's underwear together and it just went into a pile that you picked out from. But that watch was a point of pride for him, even if he never said so. Taking pride in your work is something my father taught me.

This motherfucker Newt is so good at ruining families on a personal level that he wants to implement it as federal law. Who would *want* to teach his son to be a janitor? Every father wants his children to surpass him. My father, and all the fathers on my street, would be mortified if their sons had their job. "This broom was handed down from generation to generation"? If the notion is to take janitor jobs away so kids can learn work habits, what happens to the janitors? What of those men who are supporting their families and buying homes? They're obsolete now. The family doesn't need them, and Gingrich isn't proposing retraining them. It would mean *more* families without father figures, not less. *The quickest way to get a black man to leave his home is to devalue him.*

The speaker actually said it best himself: "I don't think right-wing social engineering is any more desirable than left-wing social engineering."

Rick Santorum

I have no idea why Rick Santorum was being given airtime. By objective apolitical standards, *the man is a loser.* He lost his last senatorial campaign by eighteen points. When people think of Pennsylvania, they think of Pittsburgh and Philadelphia. But it's a huge state, and there's a lot of real estate outside those cities filled with Republicans. The rest of that shit is practically Alabama. He even lost *there.*

He's crazy, vicious, and just not a bright guy. He's like Richie Cunningham, only carrying a switchblade. I can't imagine any world figure talking to Rick Santorum. Is there *any* other country in the world where someone that unsophisticated becomes a leader? That's what *makes* a national leader: They are sophisticated and knowledgeable, not just about their own country but about the world around them.

At this stage in America, being unsophisticated is practically a choice. We don't have a monarchy or an aristocracy, where people are born and bred to be some sort of ruling class. Barack Obama is the son of a single mother. Bill Clinton is the son of a single mother. Both men educated themselves past their circumstances. Bill Clinton was as country as you got. Now he might be the most respected politician, certainly in America and maybe the world. He's still greeted like a hero no matter what nation he goes to. Let George W. Bush land in certain other countries and see if he doesn't get arrested at the airport. It's a good thing he never wants to go anywhere, because he can't. That motherfucker is practically trapped here in the United States.

Santorum has Bush's lack of sophistication, but he lacks Bush's political finesse—or at least Bush's finesse via Karl Rove. It's cynical and it's a dirty trick, but Karl Rove very effectively used gay marriage to turn out his people to vote. The way Rove figured it, if people came to the polls to vote against gay marriage, they'd probably end up pulling the lever for the Republican candidate as well.

But things have changed a great deal since those days, even though it's been less than a decade. When the Pentagon took an internal poll of the military, a majority of servicemen and women had no problem serving alongside gays. When President Obama kept his campaign promise and repealed "don't ask, don't tell," the only person who had a problem with it seemed to be John McCain—and I'd wager that's as much a function of McCain's age as anything else.

When Governor Cuomo passed marriage equality in New York State through the legislative process, not one national Republican politician attacked it. Not even politicians in the South, who one would think would be free to speak their minds on the matter. This country is in the process of accepting legal rights for gays and lesbians. The issue is a political loser—and the only politician left *fighting* against gay marriage is Rick Santorum. Everybody got the memo but him.

Santorum claims his opposition to gay marriage is based on the fact that marriage means one man and one woman, and it has meant that for thousands of years. *That is a lie.* There are many cultures on earth *today* where polygamy is practiced. Even the Bible, that book that Santorum claims to love so well, has many instances of polygamy. King David had several wives, and Jewish people revere him so much that the necklace they wear is *called* the Star of David. I'm not saying I'm for polygamy. I'm saying that to claim marriage *must* mean one man and one woman doesn't gibe with current events or the historical record.

But no one even cares about Santorum's anti-gay message anymore. The Republicans are so worried about this black man in the

White House that they've put the gay hatred on pause. A majority of servicemen were in favor of repealing "don't ask, don't tell"—and Santorum wants to bring it back. That doesn't make sense even given his theology. If the gay soldiers were being shot in lieu of moral, straight Christian soldiers, shouldn't he consider that a *good* thing?

Poor Rick Santorum. I just can't understand *what* he does well—except put his foot in his mouth. He said, "I don't want to make black people's lives better by giving them somebody else's money. I want to give them the opportunity to go out and earn the money." Let's substitute a group that gets far more from the government: senior citizens. How would that sound? "I don't want to make seniors' lives better by giving them somebody else's money. I want to give them the opportunity to go out and earn the money." The difference, in the mind of Santorum and those like him, is that black people *choose* to be unemployed and *want* to be on the dole. We are the "undeserving" poor. The argument would be that old people can't really be expected to go out and work. Well, how in fuck is a person in the inner city supposed to find a job when unemployment is approaching *50 percent*? The level of unemployment is systemic—and Santorum *knows* this. He admits to it every time he attacks President Obama on the issue. Systemic means *it ain't your fault.*

One of the worst qualities of Rick Santorum is his absolute inability to learn from history. Conservatives like to claim that they look at the historical record and apply those lessons to the present day to solve problems. Okay, Senator Shit for Brains, let's pull up a chair and have ourselves a history lesson. What Santorum and the lunatics really want in the Middle East is another Crusade. During the Crusades, Christians kept sending men to try to recapture the Middle East—and they got slaughtered. One would think that conservative Rick Santorum, someone who allegedly looks at the historical record and applies those lessons to the present day to solve problems, would have learned from the lessons of the Crusades— not to mention 2003 and Iraq. But not only will he not *learn* them, he downright *denies* them. Here he is in his own words: "The idea that the Crusades and the fight of Christendom against Islam is somehow an aggression on our part is absolutely anti-historical. And that is what the perception is by the American Left who hates Christendom." And by "American Left" he means "every history book ever written on the subject ever."

Santorum, who worships the Prince of Peace, is front and center in beating the war drums for invading Iran. He claims that Iran is seeking nuclear weapons or is about to have them, and that they will unleash them immediately upon civilian targets. He argues that there is no dealing with Iran because they will start this war for bizarre religious reasons, according to obscure prophecies intended to presage the end of the world.

All the things that Santorum alleges against Iran have been perpetrated already by the United States. One nation and only one nation has used nuclear weapons in a military context, and it's *us*. We nuked Hiroshima, a *civilian* city. Three days later we nuked Nagasaki, another *civilian* city. Nagasaki was also known for having the largest *Christian* population in all of Japan. We didn't make specific demands on Japan. We asked for *unconditional surrender*—and we got it. All the Japanese could hope for was that the nation that had nuked the fuck out of them would be nice when we took over. It wasn't a negotiation. This was fear, pure and simple.

Now let's fast-forward to 2003. President Bush was trying to get support for an invasion of Iraq. He was using almost verbatim the arguments currently being used to try to get us into Iran, at least at home. Abroad, it was a different matter. Bush got on the phone with Jacques Chirac, the president of France. Bush told him that "the Biblical prophecies are being fulfilled" and that "Gog and Magog are at work in the Middle East." I can only imagine the poor French translator sitting there, thinking that President Bush was having a stroke. There was no way Frenchie had ever heard the terms "Gog and Magog" before in any language. Chirac similarly had no idea what the fuck Bush was talking about. Only later did he learn that Gog and Magog feature in Revelation, the Biblical account of the end of the world, and that these two mythological nations presage the emergence of Antichrist. So who is the real religious zealot here?

Class dismissed, motherfucker!

Jon Huntsman

Utah is a red state, but people don't realize how red it is. It's the most Republican state in terms of party registration. So why the hell did Jon Huntsman, who is telegenic and conservative and experienced, fail to gain traction? In certain circumstances, I could even see myself voting for him. And in general, knowing that the Democrats are going to lose once in a while, I would hope that they lose to Republicans like Jon Huntsman.

By any ostensible standard, the former Utah governor and ambassador to China should have been a front-runner. So why is serving your government a sin, in Republican eyes, and being a diplomat a disgrace and an embarrassment? It's not because he worked for a Democrat; Texas governor Rick Perry campaigned for Gore, and that wasn't a disqualifying issue. Clearly, Republicans can wrap their head around something like that happening, and then having the man switch teams. It's when you're working for *this* president that you have a problem, as Jon Huntsman discovered. You would think that they would regard him as trying to mitigate Obama's "damage." Huntsman's failing is another example of the irrationality that has surrounded President Obama, an irrationality largely driven by race.

Ron Paul

Conservatives like to claim that progressives are opposed to listening to their arguments, and that black progressives especially are completely hypnotized or brainwashed or delusional. Whatever the mental condition is, we all seem to have it. But I would argue that I have never seen a conservative admit that there's any truth to the progressive position, whereas many times I can see an element of truth on the other side. In fact, I've had my mind brought around because of my conversations with Ron Paul.

I've met Ron Paul twice. The first time was when he and I were both guests on Bill Maher's show. Ron Paul basically said that the Civil War never had to be fought. This of course sounded completely crazy to me at first. "Thank God it was," I said, "or I'd be the only black guy here, serving tea."

But Ron Paul went on to point out that we could have freed the slaves and saved ourselves a lot of blood and national treasure and life. Many other countries around the world had slavery, and they didn't have to kill each other to free the slaves. What the British did, for example, was buy all the slaves from the slave owners, set them free, and then pass abolition laws. It was peaceful and it was cheaper. I had never heard it explained that way before, and I thought it was reasonable.

Then I had Paul on my CNN show, where we had a wide-ranging conversation. The clip is still on YouTube, and I challenge anyone to watch it and categorize the way I spoke to Ron Paul as anything other than respectful, if not downright deferential. At the end he confessed that he supposed he'd get in trouble for being on my show, but it wasn't bad. Had I gone on some of the Fox News shows, I would not have gotten anywhere near as polite of a reception.

If anyone doubts how far off the deep end the Republican Party has gone, take a look at how Ron Paul is regarded. His political positions have not changed for *decades*. He's got some very nuanced views, and I think that he's a principled man. But in 2008, when he ran for the nomination, he was regarded as the crazy person in the Republican Party. In 2012, Ron Paul isn't looked at as crazy anymore. He's almost an elder statesman, and his coherent, calm philosophy is being shouted out by people foaming at the mouth with anger and rage. Ron Paul obviously hasn't changed. It's his surroundings, the Republican Party, that have changed—and the thing that happened between 2008 and 2012 is that we got a black dude in the White House.

It's funny to me that I can freely admit that I would feel comfortable voting for a Ron Paul or a Jon Huntsman. But all the people on the right who view progressives as brainwashed plantation slaves can't name *one* Democrat that they would support. Ain't that a bitch?

Mitt Romney

I met Mitt Romney in May of 2007. We were both guests on Jay Leno's show one night, so the two of us sat backstage and talked for a long time. I thought he was going to get the nomination. He was perfectly tan, with sparkling white teeth. He had all his kids with him, a lot of kids, and a beautiful blond wife. Ann Romney was *naturally* beautiful; she didn't look plastic. They genuinely looked like they were a close family. Whoever was running against this dude was in trouble, in my view, because it looked like they had cast a president.

Here's the thing about Mitt Romney. If you grow up in the streets, you'll sound like the cats you grew up with. If you grow up in New York, you'll sound like a fucking New Yorker. If you're around all rich white people and you hear them talk and you go to school with them, then, when you grow up, you'll just talk like them. You would sound pretty bright even if you weren't. It's like how Americans think all British people are smart just because of their accents.

That's the impression I got from Mitt Romney. He was *entitled* bright. It's the kind of bright that you get because you attended the finest learning institutions in the world. You can get some of that shit just by osmosis. He had that white-guy "I'm superior" kind of vibe about him, that feigned kind of modesty. He seemed shallow to me. The things he was saying just weren't particularly resonant. It was all clichés and talking points. He reminded me of a very high-end used-car salesman. I didn't go away thinking, "Wow, what a bright guy." I went away thinking, "Wow, what a rich white guy!"

There's a thing Mitt Romney said that was quite telling, and everyone pounced on it. I want to quote him exactly so that it doesn't seem like I am caricaturing: "I'm not concerned about the very poor. We have a safety net there. If it needs repair, I'll fix it. I'm not concerned about the very rich, they're doing just fine." A lot of people brought up only the first part to assert that Romney, as he said, didn't care about poor people. Romney says that's out of context and not what he meant. I am going to give Mitt Romney something that he doesn't give poor people: *the benefit of the doubt*. Let's pretend that statement is not an example of utter callousness. Even so, it is clearly a statement of a man *completely* out of touch.

When he says he is not concerned about the poor because there is a safety net, he is really saying that their lives are taken care of because they aren't starving. That's what the purpose of a literal safety net is, to keep you from dying—and that's *it*. The idea that poverty is a trap, that some groups are more affected by poverty than others, is foreign. To use language familiar to Romney, a helping hand to the poor is an investment that will reap dividends in the future. But he doesn't see it that way. For him, *in his own words*, it's "Problem solved!" and let's move on to the next issue.

Rick Perry

I think Rick Perry is a complete idiot, but I think some of the criticism of him is misplaced. Rick Perry's idiocy is not a function of his poor debate performance. I know a lot of stand-up comedians who are spectacular on the stage and deliver their material with precision timing. But once the lights are off, they're dumb-asses. To me, it seemed that Perry's inarticulate nature was more a function of a man who had never been challenged and never had to defend himself in the art of debate.

A big criticism of Rick Perry came when it was discovered that his family owned a camp that had the word "Niggerhead" painted on some rock. But historically, presidents have *hated* black people. The number of presidents who liked black people and cared about their interests can really be counted on one hand. A president who is prejudiced isn't racist; he's *retro*. He's just keeping the American tradition alive.

What I found most compelling about Rick Perry is his subtle attempt to go after Mitt Romney's (and Jon Huntsman's) religion. Rick Perry always talked about President Obama's war on religion—while he let one be waged on his behalf. When pastor Robert Jeffress called Mormonism a "cult," Perry refused to denounce him. Despite what some news accounts portrayed, Jeffress wasn't being a fire-breathing nut. He described Mitt Romney as "a good, moral person, but he's not a Christian. Mormonism is not Christianity." This is a theological point that a Christian pastor has every reason to believe. A "cult" is just a minority religion based around a man who claims to be a prophet—and that's exactly what Joseph Smith portrayed himself as being.

The thing is, there are questions about Mormonism that *I* genuinely have. I don't know that Rick Perry would agree with my specific questions, but surely he's not down with their whole thing. The issue I have with the Latter-day Saints is this: Up until the late 1970s, the Mormons viewed it as a *sin* to be black. This was during *my* lifetime. I was in high school when they changed that. But if this was part of the revelation given to Joseph Smith by the angel Moroni, you can't change that just because it's politically correct. Revelation is revelation. One thing Christians won't do is change their beliefs to be popular. They believe what they believe, it's in the Book, and that's that. You can't change your theology because the United States government and society at large is uncomfortable with some of your ideas. The idea behind faith is that if you believe in something past yourself, this deity will make you a better human being—except for us black people, in this case. There are things even God can't do, apparently.

But if the God that you believe in, invest your life in, spend your life serving and proselytize for, believes that somebody's inferior, then *you* always will believe that. *Always.* You'll hear Christians say, "God said it; I believe it; and that's it." So when it comes to Mormonism, I don't know which it is: Are they Christians who will believe in what the scripture says, no matter how unpopular? Or are they a cult who change their views to fit in with the larger culture?

Herman Cain

Let me compare Herman Cain to Barack Obama by objective standards. When Obama was running for the Democratic nomination, he was facing a very impressive field of rivals. When you watched them debate, Obama always looked bright. We never saw him get asked a question that he couldn't answer. He always seemed to be abreast of what was going on.

The Republican answer to the Democrats' "black guy" is Herman Cain. When Cain was on John Stossel's show—hardly a hostile environment—Stossel asked him what his opinion was on abortion. The exchange was so unbelievable it bears repeating, because it looks more like a *Saturday Night Live* sketch than an interview with a presidential candidate:

> CAIN: My position is I'm pro-life, period.
> STOSSEL: If a woman is raped, she should not be allowed to end the pregnancy?
> CAIN: That's her choice. That is not government's choice. I support life from conception.
> STOSSEL: So abortion should be legal?

CAIN: No, abortion should not be legal. I believe in the sanctity of life.

STOSSEL: I'm not getting it. I'm not understanding it. If it's her choice, that means it's legal.

CAIN: No. I don't believe a woman should have an abortion. Does that help to clear it up?

STOSSEL: Even if she is raped?

CAIN: Even if she is raped or the victim of incest, because there are other options. We must protect the sanctity of life, and I have always believed that. Real clear.

Look at the accomplishments of the candidates that Obama defeated. You had Hillary Clinton and the entire Clinton machine; there was nobody on the Republican side even remotely close to that in 2012. The other Democrats consisted of a governor—Bill Richardson—and prominent national politicians like Joe Biden and John Edwards. Those were some major heavyweights—but note that *nobody* came from a private corporate background.

I'm not saying any businessman is intrinsically unqualified to occupy the Oval Office. But Herman Cain is *a fucking pizza salesman.* His "business accomplishments" consisted of selling shitty food to people in Georgia. That's the home of the fried pickle. How is that even remotely preparation for the White House? If you want to stick to fast food, there are plenty of better choices. At least Burger King has had to make executive decisions over his Burger Kingdom. Mayor McCheese has been fighting crime in the form of the Hamburglar for decades; he's got a résumé. Doesn't that sound ridiculous? Of course it does. And here's the catch—*Godfather's Pizza is tenth in the nation in terms of sales.* When Papa John's is an aspirational figure to you, maybe the presidency is still a bridge too far.

Everything about Herman Cain was a function of him being a pizza salesman. "I wouldn't have any bill be longer than two pages"—*which is as long as a fast-food menu.* The reason the bills and contracts are so long is because they try to anticipate as many eventualities as possible. If a bill is not extremely specific, then what the bill entails has to be interpreted by one of two groups: federal bureaucrats, whom the Republicans regard as ominous oppressors, or federal judges, who would thereupon be branded as "activist" and accused of overstepping their bounds.

The instruction manual to take some shit out of a box is longer than two pages. A school paper is longer than two pages. How are you going to fix the health care system in two pages? The fucking Constitution, which the Republicans wave around like a bloody shirt, is much longer than two pages. So does Herman Cain think the Constitution is bad law? Where should we edit that down, to get it to the two-page limit?

The very first thing I thought of when I heard of Herman Cain's 9-9-9 plan is that it sounded like a commercial for food. Not too long ago, Denny's had ads that went, "One ninety-nine? Are you out of your mind?" to promote their $1.99 price. That's why it sounded so catchy to Cain's supporters. It's sadly ironic that the rednecks who like simple shit can't remember that they've subliminally heard this song, or variations of it, their whole lives. If you'd walk into Denny's and think that *any* price is "a good deal" for the shitty food they serve, of *course* you think it's a good idea for a tax plan. A black man singing about food? That shit is *natural.* It's just too bad that Herman Cain can't get a table at the so-called restaurant that inspired his economic policy.

Cain said that "we need simple." Yet the world's not simple anymore. The world is complex, it is dangerous, and it is fluid. If you want to get fast, you race somebody faster than yourself until you can win. You don't improve by racing someone slower—or by trying to pretend that complicated things are simple. Steel sharpens steel, much the way dumb begets dumb. We're fat, we're lazy, we're ignorant—and we want somebody to make us feel good about being that way. It's like we're reverting to the animal level. When you bring a dog some food, that dog is like, "You're in charge. You've got it figured out." It's the same thing with Pizzaman for president: "Oh, this guy brings food, therefore he knows what he's doing."

Cain's candidacy really did hit close to home for me. I'm sure for many Republican voters, he's the closest thing they ever had to a black family member. He reminded me of one of my relatives. I have a cousin who could say some of the brightest things I've ever heard. He'll sound bright and well thought out and then, when he starts to explain *why* he feels that way, I get the sense that this son of a bitch is batshit crazy. Everybody has one of them cousins or uncles or aunts, someone in their family. That's what Herman Cain is.

I can tell my relatives when they're being nuts. But the Republicans wouldn't say anything because Cain was black. His purpose wasn't to represent them; it was to give them political cover. It used to be that racists would claim "some of my best friends are black." Facebook has made it easy to disprove that assertion, so in 2011 it became "I was a Herman Cain supporter." He's every racist's imaginary black friend. They didn't care when the black guy started imploding in front of them. It didn't matter that the onetime front-runner didn't even come to Iowa or actually put an organization together there to try to win. It was of no importance that he didn't have any offices or employees in Iowa, the first-in-the-nation state. Cain was just playing a role and serving a purpose for them.

That's why Herman Cain makes me more sad than anything. I

don't have an issue with him personally. I'm *sure* that Herman Cain does *something* really well. I'd like him if we never talked politics; I'd probably like him if we *did* talk politics, so long as he wasn't deluded about his presidential aspirations. I like a lot of old black cats that make me laugh. At the family reunion, that dude would crack me the fuck up.

But now that Herman Cain is done, the white people he appealed to have no more use for him because he didn't win. He's not bright, he's not entertaining, and after the music's off, why do we need to see this clown dance? Stop it, Benson. It's just embarrassing for everyone. I saved Herman Cain for last because to me he was the most revealing by far of the Republican candidates. Cain demonstrated that, when it comes to Republicans, any black man will do . . . *and I can prove it.*

## CHAPTER 5

I DON'T WANT TO MAKE BLACK PEOPLE'S LIVES BETTER BY GIVING THEM SOMEBODY ELSE'S MONEY.

—RICK SANTORUM

THE Republican Party likes to adopt the mantle of Abraham Lincoln, one of the only Republican presidents who gave a fuck about black Americans. They acknowledge that blacks vote overwhelmingly, 90-plus percent, for the Democratic Party. Republicans contend that their policies would be better for black voters but black voters don't see it. Which is another way of saying: *Black Americans don't know what's good for them.* Yet isn't that the "elitism" that conservatives decry, when allegedly practiced by the left? Why are *we* brainwashed when certain white segments of the Republican

Party, like the Southerners and evangelicals, aren't? Why do *they* not give the Democratic Party a chance? Why is the same question never asked of *them*?

I've been on Bill Maher's show a number of times and talked to these conservatives. They always think that if they talk slower, or if they're really precise with their explanations, that I'll draw the same conclusions that they do. *I don't see the world the way they do, no matter the cadence of their speech or the precision of their language.* All I am is what I've seen; we're all the sum total of our life's experiences. I *knowingly* disagree with them, and millions of other black people do too.

One political party is the most selfish, most narrow-minded, most hateful group of people that I've ever seen. The other wears rose-colored glasses and believes government can do everything and should be involved in every aspect of our lives. Neither one of those perspectives is *true*, but those are my only options. The former is motivated by a place of evil and selfishness. The latter comes from a sense of altruism and wants things to be better and fair. So who do I go with? It's like getting a ride home from a party. I'd rather go with someone who gets lost when they're driving me back than go with someone driving me with no regard to my wishes—or even intentionally driving me in the opposite direction. The Republicans want to drive me where *they* want to go. My values, and the values of people who look like me, are illegitimate to them.

To be a Republican, you really have to be more selfish and downright mean. It's a very small way of thinking. It's all about *me, my,* and *ours.* But that kind of approach necessarily means that minorities are *you, they,* and *theirs.* We're not going to have a place at the table. The Republicans are pragmatic businessmen and dwell on efficiency. Sometimes people feel that they need that type of approach. But when you look at *inspirational* political figures, can anyone name *one* contemporary GOP operative out there that would inspire people like a Kennedy, or like Clinton, or now like Obama? One person who makes Americans feel like something could be different, even though oftentimes we're disappointed?

The Republican Party doesn't even *try* to get the black vote. Anyone who wants to become president has to be able to glad-hand and persuade people on a personal level. Yet the Republicans obviously think that these black people are so fucking gone that there's no point in wasting five minutes trying to charm us, to say nothing of *persuading* us. George Bush never came to black functions because he automatically assumed that he wouldn't be welcome. He assumed he'd be wasting his time because we'd never vote for him. How can he *never* step into a room with one of our organizations, and then expect our vote? What would be his message? "Give me your vote even though I won't do anything to get it. The Democrats just use you, so let me use you too."

If we had two bright black men running for president who were ideologically opposed, *all of us* would be proud. It would be a real choice. *One* administration changed black people from Republicans to Democrats, the same way that *one* administration made us Republicans. Neither was necessarily *in love* with black people. Lincoln said time and again that abolishing slavery wasn't his priority, yet he still ended up doing the right thing. Contrary to popular belief, it wasn't FDR who brought the black vote into the Democratic Party—at least not in a unanimous way. There were still many blacks who voted Republican after he was gone because the Democratic Party was still the party of Southern racism. It took Kennedy, with his conceptualization of civil rights, and Lyndon Baines Johnson, with his political courage, to make it happen.

The reason the black community is such a lock for the Democrats is because Kennedy and Johnson took huge political risks for us. Pushing civil rights wasn't the politically expedient path for them to take. Their actions were detrimental to their political futures, so detrimental that Lyndon Johnson wasn't assured of being nominated in 1968 despite winning one of American history's biggest landslides in 1964. "We have lost the South for a generation" is what LBJ said as he was signing the Civil Rights Act into law.

Republicans have won seven out of the last eleven presidential elections. That's a pretty good record for a party that always had a disadvantage when it came to national voter registration. The reason was *race*. In 1964, Republican nominee Barry Goldwater came out against the Civil Rights Act, calling it unconstitutional. But if that were true, legally, then why did he not propose a constitutional amendment to effect the same change? Because the act alienated enough racist Southern Democrats that their votes were up for grabs. They used to be called yellow-dog Democrats before that, since they would vote for a yellow dog before voting for any Republican. Over the following fifty years, they became the base of the Republican Party. The party *based* its strength on Southern racists, on those who switched party *because* of their opposition to civil rights.

It is impossible to name *one* modern Republican who took a risk like that for black people, *one* person who put it all on the line simply for the sake of doing the right thing. It is impossible to name *one* modern Republican who ever did one thing in the last fifty years that was transformative for us—or even *tried* to. Reagan only made things better for rich, white people. The black community during that time was reeling from the crack epidemic and its subsequent addiction, crime, and incarceration.

Most important, it is impossible to name *one* modern Republican who is comfortable among the black community. Any such man or woman would be welcomed with open arms. Why would we choose to be around people who simply tolerate us or seem to have an aversion to us? Why would we go out and vote for them? How can they speak *for* us when they won't even speak *to* us?

In the Republican Party, anyone who's brown or yellow or other than white is treated differently. J. C. Watts got a House leadership position simply because of his race. Marco Rubio was touted as a vice-presidential nominee before he was even elected—literally, before he accomplished *anything* other than being a Latino. Minorities in the Republican Party are used like a spectacle. It's like the modern-day equivalent of the freak show. They think of blacks as accidental, freak Americans, and if they have one brown freak on the stage, maybe the rest of us will hop under their alleged "big tent."

All humans want to be surrounded by what they're comfortable with. The black community is no different from any other in that regard. We are naturally drawn to what we can relate to. We like the idea that someone has our same hue of skin, comes from experiences that we can relate to, has a cadence that we can recognize. Let's suppose you're interviewing two people for a job. One reminds you of your son. The other is just as qualified, but you have no kind of connection to him. Who gets the job? It's silly to pretend that's not what happens.

Bill Clinton was not literally black—but he went to our churches, talked to us, ate our food, and knew our culture. He made a concerted effort, even though it's political and it's glad-handing, to relate to us. I might only have a GED, but I still know a thing or two. One of the most basic things they teach in marketing courses is to match your product to your audience. McDonald's can't go into India, where the cow is revered, and have its menu be the same as it is in the U.S. There are entire websites dedicated to foreign companies that make unintentional jokes in English because they didn't translate things correctly for the American market. That is what the Republican approach to the black community is like. They'll make a political ad for their white voting base, and then use that exact same ad for a black audience. *Maybe* they'll change the announcer to have a deep, black voice. But their entire argument amounts to "our philosophy works for us, so it'll work for you. Not that I know anything about you, but I'm pretty sure it will." They are not tailoring their message to their audience whatsoever, so *of course* no one is buying their product.

Sadly, it's a simple fact that there are so few prominent black Republicans that I can easily discuss each one individually. One of the reasons I was so revolted by Herman Cain was his assertion that blacks hate those who stray from the Democratic plantation. Leaving aside the despicable choice of words, that's demonstrably untrue. Speaking only for myself, I never hated Colin Powell. I have always liked and admired Condoleezza Rice, *personally*. I vehemently disagreed with the way she did things and with the outcome, but you'll never hear me say things about Condi the way I said things about Herman Cain.

I very much dislike what Colin Powell *did*. He mortgaged his reputation at a time when few other people could have gotten that war started. That's how high he was held in esteem by everyone in the country. As a result of his actions, lives were lost. I think that part of him *knew* that it wasn't right. Some people say that, well, he was being a good soldier and a good soldier falls in line and falls on the grenade. But that's a myth. A good soldier, especially a good *American* soldier, is supposed to be a setter of truth. Soldiers have an obligation to refuse an order they know to be immoral. If a higher officer gives an order that's illegal or immoral, a soldier can say no. If he *does* follow through and gets caught, he can still be prosecuted.

When all is said and done, Colin Powell is still very respected. I may not agree with him and I didn't like who he worked for: I've wondered why on earth he allowed those things to happen. But he is still an extremely accomplished man who will always be held as a historically important figure. Every February, the one month when people care about blacks and their accomplishments, Colin Powell's face will be on those place mats.

Condoleezza Rice is the same. If I had a question about an international issue, there might not be a single black person who would give me a better explanation than Condi Rice. There definitely wouldn't be a black *woman* who understands world politics the way that she does. I probably would break with her when it came to her conclusions and her chosen response to an incident, but I know that her grasp of the technicalities would be, literally, world-class. She might be a Republican, but she is not a Bachmann or Palinesque lunatic. I would bet money, in fact, that she voted for Obama. She met with him and she's talked to him, and she never says anything bad about him—even though she's probably received a phone call or two suggesting that she do so for the good of the GOP.

None of their most vituperative opponents ever claimed that Colin Powell and Condi Rice got to where they are because of race. They were both extremely accomplished people and supremely qualified at what they did. Frankly, given who they were in cahoots with, I would argue that they were *over*qualified. They deserved better than what they got. So this idea that black people hate black

Republicans in general or that we hate them disproportionately to the rest of the Republican Party is a *lie*.

# # #

What I hate is hypocrisy and condescension. Every black person knows that tone of voice that white people use to make them seem conciliatory and friendly. It's the kind of tone you use when you're talking to a strange dog to make it think you're its friend. The dog might not know better, but humans sure as fuck do.

There is no greater hypocrisy between the Republican Party and the black community than when it comes to affirmative action. I get why people are against affirmative action. It's not a hard argument to make. The natural inclination for someone who isn't black is to not give a shit about others and worry about his own people. It takes someone with a higher sense of decency and a better perspective to realize that extending opportunities to nonwhite *Americans* benefits both sides in the end. It's the same as the arguments for NAFTA: Free trade between both groups enriches each partner.

But some people don't agree with that. They perceive America to be a white nation, even though my family has been here longer than, say, Pat Buchanan's or Rick Santorum's. They think blacks should be happy with the leftover crumbs we get. They regard us like guests in *their* home, and guests would do well not to complain too much lest they be thrown into the street. The fact that they don't really know what "thrown into the street" in this analogy translates to *in practice* drives them to distraction. But this is their view, and I get it. They might not say it out loud or they might not even consciously realize it, but that's their perspective.

Affirmative action does *not* mean hiring an unqualified black person over a qualified white person. That's tokenism. Affirmative action merely means that efforts should be made to find qualified black people, or to nurture environments, such as education, that allow minorities to *become* qualified. It means that if several people apply for a job, hiring a minority is regarded as a good thing. The argument that affirmative action is about racial preferences between two equally qualified candidates is nonsensical. When have two candidates for a job ever been "equally" qualified? There are so many things that go into a job interview, including candidates' personalities and how they talk to you, that to imagine a scenario where there are two equal people is impossible. The only way that could happen is if you had identical twin brothers, one white and one minority. *That's not reality.* That's the premise to some terrible Richard Pryor/Gene Wilder movie that has never been produced.

If you don't believe in affirmative action, don't practice it. But don't rail against it, and then practice the *caricature* of affirmative action that you believe to be the real thing. Namely, don't hire patently unqualified people in an attempt to curry favor with minorities. This is a *transparent* hypocrisy that fools no one. It only makes black people more aware of how stupid powerful whites think we are.

Our recent history is replete with examples of this. When Obama first got into office, the Republicans did a couple of things that were specifically designed to say, "We got us one, too." The person they chose to give the response to President Obama's first State of the Union address was Louisiana governor Bobby Jindal. Why was a *governor* giving a response, when the pressing issue on the table was the *federal* stimulus plan? No one doubts that it's because Bobby Jindal looked dark. They didn't even have *one* black dude, but they had the grown-up kid from *Slumdog Millionaire.* That was the closest they had to a person of color. He sure wasn't picked because of his inspiring oratorical skills; Jindal was so atrocious that they couldn't use him again in the future.

Right around the same time as this, Michael Steele was named chairman of the Republican National Committee. His résumé was being elected lieutenant governor of Maryland, obviously not a very powerful position—and one that he ascended to simply by being on the right ticket. When Steele next ran for Senate on his own merits, he lost by more than ten points. If race wasn't a factor, if race wasn't the *deciding* factor in his getting his job, then what was? Being a senatorial loser? Or spending four years waiting around in case the governor died?

This is not a slight against Michael Steele. He got his job because of his race. At the very same time, *I* got a job because of my race. CNN wanted a black dude to appeal to the Obama crowd, and they hired me to host *D. L. Hughley Breaks the News.* Early on, I had Michael Steele on my show, and I told him as much. "We both got these jobs right now," I pointed out on the air, "because there's a black president."

He bristled. "That's not true! I was around before Obama."

But it *was* true. Obama got him hired, and that very same interview with me got him fired. Later on the show, I asked him the same question that I had asked Congressman Ron Paul. "Is Rush Limbaugh the de facto leader of the Republican Party?"

"Rush Limbaugh is an entertainer," Steele replied.

But I pressed the issue, and eventually Steele ceded that Limbaugh was "a" leader of the Republican Party. The next day, everywhere I went it was all over the TV: Chris Matthews, CNN, NBC News, everyone was discussing the interview. And that same day, Rush Limbaugh was going in on it. He conveniently forgot his beloved President Reagan's Eleventh Commandment, "Thou shalt not speak ill of any fellow Republican," because Steele was just a tool to him and not a real Republican politician. Limbaugh started attacking Steele, claiming he was never qualified to do the job as RNC chairman. Steele quickly recanted what he had said on my show, but Limbaugh kept going after him publicly. Who knows what was going on behind the scenes; it must have been hellacious. After that, confidence in Steele evaporated, and it snowballed until he lost his gig.

If anyone has any doubt about the fact that Steele was simply brought in to be black on TV, they should look at what happened in the 2010 midterms. Michael Steele did *exactly* what he was supposed to do. Under his watch, he delivered the Republicans a profound congressional victory. They picked up more seats than in any election in the preceding seventy years. Steele certainly wasn't the cause; there was anger and a lot of missteps on the Democratic side, among other things. But if you're the head coach and your team wins, *you* fucking win. That's how it goes! You don't fire a dude who won the Super Bowl for you even if he was a crappy coach. You wait until shit falls off, and *then* you fire him.

But mascots are a completely different story. They're much more disposable. When Steele's term was done, he couldn't get reelected by his own people.

Steele, at the very least, put himself out there. He argued the Republican cause on many television shows, understood the philosophy, and fought for his team. He had a record to be judged on. But if a so-called "affirmative action hire" is about choosing race over record, is there any better example than Clarence Thomas? Let's compare Clarence Thomas's record to that of the man he replaced, Thurgood Marshall.

Marshall had argued for and won the *Brown v. Board of Education* case, easily one of the ten most important Supreme Court cases of the twentieth century, if not all time. When he was named to the Supreme Court, he had argued more cases in front of that court than any other attorney. Not only was he qualified: By that very valid standard, he was the *most* qualified candidate. It was like, "Motherfucker, you've been here so much, you might as well be one of us." He had beat them *and* he had joined them.

So when Thurgood Marshall retired in 1991, the first President Bush decided to appoint another black man to fill his shoes. But in true Republican fashion, "Any black man would do." He nominated Clarence Thomas, *who had less than two years of experience as a federal judge.* Bush had the audacity to claim that Thomas was the "best qualified." How is that even *plausible,* with so little experience? Thomas's judicial hearings immediately divided public opinion. It wasn't looking good for Clarence, so what did he do?

He played the race card.

Republicans love to get apoplectic when they claim that Democrats are playing the race card. Most of the time, it's simply a matter of Democrats pointing out that Republican policy would disproportionately hurt black people and other minorities. In one sense, the Republicans are only acting naturally. They don't view blacks as their constituencies, so they're looking after their own people at the expense of others. But in another sense, *Fuck you.* They claim that the race card is needlessly inflammatory, a low blow designed to eliminate civilized debate and introduce emotion into the discussion. *No one has played the race card more brazenly than Clarence Thomas.* No one has played it more publicly, more shamelessly, and more outrageously than when he categorized criticism of himself as "a high-tech lynching." He didn't play it in circumstances in which he was going to get the death penalty.

He didn't play it when an entire community was going to be hurt by proposed political actions. No, Clarence Thomas played it because he wasn't going to get a promotion. He played it simply because he wasn't going to get his way in the Senate confirmation hearings.

What would it look like in a boardroom if some black dude at the company got passed over for a promotion and claimed that he was being *lynched*? That shit wouldn't fly at Merrill Lynch. Everybody would be thinking to themselves, *See, this is why you can never hire these people. They bring race into everything and they're completely shameless and out of control.* Then the company lawyers would look into how they could unload this dude as quickly as possible, what the cost would be to pay him off, and how they could best get him to shut the fuck up and go away. Any of his allies in the firm would be mortified that he humiliated them like that in front of the board. "I had your back, man, and you say that they're *lynching* you? How does that make me look?"

I have never heard a single conservative thinker denounce Thomas's comments. They don't have to make a big spectacle about it. All they need to say is, "I thought Clarence Thomas got a raw deal during his hearings and I thought Anita Hill was a liar. But I think his referring to it as a 'lynching' was unfair and needlessly inflammatory." Even in retrospect, twenty years later, no one has a problem with it. Why is that? Do they really take issue with the race card being used in politics? Or is it that they have a problem with being publicly called out on their *bullshit*?

When I tell people that Clarence Thomas has never asked one single question during his tenure at the Supreme Court, it sounds like I am exaggerating for comedic effect. That is so preposterous that it seems impossible to be true. *Look it up.* When I tell people that he has not written a single majority opinion in his two decades on the bench, it seems ridiculous.

I'm not going to call Clarence Thomas an Uncle Tom, as others have done. I wouldn't call *anyone* an Uncle Tom: I think that is a needlessly offensive term thrown out too lightly. I don't know what's in the man's heart. I can make educated guesses, but that would be presumptuous. But I would *like* to know what's in his heart. How can I, if the dude won't say shit? Even motherfucking Helen Keller could tell me that she was feeling "water, water!" I, and the rest of America, have no real record to judge this judge. Being a judge is like the opposite of being a criminal. If you've got a long record as a criminal, you're probably a person who's mixed up in all sorts of crazy shit. But if you're a judge, a long record speaks to your accomplishments and the quality of your legal mind—and the opposite holds true as well.

If people questioned my intellect, my competence, and my character, I would do my best to show them to be wrong. I definitely wouldn't want to shut the fuck up. You don't have to be slick and well spoken. Even if you don't say anything, you can write things that are stellar. It's almost like Clarence Thomas is a guy who's determined *not* to be shown to be competent.

I have no doubt whatsoever that Clarence Thomas has felt the sting of racism. In fact, since he's older and since he's from the South, I'm sure he's experienced it to a greater extent than *I* have. The people who perpetrated those things against him *then* look an awful lot like the people that he hangs out with *now*. He grew up around men who looked and talked like Haley Barbour and Rick Perry—and I am sure he was not treated particularly well by them. For his conclusion to be, "I want to be more like the people who perpetrated these crimes against me," I find that really unfortunate.

# # #

I will acknowledge that it is much easier to be a critic than to offer constructive advice. After all, opinions are like assholes: They usually stink and no one really wants to hear them. Unlike the Republicans, I don't think the black community is a lost cause. So I'm going to do their job for them and tell them how they can actually get a tiny bit of the black vote. Let's suppose lightning struck and I was named Republican Party chairman. And let's suppose further that I was given the unenviable task of making inroads into the black community. It would be difficult but not impossible. Here's what I would advise:

Stop secretly playing the race card. Immediately after LBJ alienated all the racists, the Republicans saw the Southern vote as ripe for the picking (pun intended). For the first time ever, literally *ever*, there was now a possibility for the Republican Party to carry the South in free elections. The GOP didn't try to hide its agenda. It openly and explicitly refers to this as its "Southern strategy."

Though the strategy is public, the application is insidious. The Republicans do things that are ambiguous enough that they can claim that they don't know why people get offended. When George Allen said "macaca," he knew what that meant. He simply hoped that nobody else did. Can a senator, a member of perhaps the greatest debating society in the Western world, really be using epithets without knowing their application? When Newt Gingrich referred to Obama as the "food-stamp president," he explicitly claimed he did not understand why people got offended. Not that he didn't *agree*, but that he didn't *understand*. Playing dumb when you're not dumb is *lying*. Playing dumb about *race* when you're not dumb is *race baiting*.

In that exact same vein, things like having confederate symbols on the state flag are automatically nonstarters for black people. It's a way for the Republicans to talk out of both sides of their mouth, to ally with racists while claiming they're for "tradition." How can a Southerner claim to uphold tradition and then vote Republican? The GOP started as a regional party opposed to slavery and Southern economic interests. There were many places in the South where Lincoln, the first Republican president, got *zero* votes.

Why would the South revere the Civil War period, anyway? That was an ass-whupping! The human brain is psychologically designed to *repress* ass-whuppings. People who grow up beaten and abused become adults with no memories of the fact. They don't dress up and *reenact* the trauma. The Confederacy was all about *oppressing*. It was all about fighting for the right to keep black people under its boot. Who would want to recall that, *unless* you have a fond memory of it? The South harks back to this era because it's the last time that it was unfettered and got to be what it was.

Of course the rebel flag is about racism, *period*. It's like this: Let's suppose you had a guest to your home who was deathly allergic to lemons. Whenever she smelled lemons, she got sick to her stomach and felt very uncomfortable. Would any host serve a lemon dish, simply because the recipe had been in the family for generations? Obviously, you accommodate your guests and make them feel welcome. At the very least, you don't make them feel violently (and I do mean *violently*) unwelcome. That's what flying the rebel flag is like. But black people aren't "guests" in this country. We're citizens, too.

Get off your high horse. Black people are generally socially conservative. We believe in God at a level that's probably as rabidly religious or theological as anyone else. Black people dislike almost everything that social conservatives dislike. You might never know it from how many of us are sitting in jail, but from gays to drugs to pornography, black people are against it—especially black *women*, who vote in far larger numbers than black men. But they're not *hateful* about it. The tone is not one of "lock them up and throw away the key." There is a sense of compassion, which is a feeling completely antithetical to the Republican mindset.

Condemn disrespect against minorities. The best example of this I can think of is when Michelle Obama went to a NASCAR event in late 2011 and got *booed*. Not only did she get booed, she got booed while appearing with a wounded soldier and the Obama *children*. What message does that send to black people? Despite their fears that she would be Omarosa, Michelle Obama has been utterly apolitical as first lady. She isn't anywhere near as active as a Hillary Clinton, or even Nancy Reagan for that matter. She works for gardening and for healthier eating. That's not *activism*. That's some vapid Mamie Eisenhower–type shit. Irrespective of one's political beliefs, what is the message to black people when the first lady is booed? How could *any* patriotic American endorse that? Yet the Republicans didn't speak out for fear of appearing soft or alienating their constituency. All they needed to say is something along the lines of, "Mrs. Obama and I obviously have different views as to who should be the president, but to have a first lady of the United States being booed in public anywhere in this country is outrageous and unacceptable." But even that platitude is too much for them.

Attend black events. Yes, it will probably be uncomfortable. It would not be a very welcoming audience. But it would be a fuckload more comfortable and welcoming than going to some places in the Middle East, say. You *never* see a Republican presidential candidate at the *Soul Train Awards* or something similar. The crowd won't cheer for them, but they won't be booing, either. It's not like going onstage during *Showtime at the Apollo*, believe you me. Too "pop culture"? That's fine. Only someone who thinks that black Americans are unmitigated savages would believe that *anyone* would be disrespected in a *church*. No audience would do it, and no pastor would allow it.

Black people see Democrats appear at functions that are important to us. The politicians will go honor some leader that they find amazing (or they *claim* to find amazing), or they'll know somebody's name in the community, or they'll sit down and eat in a soul-food restaurant. News like that travels, and those things seem important. The same pancake breakfast that Republicans go to for the religious crowd can be had in a black community. And when the pictures run in the paper, they'll look a lot better than those corn-dog blowjob photos out of Iowa.

Stop regarding us as having a hive mind. When one black person says something Republicans *don't* like, he's indicative of all black people to them. "That's how they *all* think! They all think the same way!" But when a black person says something that Republicans *like*, then it becomes, "Why can't you be more like this guy?" Just because we're all unified against the GOP doesn't mean we're all unified otherwise.

Unbutton the collars. In 2008 I said on CNN that the Republican National Convention looked like Nazi Germany. I had never seen a whiter and more austere gathering. It wasn't simply that it was all "white"; it was *buttoned-up* white people and their buttoned-up sons and daughters. White people as a group can be pretty diverse. You've got George Bush, and you've got Kid Rock, and you've got Lady Gaga. Show it!

Stop the legal double standard. When the system is rigged to deliberately make it harder for my kids than it is for white kids, then clearly the party of "order" is fighting against me. This double standard crosses all criminal activity. I read an article referring to the Department of Justice, and it pointed out that 75 percent of people arrested in this country are white. Yet a majority of the people in jail are black. Judges, consciously or not, prefer to mete out "mercy" for their own, the white offenders, while delivering "justice" for people they have no connection to, poor black males.

Die. One of my close friends is a die-hard Raiders fan. I asked him what it would take for the Raiders to get better. "They'll get better," he told me, "now that Al Davis died." It's the same thing with the Republican Party and those who run it. All the Newts Gingrich, all the people who look like Romney, all those people who believe that there's a certain way you're supposed to be—when that mentality and that physical presence dies, the GOP and the *world* can move on.

It's like America's waiting for its grandmother to croak so we can inherit her house. We don't *want* her to die, and I certainly don't wish for the death of anyone (especially someone who I simply disagree with politically). But at the same time, just like with Grandma, it's impossible to deny that some good will come out of this death. Without a death, there can't be a resurrection.

That old mentality, those old ways of seeing the world, is a major reason why the Republican Party is anathema to the black community. The vitriol and the venom and the acrimony in our politics comes from people who never in their lives thought they would see a black man being the symbol of America. It was unfathomable to them. In many ways it *remains* unfathomable to them. It's driven them mad to the extent that they will purposefully damage this country to get rid of him.

Of course, I won't actually be waiting for a call to take over the Republican Party. There are much easier and more palatable jobs that I could be doing, like running Godfather's Pizza. But the fact that the GOP isn't doing *any* of these somewhat obvious things demonstrates that it's out of choice. At the end of the day, the Republican Party is less interested in the black *vote* than it is in the black *voter* simply going away. Don't believe me? Take a look at the Republicans' very own home page, GOP.com. Here's a screen grab as I write:

At the very top are links to subpages for RNC Latinos and RNC Women. But there's no welcome mat for black Republicans. There's not even a perfunctory page talking about Rep. Allen West taking on the CBC or what have you. I'm not putting words in their mouth. If you invite two groups into your home and are silent with regard to the third, *at best* you are indifferent to them. That sure don't sound like Abe Lincoln to me. The man may have been much more racist than people realize, but he wasn't about to let freed blacks wither away and die.

Here's where I'd like to point something else out. I began this chapter by mentioning that blacks vote overwhelmingly for Democrats, and that certain white groups vote as overwhelmingly for Republicans. These kinds of figures are discussed on the news constantly and are not controversial. It is possible to statistically predict how a certain group will behave in a given context. No one would have an argument with that. After all, demographics are the *basis* of marketing—political and otherwise. Polling is also based on this concept. But there's another, less positive term for when statistics predict how a certain group will behave in a given context: *stereotyping*. And the predictive power of these models brings me to my next point: that stereotypes exist for a reason.

## CHAPTER 6

IT'S VERY HARD TO TEACH RACISM TO A TEENAGER WHO'S LISTENING TO RAP MUSIC AND WHO IDOLIZES, SAY, SNOOP DOGG.

—JAY-Z

THE idea that stereotypes are social constructs with no relation to reality is *itself* a social construct with no relation to reality. Every nation, every group on earth, has some stereotype about some other nation or group that is different from them. I bet that even these contemporary Paleolithic societies have jokes about their women and their elderly. When something is a universal element of the human experience, it surely has *some* basis in fact.

Let me give an example to illustrate my point. One time during the filming of *Studio 60*, I was hanging out backstage with my costar Nate Corddry. Nate mentioned the song "Stairway to Heaven." I was a little surprised that white Nate listened to soul music. "You like the O'Jays?" I said.

"The O'Jays?" Nate replied. "Who're the O'Jays?"

"What do you mean? They're the cats that sing 'Stairway to Heaven.' "

He looked at me like I was messing with him. "D.L., 'Stairway to Heaven' is by Led Zeppelin. It's like their biggest song."

"Really?" I had *no idea* what he was talking about.

"Yeah, it's on the *Led Zeppelin IV* album. I can't believe that you don't know that."

"Well, I can't believe you don't know the O'Jays. Isn't it funny that you assumed that I would know what you know?"

It should come as no surprise that the black dude liked "Stairway to Heaven" by the O'Jays and the white guy listened to Led Zeppelin's song of the same name. Like I said: *Stereotypes exist for a reason*. Somehow, when a stereotype is not offensive, we can acknowledge it as a fact. Liking soul music or Led Zeppelin is not offensive to anyone. But if a stereotype *is* offensive, that doesn't make it *false*. That just makes it an *offensive* fact.

I experience stereotyping *a lot*. There have been many times when I've sat in first class on a plane, and the white passengers have questions for me: "What do you do?" "Are you a singer?" "Should I *know* you?" "What's your name? Everybody knows you, right?" If you see a white guy in first class, he can just be on some business trip for the regional branch of a cell-phone company. But if it's a *black* dude sitting in first, he's famous. He's an athlete or an entertainer. Now, how can I complain about that stereotype when I embody it? I *am* an entertainer. The stereotype, in my case, is *true*.

Why deny that these ideas exist? Someone who denies reality is a crazy person. That's what being crazy *means*: not being in touch with reality! We all *know* that black people tend to talk loud at the movies. I don't know why, but I'm *never* shocked when I hear black people yelling at the theater. I might get *annoyed*, but I don't get *surprised*. Does *anyone*?

Sometimes stereotypes are so spot-on that it's ridiculous. I've seen things that are almost a caricature of real life. When I was in Los Angeles a few years back, I witnessed the aftermath of a car accident on the street. It looked so weird to me, because it was a white dude who had run into an Asian guy. In the back of my mind, I was so convinced that it had to be the Asian's fault that I started trying to figure out how the Asian guy could have made such an accident happen. The only way it was possible was if the Asian guy had backed into the white dude—which was ridiculous. I turned to the man standing next to me, who had seen the whole thing. "Dude, what did he do?" I joked. "Back up into him?"

"He actually did."

"*What?*" I thought he was kidding.

"No, that's actually what happened. He was coming out of the parking space, didn't look, and backed up into him."

The stereotype had been justified once again. I know I'm not the only person who thinks like this. It's a shock when Asians don't know arithmetic: Everyone assumes that they know all the math. You just *do*. Every time I go get blood taken at the doctor's, it's a Filipino nurse. Every. Single. Time. The *New York Times* had a piece about how the shoeshine community is almost exclusively Brazilian dudes. Is the *New York Times* an organ of prejudice and anti-diversity racism? Let's be real.

What's amazing to me is when people get in trouble for saying things that everyone knows to be the truth. You get in more trouble for speaking the truth in this country than you do for lying. In 2010, Rick Sanchez got fired from CNN for making comments about how the Jews run the media. Is he wrong? I've been in the entertainment industry for over twenty years. Over that time period, every meeting I've ever gone to had a Jewish person in the room. Why is that? Is it just the biggest string of coincidences in history? Ben Stein, Jew, once wrote an article entitled "Do Jews Run Hollywood?" His conclusion was, "You bet they do—and what of it?" If something is acceptable for a Stein to say, it should be acceptable for a Sanchez to say as well. Facts are facts regardless of the speaker. That's what makes them facts and not opinions.

Juan Williams was another dude who got in trouble for speaking his mind about stereotypes. Juan got fired from NPR because he said he got nervous and worried when he saw Muslims board planes. Who doesn't? Shortly after 9/11, I was taking a flight. I watched as the staff kicked a Middle Eastern dude off the plane. They didn't ask him anything and they didn't say anything to him. As a black man, part of me thought that was racial profiling and it wasn't right. But another part of me had no problem with it whatsoever.

The thing is, most people are more interested in denying that stereotypes exist than actually fighting them. In the summer of 2011, the Department of Homeland Security released a public service announcement to help prevent terrorism. The terrorists in the ad belonged to every race—with one glaring exception. Old ladies? Check. Middle-aged man of unclear racial history? Yep, he's there. Guess who was missing? Here's a hint: Stereotypically, he should be driving a cab. Homeland Security tried so hard to not be stereotypical and racist that they ended up making clowns of themselves. It starts at the top and permeates its way down. When I was in

Chattanooga, their Most Wanted Terrorists poster was so hilarious that I just had to take a picture of it. It was full of white dudes! So Conway fucking Twitty has joined the mujahideen?

People always get worked up over shit like that, but I never do. Why get upset? We should try to avoid getting upset and laugh these things off. It'll be easier for everybody. So much of comedy is based on people feeling uncomfortable, because *being uncomfortable forces you to think and to question your behavior.* We can't get past racism if we can't *laugh* about it. If you're not comfortable laughing it off, at least mess with people about it. I've done it myself and the results are hysterical.

There were two times that I was out for dinner with my manager, who is white, and a similar thing happened. The first time, I ordered the Caesar salad and he got the ribs. The second time, I got the salad and he got the fried chicken. The story turned out the same way: The waiter came back and put the salad in front of the white dude, while I got the fried chicken or the ribs.

I thought it was *hilarious.* If I got offended by stuff like that, like when white people hand me their keys to bring the car around, I'd be offended *a lot.* So I decided to have fun with the waiter. "Man," I said, "I didn't order the fried chicken. He did."

Apparently they had beets on special that night, because that waiter instantly turned beet red. "Oh, I'm so sorry!"

"Why would you put it *here?*"

He got flummoxed. "I'm . . . I'm . . . I don't know!"

But he *did* know, and my manager knew, and I knew. The waiter just didn't feel comfortable saying the truth that was in front of all of us. The political correctness forced him to be deceptive instead of simply being truthful. But it wasn't like he was fooling anyone, least of all me.

All this talk of us living in a post-racial, colorblind society is nonsense, as far as I'm concerned. *Seeing* a color isn't the same thing as *hating* a color. I heard Charles Grodin say that he knew he had come a long way with regards to race when one day he looked out and all the Knicks were black—and he hadn't even noticed. My position is, he would have noticed if he had gone to a board meeting and all of them were black. Anyone would notice that, because people go where they belong. They go where you assign them. If I'm on a plane, I expect that the pilot is a white man. I only notice when it's a female or a minority.

Can anyone tell me they've never met a person that is the very embodiment of a stereotype? Not one? For us to pretend that stereotypes are these conjured-up notions that don't exist is dishonest and straight-up *bullshit*. I know Jews who act a certain way; I know blacks who act a certain way; I know Mexicans who act a certain way. I would say *most* of them act that way, and the exception is the one everybody holds up. What drives me crazy is when you mention a stereotype, and the person you're speaking to brings up that one counterexample: "I'm friends with Nichelle, and she's black. She doesn't dance." But that's the *exception*, not the rule. You notice it when a white dude dances very well. *I* especially notice it because I'm a terrible dancer and I despise dancing.

There's certain things you aren't going to see black people do. You just won't. You won't see a black dude mauled by a grizzly bear in Alaska or Montana. When killer whales turn on their trainers and kill them, you know immediately that that's not a black person. We generally get killed by drive-by shootings and the police. Who comes out ahead in the above scenarios? Which of these stereotypes is "bad"?

I can prove to everyone that stereotypes exist for a reason. I was gigging in Baltimore in 2010 when I heard this news story: Some dude broke into a house to burglarize it. While the robber was there, he decided to kill two birds with one stone. He used the homeowner's charger to charge his cell phone. Then he ran off with all the loot—and left his cell phone behind and got caught. Could that have been anyone other than a black dude? That's nigger shit, right there.

When Michael Vick got a $100 million contract, some commentator on MSNBC said that if Vick was white, he never would have gone through what he had. Well, he probably also wouldn't have been that good of an athlete, either.

As I write this, I'm working on a radio show. I headed to United Stations to do a mock episode that we could then shop around. We were taking calls, and after a while we got very tired. I asked the program director who set everything up if we had enough material.

"Oh, we've got *more* than enough," he told me. "But we've got six more calls so let's use them, because we paid for them."

"So even though we don't need them," I asked him, "you want to use them?"

Pop quiz! Was this program director:

A) Jewish
B) A Jew
C) Of Semitic descent
D) All of the above

"That's the most Jewish thing I've ever heard," I told him.

And he laughed. Of course he laughed, because my comment made sense. If he had been British and I'd said, "That's the most British thing I've ever heard," he'd just get confused. (Actually, if he were British he would have never made such a Jewish comment, but that's beside the point.)

Another example: Once I had neighbors who were two men who lived together. We've all had neighbors who are horrible, who make you wince because every time you interact with them they annoy the shit out of you. Well, these dudes were the exact opposite. Every time they said something, it was helpful: "Your dog got out, but we brought him back." "I watered your plants." "I went to the store and I picked something up I knew you would like." I don't get why they had statues of David everywhere, but that was their business. Now, I had never *seen* the two men be intimate with each other. They never said to me, "We're gay." But did they really need to?

Just like *everybody* else, I get nervous when I walk down the street and I see a group of young black or Latin dudes. I'm not being *hateful*; I'm being cautious and I'm being safe. If it was a bunch of gay dudes, the only thing I'd be worried about is if they were judging my clothes. If it were black or Latin *women*, no one including myself would be worried. That's because almost all violent street crime is committed by men. That's not a racist statement and that's not a sexist statement. That's just *math*, motherfucker!

When someone doesn't know you and treats you like a stereotype, it's not always a hateful thing. It could just be a matter of playing the odds. When I go to restaurants in the summer, the waiter often brings out a free appetizer for the table. "The chef made this special for you," he'll tell me as he puts down that plate—which is always with watermelon. I never get worked up over shit like that. How can I be upset when people are trying their best to make me a treat to enjoy, for free? Guess what: Black people like watermelon. *So does everybody else.* How the fuck can you find watermelon offensive? It's spectacular! After a hundred years, it's not even a stereotype anymore; it's an American tradition.

Are we not supposed to see stereotypes? Or are we not supposed to say what we see? As a comic and as a person, it's my job to do as the Department of Homeland Security urges: "If you see something, say something." Words are linguistic tools we use to connote things that exist. If stereotypes exist for a reason, then they've got to have a word attached to them, a name to call them. A word that is used to connote an offensive stereotype is a *slur*. Just like stereotypes, these words are very powerful. But sometimes this power can be used for good instead of evil. My wife, LaDonna, provided the perfect example of this.

Now, LaDonna is very religious and very PC. She doesn't just see the world through rose-colored glasses; she grows the roses that you can see through. When we used to drive past the building that housed the Burbank Center for the Retarded, it upset the hell out of her. It's not like it was the Center *Against* the Retarded. That's just her way of seeing things. In other words: She and I are polar opposites, and that's why I adore her.

So LaDonna came up to me all upset one day, and I took it with a grain of salt. "My father called our son, Kyle, a bitch," she said. "I want you to say something to my dad."

I have a very good relationship with my father-in-law, so I wanted to let him explain himself and hear what he had to say. He was happy to tell me what had happened. Apparently Kyle wouldn't help my wife, his *mother*, with the groceries. He wouldn't hold the door open for her. My father-in-law is seventy, so he can't always be helping my wife with heavy bags. Instead, he chose to criticize my son in the bluntest way he could.

Rather than telling the man off, I wanted to shake his hand. I immediately went to go talk to my son. "What did Grandpa say to you?" I asked him.

"That I was acting like a bitch."

"Next time you see your momma or your sister struggling with groceries, or you sit down before they do, that's exactly what you're acting like." My son definitely got the message after that. Now he races to hold the door and helps my wife carry things. He walks her to the car and opens it for her, and he walks into the house first like a gentleman should. He *gets* it. If my father-in-law didn't call him a powerful word, he wouldn't have changed his disrespectful behavior.

There are words you're not supposed to say, *ever*. I don't even mean curse words like "fuck" or "shit." I mean the fact that you can't refer to "bitches" or "hos." You're not supposed to say "retarded" and you're not supposed to say "nigger." The argument goes that these words are so powerful and hurtful that they should never be used. But power isn't always a bad thing. Power is what you use to make a bad situation into a better one. Jennifer Aniston said "retarded," and she got in a ton of trouble for it. Then Lady Gaga said it, and *she* got in trouble. Every other week a celebrity gets in trouble for saying "nigger."

# # #

But how can we avoid words when the living embodiments of them exist? That's the whole *point* of having words—to refer to things that are out there. In 2010, Alvin Greene was the South Carolina Democratic candidate for the United States Senate. The man still lived with his father. Instead of answering reporters' questions, he danced. His idea of fiscal responsibility was to sell dolls that looked like him in order to pay off the national debt.

Isn't he a retarded nigger?

I *know* niggers. I know *a lot* of them. *Every* black person does. If a fight breaks out, I don't want an "African-American." I want a *nigger*—with tight skin, ashy hands, and a bad attitude. It amazes me that it's often people who are not black who want to ban the use of that word. They don't know what it feels like—but I sure as hell do. I've been called a nigger more than once in my life. But is there *anyone* who hasn't been insulted in a nasty, below-the-belt way?

The only time being called a nigger *hurt* was when it came from a famous black comedian. He told me during a conference call, "You wouldn't have this show if it wasn't for me, nigger." This wasn't nig-*ga*: I wasn't his boy. It made me realize for the first time that someone could use the word not to be hurtful, not to be insulting, but out of the literal belief that you are somehow inferior—and the clearest way for this comedian to express that to me was to call me a nigger. In his view, I was a second-class citizen who was beneath him, and supposedly the two of us both knew it. But calling a black man a nigger is like saying "Bloody Mary" in front of a mirror. Say it enough times, and that is exactly who will appear. I told the comedian that if he called me that when I was around, I would slap the shit out of him.

When Dog the Bounty Hunter got caught using that word on a voicemail to his son, I thought the outrage was way out of proportion. He didn't want his son dating outside his race and expressed it in a coarse way. Well, my mother always said, "If she can't share our comb, don't bring her home." My wife says the same thing. Is my family's version better than Dog's because it rhymes? The sentiment is pretty much the same. We're more comfortable opposing "racism" in the form of certain words than we are acknowledging *actual* racism when it exists.

People are so scared of slurs that they freak even when the words are taken completely out of actual context. Max Bretos was suspended for thirty days from ESPN because he was discussing

Jeremy Lin and used the expression "chink in the armor." That expression is so popular that it's a *cliché*. That's how expressions become clichés—they're such a convenient shorthand for a recurring concept that people use them all the time. Bretos, *whose wife is Asian*, was clearly not making a racist reference. The term in that context has *nothing* to do with Chinese people. What possible harm could it have caused? Some Asian people winced when they heard him? I don't bug out when British people talk about their knickers. What's a bigger threat to Chinese people: an ESPN anchor's nonuse of a slur, or the massive human-rights abuses perpetrated by the Chinese government? Ain't that a "bitch"?

The NBA made an example of Kobe Bryant when he told the ref, "Bennie, you're a faggot." Obviously Kobe wasn't really commenting on the ref's sexual orientation, and no one in his right mind would think that he was. But the NBA instantly charged him $100,000 anyway. *$100,000*. There's people who *fight*, who do bodily damage, who don't get a $100,000 fine.

After Kobe's comments, the Lakers had to apologize to the "gay community." Who's the guy who they had to contact to apologize? Who's the ambassador for all gay people? Did the Lakers have to wake up Richard Simmons and get him out of his pink glittery bed to let him know that Kobe called the ref a faggot? Meanwhile, we live in a nation where until very recently it was okay to openly discriminate against gay people. It was not only okay, but it was the official policy of the United States government! It's so *hypocritical*.

We make people apologize for something that they clearly aren't sorry about—and they are apologizing for something they didn't even intend to begin with. Growing up, if two kids got sent to the principal's office for fighting, the principal would make us shake hands in his office—but we knew we were getting it on at three o'clock. We'd smile and apologize to your face now, but we all saw what happened after school. Those false apologies made things *worse*. They're not just hypocrisy; they're *forced* hypocrisy.

Eliminating certain words is part of an attempt to sanitize history, to pretend we solved the racism issue so there is no context for certain words to ever be spoken again. It's sweeping uncomfortable things under the rug. It used to be "offensive" dialects. *Amos 'n' Andy* was satirically brilliant. Groups like the NAACP thought it was so divisive and so stereotypical and so incendiary that they got the show kicked off the air. Those same civil rights groups laud Tyler Perry. How many NAACP Image Awards has he won? These people saying *Amos 'n' Andy* was extreme and dragging down our race are the exact same people saying that what Tyler Perry does is art.

Once they took care of "racist" dialects, they turned their sights on "racist" words—even if they made sense in context. Look at what they're trying to do with Mark Twain's children's books. Mark Twain was a progressive guy. He said, "Not only did you free the slaves, you freed the white man." He gave money to liberal colleges. He was raised a Presbyterian, but he was against religion. He said, "Faith is believing what you know ain't so," and, "If Christ were here now there is one thing he would not be—a Christian." So now they are taking out the word "nigger" from *Huck Finn* and replacing it with "slave." That's *not* the same thing. If you call me a nigger, I could still be very offended as I go back to *my* house in *my* car. If you call me a slave, I gotta go with you. The educators are saying they have no choice, since they're not allowed to teach from books with that word. Clearly, then, they need to change that rule and not tinker with a great classic that puts things in a historical context for kids.

It doesn't stop with slurs. Even now, Texas wants to rewrite its history books so they don't call slavery "slavery." The slave trade would be called the "Atlantic triangular trade." I'm aware of a lot of slurs against blacks, but "triangle" is a new one to me. They want to make it antiseptic because that makes them more comfortable. When Congress recently had a reading of the Constitution, they didn't want to include the three-fifths compromise. Yet the compromise was to *lessen* the effects of slavery, not to increase it. Those slaves could not vote, but were represented in Congress by pro-slavery congressmen. If they let slaves have full representation, then the South would have sent *more* representatives to Washington, and it would have become that much tougher to get rid of slavery. Failing to discuss this and forbidding certain language makes us fail to acknowledge how far we've come. History makes you look at the mirror—and unpleasant language is an important part of history. I'm not uncomfortable with *words*. I'm uncomfortable with people pretending to be who they aren't.

It goes without saying that of all the slurs out there, there is none more incendiary and yet more perfectly constructed than the word "nigger." If something can stand the test of time, fighting off weather, erosion, and social upheaval, then you know it's well built. The Great Pyramid was the tallest building in the world for close to four thousand years. You don't need to be an engineer to know that building is well constructed. That's what the word "nigger" is. It's like the *Mona Lisa* of slurs.

The only thing I don't like about the word "nigger" is that we haven't found a word that makes white people just as uncomfortable. When America and Russia didn't get along, they had enough nukes to kill each other off if shit went down. The policy was called "mutually assured destruction." That's the sort of weapon black people need. We don't need detente. Instead of working to eradicate the word "nigger"—which will never happen—we need to get linguists together to find a word that's just as incendiary for white people. "Cracker" is not going to cut it. White people from the North don't get it, and it sounds too old-fashioned everywhere else. Meanwhile, "nigger" keeps feeling new and improved. By my math, we're up to Nigger 4.0.

People forget that the definition of a racist isn't "someone who uses the word 'nigger.' " I knew a black dude who said that he was going to stop using the word "nigger," or even "nigga," because it made him sound ignorant. What is that, a baptism? "I'm going to dunk you in this water, and all the shit you did before is going to be washed away"? Only a kid believes something as stupid as that. If you stop saying "nigger" but still keep treating people like one, you've just gone from being racist to being a racist hypocrite. *That's not an improvement.*

It works the other way as well. There are plenty of despicable racist jokes that people circulate around e-mail. Those people then say with a straight face, "I didn't mean to be offensive. I had no idea that a black person would get upset that I said he looked like a gorilla. I mean, it's not like I used the n-word."

Racism is an attitude, not a vocabulary test. People want things to be different from the way they are. Well, that's life! It's not what you *want* it to be sometimes. This PC shit is new, but slurs are old. How can a four-hundred-year-old word still be so controversial? "Nigger" has stood the test of time. It's outlasted civilizations—and, I guarantee, it'll be in the dictionaries long after all of us are in the ground.

Using the word "nigger" is the easiest way for a racist to identify himself. It's like a badge of honor for them to say because they're breaking a taboo. They feel strong and defiant—so why the fuck should we be giving these people tools of empowerment? *Suppressing* the word won't suppress the *thought*. But expressing the word might be an opening for a conversation. How can we change minds unless we know their contents?

From a selfish perspective, I'm glad that people are so uncomfortable around slurs and stereotypes. It makes my job as a comedian that much easier, since discomfort is such grist for the comic mill. The entire show *The Office*, for example, is based on awkward, uncomfortable moments. It's like that old line about stand-ups "saying what we're all thinking." When I discuss slurs or stereotypes and people laugh, that's a bit of their tension being released. They are acknowledging thoughts they don't like having but nevertheless cannot deny. *Nothing makes Americans more uncomfortable than race*. I experienced that firsthand when I came to the defense of Don Imus—and instantly became a black sheep.

## CHAPTER 7

IT'S THEIR HUMANNESS THAT HE'S BELITTLING AND DEGRADING, AND IT'S NOT JUST A JOKE.

—PASTOR KYEV TATUM
(ON D.L.'S DEFENSE OF DON IMUS)

TO me, saying someone is a "black comedian" can mean one of two things. It can either mean that a comedian is of African descent, which is simply a genetic fact. But it can also mean a comedian who plays solely to a black audience—and that is not something I ever wanted to be. To be a black comedian in the second sense would really be like being a "black chef." A good chef, just like a good comedian, can tailor his product to a variety of audiences. He should be able to improvise and not have a narrow purview to draw from. Thankfully, I've never been a "black comedian."

Early on in my career, I was supposed to go on a twenty-city tour opening for Harry Belafonte. The first gig was at the Melody Fair in Buffalo, New York. The venue was theater in the round, and to get to the stage I had to walk down this very long ramp. As I was making my way to the stage, I looked over at the crowd. I had never seen so many old white people in my life. It was like a *Golden Girls* rally. Finally, I made it up to the mike. I stared at them, they stared at me. "What the *fuck* are we gonna talk about?" I said.

I killed that night. I probably did end up *actually* killing at least one person there. Statistically speaking, *someone* must have died during my thirty-minute set. But after everyone had a great time and they were all applauding, Harry Belafonte called me into his dressing room. He sat there in a chair, with his back to me. "You're a funny man," he said in that famous raspy voice. "A very funny young man—but you're not for my audience. You won't come back with me for the rest of the tour. I put a call in to Jeffrey Osborne. Tomorrow morning, you're going to get on a plane and you're going to go to Vegas to perform at the Golden Nugget."

The next day, I was staying at a suite at the hotel. I brought La-Donna out with our three small kids, and my mother-in-law came too. I wasn't going to be making much money, so when we ordered room service we were very conservative. When the food came and I went to sign the bill, the room-service dude waved it away. "It's gratis," he said.

"What do you mean?" I asked him.

"It's *gratis*," he repeated. "You don't have to pay, as long as you're performing here."

After that, all fucking bets were off. We ordered so much shit that the *manager* of the Golden Nugget called the room. He gave me an *intervention*, and that too was *gratis*. "We love that you're performing here," he said, "and feel free to order what you want, but you have got to relax. Just *relax*."

That Harry Belafonte show was a learning experience for me. First off, I learned what words like "gratis," "prix fixe," and "per diem" meant. But I also proved that I could perform in front of an entirely white crowd—an entirely white and *old* crowd—and make them laugh. So when I got approached to do a part on *Studio 60 on the Sunset Strip*, I wasn't scared at all. The show was produced by Aaron Sorkin and was supposed to be the Next Big Thing. The series was very insider and was trying to appeal to the type of urban sophisticates who read the *New Yorker*. Clearly, it was going to be a show only watched by white people.

I was on the road when my manager gave me a call. Sorkin was casting the series, and he was red hot after the success of *The West Wing*. "But he can only meet you today," my manager said. They didn't even send over the script. Aaron's assistant called me while I was on the treadmill at the gym. I put my cell on speaker and the guy read me the sides, which was basically the breakdown of the character and the overview of the series as a whole. After I was done with my workout and with the call, I quickly grabbed a shower before heading down to meet Sorkin in his office. I was excited because the cast on the show was spectacular. They had Matthew Perry in there, Amanda Peet, Steven Weber from *Wings*, and Brad Whitford from *The West Wing*.

Sorkin and I talked for about an hour, and he reiterated what the character was. I knew that I could deliver what he wanted, so I bullshitted my way through the conversation as though I had read the whole script. After it was over, I not only got the part but I got named as a producer. I'd be writing some of the comedy, since the series was about comedic actors. I never had to audition, and I know that there were a *lot* of actors who were hungry for the part. I actually didn't end up reading the script until the first day of shooting, and that fact got out somehow. Even now when I take meetings, people will sometimes ask if I read the script this time *for real*.

One of the highlights of the run was working alongside John Goodman. Everyone knows that John is a tall, huge dude, but he is also a superb actor in every way. His character was this racist judge who kept disrespectfully calling my character "Sammy" when his name was actually Simon. This was when John was close to his heaviest, and he kept falling asleep in his chair as we filmed—but it worked for the character. It was a two-part episode, so he and I ended up working together a lot. I thought he was going to die in the middle of shooting because he kept falling asleep and sweating so much; it was horrible. But not only did John not die, obviously, but that performance of his was so outstanding that it garnered him an Emmy nomination.

After the episodes aired, I found out that a really good friend of mine *had* died. Growing up, he lived across the street from me. The funeral was attended by everyone from the old neighborhood. After the service, we all did what black people like to do at these times: We headed to the repast where everyone can eat, laugh, and remember their friend who passed. It's like a big party.

In the back of the house sat my father with all his old cronies. His group is full of the kind of old dudes who put their napkins in their shirt and just hang out talking shit. I ventured over, making conversation, and then my father caught my attention. "I saw your show," he informed me.

"Oh, okay."

"You let that white man talk to you like that?"

"What are you talking about?" I had no clue what he meant—*none.*

"I'm talking about your show. He kept calling you 'Sammy' or 'nigger.' You let that white man talk to you like that?"

Now I realized "that white man" was *John Goodman.* "Daddy, it was a *script.*"

"But it made you mad, didn't it?"

"*Not at all.* I never even thought about it. I promise you it was something that didn't even register, not even a little."

"I can't believe this," my father said. "Are you going to tell me that man is going to keep calling out your name, and you didn't care?"

"Daddy, it's a *script.* They wrote it; I was the guy; I did it. I thought it was great. It was some of the best and most challenging acting I've ever had to do, and I was working with the pros. It was *great.*"

My father is not a funny dude. He's *never* been a jokester. The way he speaks to people, especially me, is gruff. When I visited him in the hospital one time, the *first* thing out of his mouth was a sarcastic: "Wow, the superstar is here to visit his dad." But what he was saying was *absurd,* even given my relationship with him. I knew that he understood that a television was not a window, that he wasn't looking through the glass at something that was happening outside at that exact moment. Yet I started to realize that, crazy as it sounded, he was actually serious about what he was saying.

I looked at his buddies to see their reactions. All I saw was a bunch of old dudes eating and looking around, drinking their beers as if nothing was going on. "I bet it pissed you off," my father insisted.

"Charlie," old Mr. Russell said, "that's *enough.* Leave the boy alone"—"the boy," of course, meaning me, a grown man in his forties with his wife in the other room helping people serve food. I talked to Mr. Russell for a little while and then I just left them all sitting there. I told LaDonna what had happened, and she wanted me to let it go. "Oh, come on," she said. "He's an old man. Leave him be, he's set in his ways."

He was older, sure, but he wasn't feeble. He wasn't suffering from dementia, where he wasn't aware of what he was saying. I don't think age is an excuse for bad behavior in general and it certainly wasn't in this case in particular. My relationship with my father hadn't been great before that, but this was the first time he'd ever been *mean*. He wasn't just mean, he was *insistently* mean. He usually didn't give a fuck and eventually kind of let me go, but not this time. This time he dug in and he wasn't going to back off. To this day, our relationship hasn't recovered.

My wife was wrong about why he said what he did. It wasn't that my father was set in his ways. He and I simply had a fundamental difference of opinion. When I was the only black guy on *Studio 60*, I viewed that as a source of pride. I could be myself in South Central, and I could be myself in a meeting with Aaron Sorkin. The more rooms a man can feel comfortable in, the more places where he is welcomed in as a person, the greater the opportunities for him to see the world and to explore and learn about it.

My father clearly didn't see things that way. I wasn't "crossing over." In fact, I don't think he even had a concept of what "crossing over" would look like to him. It *bothered* him that I was on that series. He wasn't alone. It bothered *a lot* of other people to a greater or lesser degree. From their perspective, I was simply a token. I was Isaac on *The Love Boat*, and I had promised myself that I would never be Isaac or some other sort of caricature.

# # #

I've experienced this sort of narrow thinking at various points in my career. When I got my show on CNN in 2008, I was proud that I had become the first comic to have a series on that channel. Yet when I called into Al Sharpton's radio show to promote it, I got heat for my choice. "Why you got to do it on CNN? How come you can't do it on BET?" Well, why am I talking to you about what I want to do with my career? How come I can't do what the fuck I want to do?

No matter who you are, freedom means having more choices *by definition*. It doesn't mean going from having one, and only one, shitty option to having one, and only one, *great* option. I am certain that later in her life, Rosa Parks *sometimes* sat in the back of the bus. Maybe she liked the view or whatever. I am certain that after segregation laws were repealed, black people *sometimes* sat in the back of the Woolworth's counter. Maybe those were the only seats available.

I've had this kind of racial criticism several times in my career. I understood it, but I have never agreed with it in the slightest. Early on, I did BET's *Comedy View* and then *Def Jam*. Both were all black. Then I was an actor on the series *Double Rush*, which was created by *Murphy Brown*'s Diane English. When we first did *The Hughleys*, it was on right before *Home Improvement*. Depending on what TV series I was on at the time, my stand-up crowd would change color. When I started doing frequent appearances on *Politically Incorrect*, for example, the audience got whiter. Picasso had his Blue Period, and I would have my white periods.

All the varied contexts I was involved in informed my perspective. I read different things from what I'd read before. I started including more jokes about current events in my set, and a lot of political material. My scope was not as narrow. It wasn't as much about "being black" anymore. My focus was on experiences that I had and that I thought were interesting.

After one set with a mixed crowd, my road manager pulled me aside. "Man, you see this?" he said.

"See what?"

"You're losing your black audience, man. You should just stick to the shit that we've been doing."

It would be one thing if I was losing my audience, period. If I wasn't selling tickets, then something was clearly wrong with my material or my performance or my publicity. But to claim that selling tickets to a whiter crowd was *bad* made no sense to me. If I made a person laugh, if I made them get in their car, buy a ticket, and sit down and listen to me talk—and they enjoyed the experience—*then I've done my job*. As a black man, am I somehow not entitled to enjoy Spanish food or sushi or Italian food? That's an absurdity. But I would argue that humor is *as* universal as food is. You can judge how content a community is by how easily its people laugh. Laughter is much more indicative of a thriving society than material concerns.

My loyalty is always to the truth, not to a race. I don't think of myself primarily as a *black* comedian or as a black *comedian*. I think of myself primarily as *myself*. And sometimes, being yourself can cost. I learned *that* the hard way.

# # #

I am no stranger to having jokes backfire. In the early '90s I was a sidekick on an L.A. radio station run by Stevie Wonder called KJLH. One day on the air I made the mistake of saying, "Do you think this station would be this raggedy if Stevie Wonder could see?" Forty-five minutes later, Stevie Wonder came barging through the door and he was *livid*. He must have driven his car down to KJLH as fast as he could, honking at all the people on the sidewalk to get the fuck out of his way.

He started dressing me down. Of course I'd always loved Stevie Wonder, so to have an icon like that yell at you was more weird than anything. He kept going on about how it was disrespectful and it wasn't funny, and that I don't understand. Maybe I shouldn't have pointed out that I was sitting over *here*, and not where he was yelling over *there*.

I was so fired.

As a comic, I say incendiary stuff *all the time*. I have the right to tell a shitty joke or to be offensive, and I refuse to take away a right that I enjoy from somebody else. I've defended Tracy Morgan and I've defended Rush Limbaugh. Going back further, I defended John Rocker in *The Original Kings of Comedy*. I am *consistent*. But when I defended Don Imus, shit hit the fan.

Imus had called the Rutgers women's basketball team a bunch of "nappy-headed hos." They weren't hos, but they sure were nappy-headed. I defy a sister to play basketball for four quarters and keep a perm. You start out looking like Halle Berry, and by that fourth quarter it's Ben Wallace. But America wasn't interested in hearing any more jokes. A women's college basketball team had been insulted! Our country was in *crisis*! A joke? *Women's basketball?* Those terms should *never* appear together!

My defense of Don Imus was as follows: I thought that what he said was hurtful; I thought it was malicious; I thought it was a bad joke on a slow news week. I wasn't defending Don Imus the *person*. I was defending his *right* to say something dumb. If

Americans have earned no other right, it's the right to say something dumb.

I've been asked, "How would you like it if your daughters got called that?" My reply: "My daughters would know what they were and what they weren't. I didn't prepare them for the world that I wished existed; I prepared them for the world that I believed *did* exist. I always told them it's never what you're called, it's what you answer to." Is it more prudent to prepare your children for real life, or for a made-up fantasy world where everything is great and people love each other and respect each other? If I'm wrong, even better. I've prepared them for a bad scenario that will never come. It's a *good* thing if you have a fire drill but no fires. That's just insurance.

But few were hearing what I was saying. I had to argue with Al Sharpton about it. Everybody was angry and no one would talk to me. It was the first time I'd ever had any kind of interaction with the black community where I wasn't their darling. Yet it never occurred to me that saying what I believed would draw this kind of ire. Steve Harvey wouldn't let me on his show, because he said black women were mad at me. I could see why. He plays specifically to that audience, and he wasn't about to have it jeopardized.

Many people wanted me to apologize, but I didn't feel like I had done anything wrong and I wasn't going to. I knew I could take it. What I now know about myself is that I'm tough. I can last. I'm not scared to give an ass-whupping, and I'm not scared to take one. I'm not scared to be wrong; I'm not scared to be right. Even now, if you Google my name you'll see people are still talking shit about it—and I don't care. Any fear or reservations that I had about saying *anything* that I wanted to onstage died during this period.

If I *had* apologized, it would have made my comments more

sinister than they were. It would have meant that I had something to apologize *for*. To me, I was being more *ironic* than I was *malicious*. Apologizing would have given my critics credence. It would also have changed my whole mindset—a mindset based on feeling comfortable being uncomfortable.

Apologizing is not the answer to controversy. *Honesty* is the answer. I defended Tracy Morgan when he went on about how he'd stab his son if the kid turned out gay. I said Tracy should have never apologized. Not only did he end up apologizing, but he had to do it more than once. Every week it seemed like he was sorry again. But was he sorry for his views, or for the reaction that they caused? He may have expressed himself in a particularly incendiary way, but what he meant was pretty straightforward and uncontroversial.

A similar thing happened in my family. In 2011, my nephew came out of the closet. He came out to his mother, and then he came out to my wife. He came out to his father and my kids and his sister. I don't know why he felt the need to come out, because he goes to Morehouse and he designs women's dresses. I've *known* he was gay. I've never judged him and I've always loved him. He and I are very, very, very close. Yet the last person he came out to was me. "Why am I the last person in the family that you're telling?" I asked him.

He didn't really know what to say. "It was difficult to tell you," he finally said.

"There's two things I want you to understand," I told him. "First off, I will love you no matter what you do. I want you to be safe and happy. I want you to know that. And second, I'm glad you're not my son." He stopped and he laughed. Then I called his father to tease him about his son making dresses. That's all I could do.

I meant both things that I told my nephew. I *am* going to love him unconditionally. It's just the extra bullshit I didn't want. *Everybody* wants it easy. The coward lives to tell how the brave man died. It's *easier* for my kids to marry people of the opposite gender. Everywhere in the world, everything seeks the easiest route. The lion goes for the easiest gazelle to kill. Even water automatically finds the easiest path to flow, that of least resistance.

Forcing comedians to apologize doesn't even make sense on a strategic level. Everyone remembers Imus's comments and the brouhaha, but people forget what the consequences to his actions were. First of all, they had to pay off his contract. I don't give a fuck what you did that caused the networks to succumb to public pressure. You still get your money. Even Charlie Sheen got paid off. So Imus didn't lose any income.

Six months later, Imus got a new show with a bigger audience on more stations than the show he had before. His *agent* couldn't have done as well by him as his critics did. Every radio show's *goal* is to have as much of an audience as possible. In other words, a show's success is directly tied to how much *attention* it gets!

There's a reason comedy and tragedy are so often tied together, two sides of the same coin. By trying to destroy Imus, his foes ended up making him a bigger success. Isn't that absurd? Isn't that ironic? *And aren't absurdity and irony two of the greatest sources of comedy?* We really only have two choices in life: We can either take a joke—or we can end up as the punch line. Sadly, the more contemporary civil rights leaders focus on frivolous throwaway comments like Imus's, the less powerful they are in fighting actual grievances. It's exactly like the Boy Who Cried Wolf.

The attacks on Imus set a terrible example. The message was: *If you say the wrong thing about race, then you will be vilified.* Even though it worked out for him, I'm sure Imus didn't like the gauntlet he had to run to get there. But since this is such an uncomfortable subject to begin with, many aren't sure what "the wrong thing" *is*. As a result, they avoid the subject altogether.

It wasn't always this way. Black sitcoms, for example, were universally beloved. But nowadays there are *no* black shows on network television—and I would wager that there probably won't be any in the near future. My show, *The Hughleys*, was among the last of this dying breed.

## CHAPTER 8

THE NAACP SUPPORTS A PERSON'S RIGHT TO DO WHATEVER THEY FEEL THEY MUST DO.

—KWEISI MFUME

ORIGINALLY, the civil rights movement was focused on getting minorities a place at the table. That was the case literally, as in segregated public establishments, and it was the case figuratively, with regard to business opportunities. So extending civil rights boils down to one simple and easy question: Does a certain action make it *easier* for a group to achieve, or does it make it *harder*?

People realize intuitively that getting your own television show is very hard. But have contemporary civil rights leaders made it easier for minorities to get their own shows—or have they made it harder?

In other words, have they maintained the spirit of the movement, or have they turned the movement against its own people? I know how I would answer that question, and I am speaking based on my own experience.

In 1992 I didn't have my own show yet, but I did have a family and I needed insurance. To get insurance from AFTRA, the actors' union, you have to make a certain amount of money in a year. I found out that *The Fresh Prince of Bel-Air* was looking for a comedian to warm up the audience before taping and during breaks. It wasn't a great gig, but it was a *paying* gig.

I was waiting in the production office's lobby when Myles, one of the writers, came walking in. "What are you here for?" he asked me.

"I'm here to audition for the warm-up job," I told him.

"I've seen you on TV, and I've seen you out in Philly. You got the job."

My primary gig was to keep the audience abreast of the script. "In this scene Will's going to make fun of Carlton's dancing again." If the script wasn't funny, I just started telling jokes. Pretty soon, the crowd would be laughing so hard that the writers had a problem. "Hey, man, you're funnier than the script," one of the staff told me. "You just need to keep the audience abreast of what's going on. Don't do any jokes."

But I wouldn't listen. It was the audience to a *comedy* show and I had a microphone; I'm going to be telling jokes. That's just all there is to it. I would have at it and I was *slaying* them, Jack. I didn't care who walked around the stage; I would call them out and tease them mercilessly. It was completely in good fun and there was never anything malicious about it. But people in Hollywood have thin skins and inflated egos, and it often takes just a pinprick to pop that self-important balloon.

Myles would let me know that it was driving the show's writers *nuts*. "I hate him! He's vulgar." But we all knew it wasn't my foul mouth that was the issue. It got to Will, too. It was *his* show, after all, and he didn't like that his opening act was upstaging him on his own set. One time he and I started going back and forth right in front of everybody. He started coming up the stairs to me so we could battle. "Stay down there," I told him. "That's your world. Up here's my world. Don't mess around."

"Give me a microphone," he said. "Give me a microphone!"

Quickly they scurried to find him a mike, and I just stood there amazed. "Before that thought gets finished running around in your big-ass fucking head," I told him, "come over here and ring the starting bell. *Ding!*"

The audience just erupted, and Will was paralyzed. There was nothing he could say, but I can't imagine this kind of thing was appreciated. The show was like one big family, but I already had a family and I didn't need another one. I even refused to let my kids visit the set despite how much they were dying to meet the Fresh Prince. LaDonna thought that was petty. She thought everybody would love the kids, but she thinks everybody loves everybody anyway. But from my perspective, my children are *my* children and *my* responsibility. I heap love and praise on them. I didn't want to expose them to the industry, and particularly people who make a living pretending to be somebody else. I don't mean Will, I mean actors in general. Their gig is to pretend to be someone that they're not. That's not only a skill set, it's a character flaw.

Will would make everybody come into the office to do cheers and that kind of stuff, but I wouldn't do it. I would get the script, go sit in the bleachers, and read it. Obviously my attitude didn't endear me to the higher-ups. After a while they started playing music between scenes so I couldn't talk. They thought I was being insolent, and I thought I was doing my job and being funny. Maybe there was some truth to both of our sides.

The last straw was one day when I was doing introductions. When it came time for me to introduce Alfonso Ribeiro, his father told me to roll the R's. I didn't, because I *couldn't*. The producers thought I was being a dick, but I really couldn't pronounce it. That gave them the excuse they wanted to fire me.

One month later, Will called me back himself. "Come on, D.L.," he said, "I want you to come back."

I knew that meant that whoever replaced me had been *horrible*. But the experience had been needlessly shitty for me, too. "No, man," I told him. "They treated me fucked up."

"Just give it a try."

I knew that if the star of the show was calling me back, then no one else really had the power to fire me. After that, I could do whatever I wanted. I wasn't taking a lot of shit, but I had insurance. The experience really soured me on getting my own show, which is purportedly every comedian's dream. But I always wanted to do a late-night talk show, not a sitcom.

Sure enough, the opportunity presented itself. NBC's *Later* was going through guest hosts, and I threw my hat into the ring. The network execs were hesitant. They said that they couldn't understand me because I talked too bad, so my manager set up a meeting simply so they could hear me speak. As I was chitchatting about my recent experiences moving into a white neighborhood, my manager slammed his hand on the table. "Fuck that," he said. "You got an idea for a series here. They're going to let you guest-host this, that's fine, but I'm going to get you a series."

And that's exactly what he did.

The way we pitched *The Hughleys* was by telling the executives stories from my life, and that strategy worked. Every network bid, and we ended up going with ABC. We shot the pilot, and it got picked up for a full season. In many ways it was like a traditional sitcom, although in our case *everyone* was everyone else's wacky neighbor because of the differences in race.

After the first season, we were doing really well and we thought we were going to get renewed. While I was waiting to hear, I found out that another new ABC show called *Sports Night* had gotten its order in for another season. An Aaron Sorkin series, *Sports Night* was critically acclaimed, but it just wasn't doing well ratings-wise. ABC renewed it as a token of goodwill to Aaron, who's a brilliant writer (and who I would later work with on *Studio 60*, as I mentioned).

I had lunch about this time with Jamie Tarses, then head of ABC's entertainment division. She was talking about *Sports Night* but wasn't letting me know shit about *The Hughleys*. "We're the number-one new comedy on ABC," I reminded her. "Am I gonna get picked up?"

I guess that's not the typical Hollywood approach, to flat-out ask an executive like that. "I can't guarantee you," she said, "but I'd be *shocked* if you weren't picked up. You know how it is." She started to explain the process.

"Jamie, I've been a nigger for a long time. It's just new to *you*." I was used to living on the periphery, living as an afterthought. It wasn't surprising that a white show that we were outperforming would get picked up, and would get decided upon *first*.

Eventually, though, we did get the order for another season. But before we could start shooting, there was another major problem for me to address. I had created the show, and I was the producer.

As the producer, I was privy to the show's budget—and I saw that *everybody* was making more money than me. I had no idea what was happening, but that didn't make sense to me. The show was *The Hughleys*. It was *my* show about *my* life, and I needed to make more money than everybody—not the other way around.

My lawyer called the network and told them that I was too sick to go to work. I wasn't coming in until the budget was adjusted in a way that made more sense. The network said no. They said they couldn't pay me more, so sure enough I didn't come in to work. They could have made it happen if they just gave me what I wanted. But instead, they gave me something I *didn't* really want.

The Cadillac Escalade had just come out, and *everyone* knows black men like Escalades almost as much as we like smoking crack and raping white women. The next morning, sitting in my drive-way was a brand-new Escalade. At first I couldn't believe that the network thought that would work. Then I realized that for some other people, it *had* worked. Don King made a career out of moves like that. He would show up to meet poor, black athletes with a briefcase full of money and a contract. They would get the money if they signed on the spot—but the contract had a stipulation that the briefcase of money was a loan to be paid back. So sometimes, flashy bribes worked.

This wasn't one of those times.

I kept the Cadillac but never drove it. ABC ended up taking cash from everybody who was making more than me and gave me a pretty big raise. My illness miraculously cured, I returned to work. This was the era when audiences started getting more and more divided, and they didn't really know what to do with a show like *The Hughleys*. It wasn't a black show but it wasn't a white show, either. That caused a lot of drama, which is not a good thing for a comedy.

Of course we had creative differences, but that's part of the process. It's those kinds of arguments that drive you crazy at the time, but you look back upon them fondly. The writers kept wanting to put me in a dress on the show, and I kept saying no. That battle I won. They wanted me to chase a chicken, and ain't no way in the fuck that I'm chasing a chicken. For that one we compromised and my costar chased the bird around. They had a musical episode, and they got me over on that one. We did the whole song and dance, literally. But at the end I got to hold up a sign that said THE WHITE MAN MADE ME DO IT!

We moved to TGIF, ABC's family night that featured *Full House* and *Step by Step*, but we were an edgy, urban show. On the one hand, our "Why Can't We Be Friends" episode was shown as part of an army department's racial-sensitivity training. On the other hand, I got death threats because we did a show about guns, and people didn't like what we had to say. This was before Twitter and Facebook, so people couldn't contact you directly. You had to go out of your way and read the message boards to find out that someone was calling you a nigger.

People got upset with us *all the time*. We had a Christmas episode, and the story flashed back to when I was a little boy and the first time it snowed in L.A. I dreamt that Santa Claus came, and we had Isaac Hayes playing St. Nick. Later in the story, my son had the same dream and Isaac Hayes came back. The posts were immediate: "My children woke up and they asked me if Santa Claus was black!" What can you tell people like that? *Of course* Santa Claus is not black. He's not *Jesus*. But Santa isn't white, either. *He's not real.*

For four years, working on the show was a struggle. I don't mean there was more bad than good, because there wasn't. One of my writers put it best: "There were too many people making an easy job hard." I had the best crew, the best support people; people I'm very close to to this day. I loved coming to work to see the people, but I *despised* the process. It drained me and took everything out of me.

I'd always kind of thought of myself as a freethinker. And as bright as I thought I was, they just didn't agree. They would humor me, smile, and then do whatever the fuck they were planning on doing. There wasn't a discussion; it was a placating, patronizing situation. From what we ate to what we wore, we would have these internal skirmishes that made me feel like a child.

No one made it harder than the president of the studio that produced *The Hughleys*. George was gay, but specifically that very bitchy type of gay. He wanted me to change the way I pronounce my name. He thought *Hewg-lee* was too hard for marketing, so I should pronounce it *Hew-ley*. He wanted to cover the birthmark on my cheek. Whenever George wanted me to not do something, he would act as if it didn't come from him but from the network. It took me a while to figure out that game. I was hands-on, so I would go to the writers' meetings and the table reads. If I got a note from "the network," I would tell the director or the writer why I wanted to do things differently from their note.

"What note?" they'd ask.

"Didn't you just tell David to move the sofa?" I said, or whatever it was that week.

"No . . . "

The problems kept coming whenever group decisions had to be made. In one episode in particular, my character's son was supposed to have a crush on a girl who was his babysitter. When it came time for casting, I thought one girl was *stunningly* beautiful. Not only did little boys have a crush on her, but this here big boy did, too.

Yet according to "the network," she was too dark. George

thought that wasn't beautiful. I was like, "Why am I arguing with you to decide what's hot? You're *gay*. When I see that girl, I want to fuck her!" They brought a lighter woman in, and it *killed* me. I knew that that dark, gorgeous beauty had heard the same thing a million times before, and my show was just the latest in a long line of unfair and outrageous rejections.

When I started to grow my hair out, George didn't want me to. He wanted me to cut it and kept telling me so. I did the smart thing: I got a doctor's note saying that I had alopecia, and that my hair was covering up my bald spots. *George wanted to look at my scalp.* He just wouldn't let my haircut go. Week after week, he wouldn't let it go, wouldn't let it go, wouldn't let it go. It was constant snide, bitchy comments from him. In September 2001, we were doing a table reading. Out of nowhere but as usual, George asked, "Why do you do your hair like that?"

I lost it, like for real. I didn't just lose my temper; I lost my fucking mind. I jumped up and slapped that table. "Goddammit!" I screamed at him. "I'ma fuck you up!" I literally chased him out of the building. If I'd have caught him, I would have beat the shit out of him. Security had to get involved.

That was a bad day.

To George's credit, he ended up apologizing. He said if he had to do it all over again, he would never have handled me that way. I can't imagine what the look on my face was like when I was chasing after him, but let's just say that I imagine it wasn't very family-friendly.

But there's no way a show like *The Hughleys* could be on network TV today. The culture won't allow it. Before cable, some of the biggest TV stars were black. Emmanuel Lewis, Gary Coleman, and Redd Foxx were huge celebrities for *all* Americans. At one point, Sherman Helmsley was the highest-paid actor in television. Now

TV has become very divided and myopic. We don't all watch the same type of shows, and we don't all have the same popular culture. It's more segregated than it's ever been before, with very, very micro audiences. Those were probably more turbulent times politically and socially, but people were more accepting from an *entertainment* standpoint.

# # #

Nowadays, the black community can be our own worst enemy with regard to entertainment. The NAACP will declare something a "stereotypical" show, say that they don't want to see those types of images—and basically get a whole crew of people fired. After two years on ABC, *The Hughleys* moved to UPN. UPN was in many ways a black network and part of the growing segregation of television. One show that the network had green-lit at the same time we were on was called *The Secret Diary of Desmond Pfeiffer.* The title character was a slave who was smarter than everybody in the room. *Nobody got the point.*

To produce a show that "makes light" of slavery was regarded as such a blunder that the series is held up to ridicule to this day. But if humor is based on the absurd, is there anything more absurd than the idea that one grown man can own another grown man? The very premise is preposterous. Though slavery has been over for more than a century, 1998 was apparently too soon to poke fun at it. Yet while Europe was still coming to terms with the Holocaust, Americans were laughing at the bumbling Nazis in *Hogan's Heroes.* *Desmond Pfeiffer* was so controversial that it was taken off the air after less than a month. The network never let it breathe and never let it grow.

I had to deal with the same kinds of issues over the four-year run of *The Hughleys*—as if there wasn't enough to deal with from the studio. Every season, they would roll the show out and the media would come and ask us questions. They had these up-fronts in New York and in Los Angeles. Many times it was more like I was being interrogated and asked to defend myself. There was one particular black *Los Angeles Times* reporter who just didn't like the way that I was portraying things, and we developed a very antagonistic relationship, arguing with each other. It was always "Why is *this* black?" and "Why is this *not* black?" with him.

It was the same thing with NAACP president (and former congressman) Kweisi Mfume. I got into it with him and with a lot of other civil rights people. Their position was that we had to "protect" what images people see on the screen in an entertainment. My position is that the NAACP should concentrate on making thing better through civil rights and not through what entertainment we see. I don't know of any NAACP board members or civil rights leaders who ever wrote scripts. They have as much business telling me how to write a sitcom as I do telling Kweisi Mfume how to petition the government.

What do civil rights leaders have to do with art? What do they have to do with perception? Art *by definition* is supposed to make people uncomfortable. Art, true art, by definition is open to different interpretations. I remember when Gabriel Byrne played the devil in *End of Days*. If Denzel Washington had played the devil, there would have been mayhem. "Why a black man gotta be the devil?" Well, why can't a black man be an *actor*? Or a writer, or an artist, or whatever? Why does Kweisi Mfume or *any* man get to decide what is "black" for somebody else?

If a producer hires an actor, that actor should be allowed to succeed or fail based on his own merit. Instead he's set up to fail by his so-called "brothers." One thing activists do is they get *loud*. When you're working on a show, it's enough of a pain in the ass to get notes from the network. Now you've got to get notes from Kweisi Mfume? It's no wonder why every single time there is a television show involving race, even a sitcom, there's a level of controversy associated with it—which means some network president now has to explain himself. After a while, the executives get tired of it and it's easier just to not have black actors there. When you look at why black people aren't represented on television, civil rights leaders have a big hand in that. They are participating in our removal from television. We haven't had a black drama in *decades*, if ever. It's too serious and too touchy. *Roots* was the closest thing. They technically classified that as a miniseries, even though it sure as hell was a drama to *us*.

These leaders try to pretend that current crimes perpetrated by black people don't exist *now*. If the only black images you see on TV are nice, professional, yuppie black people, that's a false kind of racism. In real life, human beings see black people at their best and then black people at their worst. We're Barack Obama *and* we're Flavor Flav. Both are *real*. To claim that Flavor Flav or representations of his type shouldn't be seen in media is to render a whole section of the black community invisible. That's how our *opponents* wanted it, for decades.

To suppress harmful imagery in the media is straight propaganda. It was the case when President Bush stifled pictures of the body bags coming out of Iraq—and it's the case when the NAACP stifles images of inner-city crime. If a person from a foreign land turned on our television, he would conclude that every white person had a black best friend . . . and every act of crime is committed by a poorly dressed WASP.

I know more cats who are hustling out there, trying to do whatever they can to get by, than I do people with MBAs. I probably know more dope dealers than I do doctors. Mind you, both of them do well and both serve a purpose. Just because an image of a black dope dealer or a black doctor is on TV doesn't mean the show's creators are supporting it or endorsing it. It just kind of *is*.

When Jamie Foxx did *Booty Call,* everybody talked about how stereotypical the movie was. People forget his silly Wanda character from *In Living Color.* Yet that was part of his journey on the way to doing *Ray.* If he had stopped with *Booty Call,* it would have cut his career short. His path almost exactly parallels Tom Hanks's. Hanks got his start doing drag nonsense on *Bosom Buddies.* Now he's a multiple Oscar winner. The stupid stuff paves the way for the great stuff. You can't eat fancy food all the time; sometimes you just want a burger and fries, and it's perfectly okay. There is a lack of consistency between how black actors are treated compared to white actors, by the very people who supposedly care for them. This schizophrenic approach even fights against itself. When *The Color Purple* came out, it was extremely controversial. Nine months later, activists were just as angry that it didn't win any Oscars.

When I had my CNN show, one of the skits I did was about Fannie Mae and Freddie Mac and how they were pimping us. The reaction was extreme and immediate. It's gotten to the point that you have to be so literal that you can't even tell a joke that's nuanced. It's like how McDonald's coffee has to have a warning label that lets you know that the hot coffee is hot, and that hot liquid and your bare skin are not friends. We're coming to a point where every joke has to have a disclaimer on the screen that announces, "By the way, I'm joking!" That's even more insulting than telling an offensive joke. I was on Facebook during Hurricane Irene, and I was talking about how the authorities were having problems with evacuations. People were refusing to leave, thinking nothing bad was going to happen to them. Well, I posted, that's because Irene is not a threatening name. My favorite aunt is named Irene. They should have called it Hurricane Mohammed and watched the people flee.

The comments came immediately: "That's not funny!" "Being black, you should understand that that's hurtful." Well, something can be hurtful *and* it can still be funny. Laughter is involuntary, just like tears. When you see someone fall, one of the first things you do is turn around and cover your mouth, because you don't want to laugh right then and there. That laughter just snatches itself from your mouth involuntarily.

My father got hit by a train when I was a teenager. He was on his way to work at Crenshaw and 120th. *Somehow* the train came behind the factory, he went across, and the gate didn't go up. Whatever it was, it was a perfect storm of bullshit. I came home and my father was in bed all bruised up, with a sling on. "While you was out fucking around," he told me, "I got hit by a train." I couldn't stop laughing. I didn't know if he had internal bleeding, or a broken leg, but I knew this motherfucker got hit by a train. He gets mad at me to this day because of that reaction, but it wasn't like I did it *intentionally*. It wasn't like I *wanted* my father to get hit by a train—not that night, at least. It was just a reaction. We're not that delicate as a society that jokes are going to do us in. I've never thought black people were that delicate as a community. We survived beatings, discrimination, and lynchings. We're not going to be done in by *punch lines* and *pictures*.

There most definitely is a role for civil rights leaders in our society. They should do what they do best, which is making the world

better for whoever is getting discriminated against at work. If someone tries to introduce a rebel flag somewhere, they should be on
the scene like the motherfucking fire department. That's their bai-
liwick. But in terms of trying to force perceptions on TV and film
that they believe to be redemptive, it's impossible. It's like grabbing
smoke. Who the fuck can do that? My community suffers far out of
proportion to any other American community. We need help. But
leadership is a function of the times. FDR, Lincoln, and Washington would not have been as great as they were if they didn't have
these profound crises to navigate us through.

It's the same thing with civil rights figures. America as a nation has gotten slower, stupider, and softer. We've regressed—and
the people representing our civil rights leadership have necessarily
regressed too. Their causes are not clear-cut, and their goals are not
as transparent. This brings me to my next point: the moral decline
of black leaders in America.

## CHAPTER 9

DR. KING'S GENERAL PRINCIPLES ARE UNIVERSAL, BUT THE THINGS HE CONFRONTED TOOK PLACE IN ANOTHER ERA.

—AL SHARPTON

G REAT men are a function of great moments in time—and no one doubts that Martin Luther King was the greatest of our civil rights leaders. His greatness was a function of his era. Imagine being surrounded by all those transformative, historical figures: Earl Warren, Thurgood Marshall, the Kennedys, J. Edgar Hoover. All these people were *transcendent. Everything* was in flux. It was the fork in the road for this country. America was choosing whether it was going to be what it said it was. One way or another, we were having it out. It was the battle for the soul of our country. King was the right guy at the right time in the right situation.

I think that he understood the importance of his moment, and it overwhelmed him. He felt called to duty by the times because he knew that he could actually pull it off. But he also saw the flipside of the situation. Generally, people who change the world and make it better for all mankind don't live to be ninety-something years old. Look at how messed up Chairman Mao, Pinochet, Mubarak, and all these people are. They live a *long* time. They live longer than the average black male lives in the United States. When you're changing the status quo and bucking the trend, you're doing something different. And if you try to make things different, there are going to be people who like the way things are just fine. They're going to make sure things happen to you—and often, those things have the most dire consequences possible.

So when King said, "I may not get there with you," he understood what that would mean. It wasn't just a figure of speech for him. He knew that he would die for what he was doing, and he was willing to pay the cost. If you know that something will cost you your life and it ain't worth it, you stop. I don't mean cost you your life *eventually*, like smoking cigarettes or driving drunk. I'm talking about either you quit this shit right here, or somebody is going to put a bullet in your head *for real*. They weren't fucking around with him. And that attitude, that defiance at the greatest possible cost, is generally what it takes to make the world move forward.

King framed what had previously been a political issue as a *moral* conflict. Protecting people's right to vote, like protecting their right to speak or to worship, is a moral issue. That's why it's referred to as the "right" to vote, in the same way we talk about the right to free speech and religion. It's not a voting *privilege* or a voting *waiver*.

Rights are not up for political discussion. Politics is what happens *after* everyone has a seat at the table. Once everyone's inside, *then* discussion can begin. King realized that, and he realized that he had to paint matters so vividly that any decent person would know he was right. Eventually even *indecent* people knew he was right. They got it—they just didn't care.

It's very easy for someone on a moral crusade to sound pompous and off-putting. The very word "crusade" has a negative, hostile connotation. So King needed to make sure people would listen to him—and he accomplished that with his humility and his very public and explicit appreciation for his predecessors. The thing about being American is that we generally believe history begins and ends with us. But King had read about Gandhi and other movements that had situations similar to his, and he learned from them. He applied foreign thinking and refined it for an American context—much the way the founding fathers did with the writing of the Constitution, right?

In one sense, Gandhi's task was more impressive than King's and more difficult to pull off. If you can make the mightiest empire in the world leave your country without fighting it, then you're a bad motherfucker. The British Empire was so massive that they brazenly pointed out that the sun never set on it—*and they were telling the truth*. It spanned the whole globe. Gandhi defiantly told them to GTFO, and that he was willing to do whatever, *peacefully*, it took. If *that* great achievement was possible, then surely making some rednecks back off was feasible—and you can keep your shirt on, and you ain't got to wear that robe or go on a hunger strike. No other black leader had such a grasp of what came before him as King did.

Martin Luther King was as bright as the people who were competing against him. He was not only an intellect but an orator. At that time it was very, very rare to have a black man that well-spoken, someone who changed minds regardless of the listener's background. The people who were opposing him were degenerate rednecks. People heard them, and then they heard him, and it was like, "Wait a minute . . . "

Sadly, nowadays King has come to be known as "white people's favorite black person." I think there's two big reasons for that. On the one hand, he is such a popular figure. You don't need to know anything about him other than his name, and no one will question you. You can pretend you admire him, because admiring him is a given. On the other hand, many of the things he was saying were profound, universal truths. Republican candidates are quoting Martin Luther King. His words weren't specifically for a group or for a person or for a slogan. They were for *human beings*.

Yet when Martin Luther King was alive, the parents of some of those very people who now celebrate him regarded him as a troublemaker—and that goes for black *and* white. People who are so close to it don't have the power of perspective. They released Jackie Kennedy's tapes in 2011, and she didn't necessarily like King. It's like how chemo makes you sicker before it makes you better. When people do something selfless and good, sometimes they have to be dead for a little while before they're appreciated. History has to have time before someone's contributions can be fully appreciated.

That certainly is the case with Martin Luther King's counterpart, Malcolm X. Martin Luther King was very general. He wanted the world better for *everybody*. For him, you shouldn't judge a person by the color of his skin but by the content of his character. Malcolm X's agenda was much less universal. For black people, he was that same sort of romanticized figure as Nat Turner. He was a man of the people, and those "people" were *us*.

From what I have read and understand, Malcolm X wasn't big on integration. He never thought that was the way forward. His stance was, "You leave us alone, and we'll find our way." That's why for whites—and for many blacks at the time—he was the boogeyman. It's no accident that there's that iconic photo of him looking out the window, holding a machine gun, saying, *By any means necessary.* Malcolm X was another man who knew he would die for his beliefs, who knew what they would cost him.

Malcolm X was as intellectual as King, and equally aware of history. He just came up with a different conclusion. History taught Malcolm X that you fight fire with fire. History taught him that you should be feared, and that fear begets respect. He didn't want black people to suffer abuses at the hands of outsiders. He wanted to fight and let his opponents know that there wasn't going to be an easy win. There are a lot of people who argue that King was starting to think more like Malcolm X toward the end of his life. I find it hard to believe that he wouldn't have at least toyed with Malcolm X's ideas and given them serious consideration at various points.

I think that King and Malcolm X are equally historic men. But because peace is more convenient and easier to wrap your head around, Martin Luther King is regarded as a bigger figure with the public at large. In our community it's a little different. I grew up always hearing about who Malcolm X was (and who Marcus Garvey was) and respecting them. They were held up as role models of strength, intelligence, and passion.

Malcolm X's legacy has been carried on by white people's *least* favorite black person, Louis Farrakhan. I think it's fair to say that Louis Farrakhan has probably been the most consistent black leader of our times. His message has never really changed. He was a polarizing figure, and he remains so. In many ways, his philosophy has become accepted and endorsed in my community. He speaks of self-reliance. He reminds us that no one is coming to save the inner city, so we'd better do the best we can with what we've got.

People are loath to give Farrakhan credit when they proclaim his ideas. Part of that, I'm sure, is about Muslim versus Christian. Another reason is his needlessly provocative approach. I obviously have no problem with harsh language, but glib antagonism engenders hostility in return. If you don't explain the less palatable aspects of your perspective, people tune out the good things you have to say.

At one time in the late '90s, Farrakhan sent word that he wanted to meet me and a few other black celebrities. They put us up in a hotel in Chicago and took us in black limousines to visit him at his house. At that time, Farrakhan had prostate cancer and was having a really bad reaction to the radiation treatment. I'm sure his mortality was weighing heavily on his mind. He was trying to gather a group of people who he believed could be influential.

When we got to his house, Farrakhan told us a bunch of stories. The point was that he was trying to find solutions. He basically wanted us to get black men to be black *men*: to take care of their families, to stress education, to keep their neighborhoods safe. There was no incendiary language or so-called "hate speech." This was done privately, without any attempts at self-promotion or anything like that. It really was a meeting of the minds to see how we could make things better.

Some of the things that he said were the very things I heard *opponents* of black people saying: that we need to be more self-reliant, that we need to take education more seriously, that drugs were bad. But when Farrakhan was saying these things, they weren't being raised to attack and to diminish. There was always a tone of compassion in his words. Despite his illness, I was impressed by how powerful he seemed. He just seemed like a strong guy.

I've seen and talked to him at length on several other occasions since then. I never saw the hateful, anti-Semitic rabble-rouser that people accuse him of being. I saw a guy who was *honest*. I can't say I've agreed with all of the things that he's said. I think it's obvious that he may make statements whose controversial nature detracts from any truth that they might contain. But I can say some people have a part to play, despite their flaws and weaknesses, and he is definitely such a person.

For all his flaws, people forget his accomplishments. It's almost unbelievable that he was able to pull off the Million Man March. No other leader could have done that. You can't get black men to all go to the same *game*, to like the same broads, to see the same movies. But Farrakhan got more than a million black men from all over the country to come see an event because they wanted to be a part of something larger than themselves. There were grandfathers and fathers and sons. It was three and four generations of men together. They all wanted to be connected and, somewhat, to be given direction.

Farrakhan didn't get them there for fun or to throw some sort of party. He told them about being men, and that gave him some credibility to the media. It felt like a movement, like something spectacular was going to happen as a consequence. We showed up—but we didn't know where to go after that. He started something, but he just never finished it. Those black men got disenchanted and moved on. If we had followed through, now, many years later, there would be a generation of boys going to college, raising their children, and not going to jail. That could have seeded a moment that turned our fortunes around. But the moment passed, and what a shame that was.

As I said, *Greatness is often a function of the times.* Muhammad Ali was a great boxer and is a great human being. But there have been other men who were equally as physically gifted who do not get anywhere near the reverence that he gets. It was all the things *around* him that helped us to see those facets, to see him as so much more than an athlete. It was a combination of the times, and his talent, and his political stance. Here was a man whose fame came from a nonpolitical context—sports—taking a stand against the war. He was folksy and he could articulate how he felt about things: "No Vietcong ever called me 'nigger.' " The moment called for a guy like that, and he rose to the challenge. Even then, many Americans couldn't love him until he was shaking, holding that torch in the Olympics. It was only once he was so feeble that they didn't fear him anymore that they felt comfortable embracing him.

Ali, King, and Malcolm X were men who never *looked* for causes. The causes found *them.* But imagine being around men and seeing what causes could do for you; being around men who were so passionate about what they believed that it cost them everything. Imagine wanting that—and it never finding you. That's what I think of when I think of Jesse Jackson. He was a great orator. He had seen a lot of things firsthand. He was a man in search of a cause that would raise his standing. He was a guy in search of a reason to be great. He came from greatness, saw it every day, was around it, saw what it cost, believed that he had it in him. But for some goddamn reason that cause—the cause that could have solidified him, that could have catapulted him—never happened.

Later on, he kind of realized that it wasn't going to find him, so he started trying to somehow *manufacture* it. He gave what I consider one of the greatest speeches in American history with his "It's morning time" speech. But that was *it.* He was reduced to running around with chicken blood on his shirt, claiming that it was Martin Luther King's. He enriched himself by going to the corporations and telling them, "I can make your black problem go away."

I've been in meetings in Hollywood where certain TV shows had people mad at them. The shows were being accused of racism because, say, they didn't hire black writers. Whatever the case may have been, the first thing the executives did was reach out to Jesse Jackson. They believed that if you gave him some money, all your negative racial press would go away. Can anyone say they were completely wrong in their thinking?

I know for a fact that Jesse succumbed to venality, because it affected me directly. In 1999, I had a house that I wanted to sell in Baldwin Hills. I had a property-management company taking care of the sale for me, and we got a bid on the house from a young woman. "She really wants the house," the broker told us. But the bid was significantly less than we wanted—I'm talking forty grand less. At that time, the market was pretty solid. There was no need for us to take a bath on the sale.

"No," I told the broker. "If she really wants it, you tell her that the asking price is the actual price."

A couple of days later, the buyer matched the price. There was a check from the Rainbow Coalition making up the difference between her original offer and our final price. I instantly thought that *somebody* down there at the Coalition had himself a little chippy on the side, but I didn't care one way or another. What mattered to me was whether the check cleared—which it did.

Several weeks after the sale closed, I was on the set of *The Hughleys*. "Is that your house?" someone asked me.

"What are you talking about?" I said.

"That's your house on the TV news!"

And it was. Everyone from the show gathered around to watch the TV set. The reporters had cameras in front of my old house, and the newscasters were proclaiming that this was the home of Jesse Jackson's love child. His mistress had had a baby, and they were saying that he had bought the house for her.

At some point in the following days, the government even called me investigating whether Jesse had used funds improperly. Obviously, I played dumb. "I don't know," I said. "I've never seen anything and I don't know what you're talking about. Talk to my lawyer." I kept my mouth shut about the whole thing—with one glaring exception.

In 2002, Jesse got mad about some of the jokes Cedric the Entertainer made in *Barbershop*. One of the lines that bothered him was a quip about how Martin Luther King "got more ass than a toilet seat." Now, let's be honest. No one who admires King thinks that his alleged womanizing detracts from his accomplishments. The people who *do* bring that up are only using it as an excuse to denigrate a man whose goals they have always opposed. Besides which: *It's a joke.*

I was at the Trumpet Awards in Atlanta that year, and so was Jesse. He was standing near me when he started being very vocal about the film and how offensive it was. He wanted them to censor some of the dialogue. He was complaining loud enough for me to hear him.

"Well," I interjected, "*some* people need to not have those kinds of moral views." Meaning, people in glass houses shouldn't throw stones.

He's no dummy. He instantly knew what I was talking about, and he dropped the matter right then and there. I maintain that if he hadn't had "Reverend" in front of his name, none of that stuff would have mattered—and his downfall would not have been as severe as it has been. That title provided a moral component to his views, but it also held him to a higher standard.

Back then, there wasn't the concentration on people being exposed to everything that you did. There wasn't TMZ or Media Takeout or all these kinds of blogs that exposed behind-the-scenes goings-on. Even someone as well-known as Jesse Jackson could still have some auspice of anonymity in certain contexts, which I am sure he took advantage of for years. So when it came out publicly that he was saying one thing and doing another, people were disappointed. He was very well regarded in the black community. Many white people, of course, thought his comeuppance was long overdue. The animus toward him in certain pockets was intense. Bill O'Reilly basically made his name by taking Jesse Jackson to task on the air, for example.

Yet the proposition that Jesse Jackson was shameless in his actions was demonstrably false. When all his dirty laundry got aired in public, it was *shame* that immobilized him. He didn't sweep it under the rug, make an insincere apology, and pretend nothing of importance had happened. He really fell back in his public persona—and that allowed Al Sharpton to basically take Jesse Jackson's place.

# # #

If Jesse Jackson was a reduction of Martin Luther King, then Al Sharpton was a reduction of Jesse Jackson. He was a copy of a copy. When Sharpton started out, he was less crisp, less focused, less sure, less sharp than Jackson was. But as their careers went on, they sort of switched roles. Jesse went down and Sharpton got more nuanced and much more sophisticated. The copy actually started to be crisper than the original. Sharpton transitioned from being this black-radical marcher to someone who wants to talk about education with Newt Gingrich and meets with Hillary Clinton. Hillary Clinton would not have been caught dead with the early Al Sharpton, the fat man in sweatsuits and gold chains. Newt Gingrich probably wouldn't even have wanted to be in the same *state*.

I watch Sharpton's television show all the time. Clearly, he is trying to be seen as much more than a civil rights leader nowadays. The more Sharpton becomes a statesman, the more of a dance he is going to have to do. He is always going to have to work his answers so that people who have loved and supported him for years will be comfortable—or at the very least, not put off. You can't be a civil rights leader/political player and not have that connection to your base. But as you broaden your appeal, you necessarily broaden your focus. It wasn't "black rights" for Martin Luther King: It was a *human* rights issue. It was something *everyone* could get behind, even though the problem was primarily hurting one group in particular.

That's why I think that Jesse Jackson and Al Sharpton have focused so much on racial discrimination as a cause. The 1960s were the last time we had a national consensus on race. They were probably the *only* time we had a national consensus on race. Those who opposed this consensus had their views driven out of civilized discourse. A person can openly argue for colonies on the moon, shutting down every U.S. embassy abroad, and defaulting on the national debt. But racist views have to be couched in code words and deceit. So to fight discrimination is a winning fight, because no one will fight with you openly.

But the consensus means that the fight has been *won*, at least ideologically. Of course racism is a huge problem, but it's not the only problem—and it's not the biggest problem. It doesn't stop black women from going to school in record numbers, for example.

If there's a problem with a company that discriminates, that shit doesn't fly anymore when exposed to scrutiny. It's very easy to point the finger when the danger is external. "Us versus them" is a common human mindset.

But what about when the dangers are *internal*? Civil rights leaders can't be as candid. They can't alienate their own audience or they will lose their power. We are at a point in America when every community, every *person*, can create their own reality. If something makes you uncomfortable, you can successfully avoid hearing it. The thing is, it is *truths* that make a person feel uncomfortable. Some part of your mind registers the fact they are trying to deny, and that's where the unease creeps in.

I am not a civil rights leader. My constituency is fluid, and I do not claim to speak for anyone but myself. If the NAACP types often want to suppress what they see on the *screen*, it's no wonder they are uncomfortable with what they see on the *streets*. Fortunately, I don't have that problem.

## CHAPTER 10

PRESIDENT OBAMA ONCE SAID HE WANTS EVERYBODY IN AMERICA TO GO TO COLLEGE. WHAT A SNOB!

—RICK SANTORUM

NOT even the most virulent racist would argue that older black men are as involved with unsavory activity as younger black men. Clearly, *age* has something to do with the problem. What is it that all young people of *all* races have in common? *They're fucking stupid.* And if stupid kids are encouraged to act in stupid ways, then they *will* act in stupid ways. I myself learned one of these very stupid ways of acting at a young age. I learned it the same way many kids learn their stupid ideas: on the school bus.

It doesn't matter what your background is: *Every* kid in America knows the seating hierarchy of the bus. The youngest and the nerdiest kids have to sit in the front. The farther you sit from the bus driver, the cooler you are. But that school bus could be a very dangerous place. People would be bopping you in the head and messing with you, so you had to have some protection. That's why, in seventh grade, nerdy li'l Darryl Hughley planted his black ass directly behind the driver every single day. I was so far up that dude's butt, I could have charged him for a colonoscopy.

On the other end of the bus, *way* in the very back row, sat Catherine Bogatz. That part of the bus was so different that it wasn't even a seat anymore; it was more like a long bench for the rulers of the bus kingdom. Gorgeous Catherine sat right in the middle of that bench like the queen that she was. She was *stunning*. To this day she remains the most beautiful creature I've ever seen.

Our bus driver was very young, about nineteen or twenty, and wore these half gloves that all the broads dug. He was clearly new at the job, because he had the shitty route that nobody wanted. It was my route—and Catherine's route. Back in those days, radio stations worked on a cycle and you knew what song would come on when. So every day on that bus, we heard the song "Gloria" by a group called Enchantment.

Whenever "Gloria" came on, I was under the belief that Catherine and I had an unspoken deal: I would look at her with utter adoration, and she'd cut her eyes a little bit and give me a smile in return. Even though it wasn't even a *real* smile but more like a smirk, it fucking made my day. It was like the queen was acknowledging that I existed. It was *beautiful*. It fueled me.

So one day, "Gloria" started playing. I did what I was supposed to do and turned around and looked at Catherine. She saw me and yelled down the length of the entire school bus, "What are you looking at, motherfucker? Stop looking at me, you nappy-headed fucker!" Everyone on the bus laughed. It was the most graphic representation of the power of a woman over a man's psyche that I would ever experience.

The driver tilted the mirror back so he could see me and said, "It's all right, little man."

The bus driver knew what I had yet to learn: I was what I later identified as a "pussy-later" type of cat. The black community is probably 90 percent pussy-*now* guys. They're the guys who won't go to school; dudes who sell a little weed or dope on the side; people who quit school to rap. Or they're going to be basketball stars. Or they get a college scholarship but don't go to class—so they get kicked out. Or they get a job, complain about it, and are always quitting. When these guys get money, they buy rims and shit that will impress broads. They're Eddie from *The Five Heartbeats*, the lead singer all the ladies loved.

There's *pressure* to be a pussy-now type of dude. When you're young, the whole thing is being cool to the people around you. It's very hard to realize the costs of being a pussy-now dude—especially when you're getting all that pussy and when everyone thinks you're the greatest.

Pussy-now dudes play checkers. But pussy-*later* dudes play chess. One is short-range: "*Jump the king—I'm the shit now!*" The other has long-range implications, where every move predicates and decides the next set of options. You have to think steps ahead. That's how life is! It's like choosing retirement funds or college funds, deciding which choices will enrich you and which won't. When you make a mistake, there are ways to recuperate from it. It takes a whole bunch of bad shots to try to get to a goal. The whole game is about trying to minimize the bad shots, *not* trying to have great ones. That's what pussy-now guys don't get.

When you look at your life, you've got some really shitty days, some fucking *spectacular* days, and most days you don't remember. You remember the great ones and the really shitty ones—and you've had more shitty days than you've had great ones. But the great ones make up for it. You *live* for them great days, like a sunny day in a New York City winter. Those great days are spaced out, and you can only have so many in your lifetime. That's why these pussy-now-type dudes burn out so quickly. They use up all those great days very early on.

When I was growing up, there were a lot of kids that had to be home when the streetlights came on. It was a universal, totally black experience across the country. In the winter it was early, and in the summer it came later. But whatever the season, when it got dark, you got your ass home. When those lights came on, you saw everybody literally breaking toward the house. But then there was that dude who never had to be home, and *everybody* thought he was cool.

That dude is the one who ends up going to jail. Now he doesn't have a home to go to at all. Jesse got to stay up all hours of the night, and all the girls liked Jesse. Now Jesse is homeless. Those pussy-now dudes are cool from junior high to high school. Seven years! In terms of a life, that's *nothing*. Yet those seven years are all they live for. They come to the high school reunion. They hit you up on Facebook with old high school pictures and memories. Everybody remembers pussy-now type dudes. They had all the fresh shit, went to all the parties, got to stay out late. Everybody loved them. Pussy-later motherfuckers, people don't even know. "He went to this school? I never saw that motherfucker because he was in the library."

When you're a kid, pussy-now is where it's at in my community. I used to hang around with these pussy-now dudes, hoping it would rub off on me. They managed to teach me a lot about life. For some reason I couldn't explain, I felt bad for them. These dudes had low riders and money and broads. I could never figure out why I felt bad for them; it didn't make any sense. I wanted to *be* them! All through life, those dudes guided me. They'd do shit and tell me, "Nah, nigga. You go home. This ain't your thing." Even they knew I wasn't cut out for it—before *I* knew. They kept me away from all the bullshit that they did.

One time, when I was twelve or thirteen, I wanted some money. I asked this cat if I could sell some weed for him. In front of all the other dudes, he said, "Nigga, you ain't built for this shit." Everybody laughed, and I thought he was disrespecting me. Later on, he *gave* me twenty dollars. I thought he was fucking with me some more. But it was actually respect, and I didn't even know it. I *wasn't* built for that. He was saying I was *above* what he was doing. That was a compliment, and I didn't fucking get it.

I *wanted* to be a pussy now type of dude more than anything. I wanted pussy and I wanted it *now*. To lose my virginity I had to fuck a girl who was hideous, that's how bad it was. It wasn't *romantic*: I just needed to get this thing off. I never masturbated, but I sure had dreams. In the dreams, it was so spectacular that I was like, *Wait until I get somebody to do this shit!* But all the chicks that inspired my hormones to go crazy, all the Catherine Bogatzes, those bitches wouldn't have shit to do with me. You've got to be cool, or they won't fuck you. They don't fuck *nobody* people don't think is cool.

But there was this one girl down the street who *would* fuck me. So what if she was so hideous that she looked like me? The important thing is that she was a loving human being. She was a sweet woman, and when she gave me some I couldn't even believe it. Today I realize that I was having my first orgasm with a woman, but

I had no idea what was happening at the time. I almost started *cry-ing*. I loved her so intensely for ten seconds, a feeling of love I can't even explain. I *instantly* knew what this sex stuff was about, and I knew that I wanted to be doing it *a lot* for the rest of my life. In that moment, that she–D.L. was radiant to me. She was beautiful and warm and just *everything*. But after the ten seconds passed, I liter-ally wanted her to leave. She couldn't get out quickly enough. I can't even describe how fast it shifted. I was like, "Oh! *Oh!* Bitch, leave."

# # #

I was one of the fortunate pussy-later dudes because I actually managed to get one in. I'm sure a lot of my pussy-later brothers weren't as fortunate. Take Tiger Woods. When Tiger Woods was in school, he was a buck-toothed chigger playing a white man's game. No broads were trying to fuck him. His very name must have been sarcastic to them. "How's it going, *Tiger*?" Now he gets so much pussy that they write articles keeping track of the number, which is another argument for pussy-later: On average, you'll end up getting *more* pussy in the long term.

This pussy-now/pussy-later dichotomy is one I constantly see validated. These days, I'm friends with John Witherspoon. When people think of John Witherspoon, they often think of his charac-ter in *Friday* talking about how smelly his shits are. But don't get it twisted: In real life, John Witherspoon is a very fancy dude. I'm sure his shits smell spectacular, like strawberries and champagne.

John and his wife always have really high-class social events at his house, and *my* wife always drags me there and to other fancy crap like that. LaDonna's on the phone asking me to buy tickets to the Pasadena Playhouse so she can see August Wilson's *Fences* or whatever the latest bourgie Jack and Jill Links thing is that month.

I couldn't care less about some party for a play, but I love John so I go to his events. When John has his events, his wife takes care of the hostessing and he isn't even there half the time. He and I will go back to a separate house that he's built on his property so he can be by himself. He pours me wine that he don't pour nobody else, and he shows me all sorts of cool shit.

In 2009, John was having one of these hoity-toity parties. I pulled up, and the dude who was the valet used to be the coolest cat in my neighborhood. I recognized him right away, and he recognized me right away. Now, you know you're doing bad when you're a black valet dude in Los Angeles. They're *all* Latin. In all the years I've been valet parking, I'd only seen one black dude with a red vest on—until I pulled up to John Witherspoon's house and saw the second.

It was the most awkward thing imaginable. I didn't want to give this dude my key and a tip. I was immediately thinking back to high school, when pussy-later me was begging pussy-now him to let me smell his fingers. I *loved* the dude. I was very glad to see him—just not as a valet. It was hard, but proved my theory.

Pussy-now-type motherfuckers become valets, janitors, or factory workers. Pussy-later-type motherfuckers have different kinds of gigs. They're managers. They're referred to as "your honor" or "Mr. President." Nobody was really trying to fuck Obama growing up, with those big ears and that goofy smile.

In 2010 I was getting my hair done in New York. On the TV this cat named Judge Kevin Ross came on. Just like me, Kevin Ross was a pussy-later dude. I know this because he also went to my high school. I said pussy-later-type dudes play chess, and Kevin Ross was *literally* in the chess club. Kevin was the student-body president of a school where it was all white and Asians—and us. Everybody thought he was a nerd. And we went to school with Japanese kids;

we're talking about smart people from the *tap*. Kevin grew up to become a superior court judge in Inglewood, and now he's on TV doing what he did, being exactly him: a pussy-later-type motherfucker.

White people don't have to make a choice. They can be pussy-now *and* pussy-later. JFK, Donald Trump: They had pussy day in and day out. You can be a fucking loser your whole life, and then your father dies and leaves you a company or somebody hires you. But no black dads are dying and leaving real estate empires to their kids. The things young black men have to do to get pussy *now* are the things that prevent them from getting pussy *later*. We have to work that much harder just to compete with everybody else. At the end of the day, we have to make the choice: Are we working our minds? Or are we working our dicks?

There's this mentality in our community that proclaims, "This is as good as it gets, so I better have it now. I can *only* have it now." You don't think you're going to live a long time. When I grew up, *nobody* really thought about going to college. What was the point? Why *not* go to jail, when there ain't nothing else out there for you?

But like me, Tiger Woods, Judge Kevin Ross, and Obama demonstrate, *It gets greater later.* I didn't get that broad in high school, but I've got a great apartment in New York. I've seen the world, and on my terms. I didn't get to go to a lot of parties, but all them girls would fuck me now. The bus driver knew what he was talking about: It *is* all right. I wouldn't trade my life for his, even though he fucked Catherine Bogatz when she turned legal.

This pussy-now/pussy-later dichotomy isn't original to me. Sociologists and economists have the same concept, only they call it "time preference." It's the basis of finance and the reason we pay interest rates. It goes a little something like this: If I offered you a dollar now or a dollar a year from now, everyone would prefer the dollar now. I might be lying and I might not have the dollar next year. Thanks to inflation, that dollar will be worth very slightly less next year, too. But what about if it was a dollar now, and $1.50 next year? Or $2? At *some* point, people choose to wait.

The pussy-now, short-time-preference mentality means that people don't think about the future *at all*. It's like buying a TV with a credit card—and then owing the cost of two TVs in a year due to interest. These pussy-now types get four years of coolness and pleasure—and owe forty years of emptiness. This is a mindset that they are *taught*. If you believe that you have no future, then that belief will certainly come true. With black girls, that comes out as teen pregnancy. With black boys, it sets them down a more compli-cated path.

Even though they might not be thinking about the *future*, these boys can make their *present* better. But to do that would entail mak-ing the most of what they have now—and that is something else that they are discouraged to do. Then they would lose their ghetto pass.

## CHAPTER 11

YOU LOSING YOUR GHETTO PASS, MAN.

—THE GHETTO POLICE

THE best way to better yourself is to get an education. There will *always* be a need for educated workers. You might have to take a pay cut in horrible economic times, but you're not going to be out on the street. A landlord will be a lot more understanding if an educated man is late with his rent than if an uneducated man misses it. Being educated naturally engenders respect.

This is one of the things I feel most passionately about, and one of the biggest regrets of my life. That's why I made damn sure that my kids were going to get an education. In May of 2011, my son Kyle was going to graduate from college and wanted me to give the commencement address at his school. Yet I hadn't even graduated from *high school*. I felt like I would have been a hypocrite, telling the kids to take advantage of their education when I didn't avail myself of one. I was flattered, but I turned Kyle down.

My son went back and told the school my concerns. They said that they would give me an honorary doctorate if I spoke. A *doctorate*? Man, I was going to be Cliff fucking Huxtable alongside my graduating son. I might have only had a GED, but even I knew what a two-for-one was. I told the school that I would do it.

When it came time for me to give my speech and tell my jokes, I realized that Kyle was the very first male in my family to ever graduate from college. Standing there up on that stage in front of all the kids, I grew very overcome with emotion and started to get choked up. I was really tearing up when it hit me: A few minutes before my son had gotten *his* degree, *I* had gotten *mine*. My son was the *second* male to get a degree. *I* was the first! *Wow.* Me, a college graduan!

I went up to Kyle after the ceremony and showed him my certificate. "You went to school for four years," I said. "I told jokes for fifteen minutes in front of some white dudes with collars on—and we got the same thing. I didn't have to spend thousands of dollars. *I* got paid! I'm a *doctor*. It's D.R. Hughley now!" Of course I was being absurd. My prize certificate was nothing compared to the knowledge and skills Kyle had developed to get his diploma.

Just like many, many black boys in this country, I took a wrong turn very early on. When I was in the third grade, they came to Avalon Gardens elementary and tested all the kids' skills. They told my mother that I tested very high in language, reading comprehension, and reasoning. After I got those scores, every week these people would come take me out of class and take me to special studies. All the other kids would look at me like I was crazy. "Where are you going?" my friends asked me. "What are you doing? What, you think you're smart?" The fact that I was trying to learn was insulting to them.

Because of their reactions, I started messing up. I knew that if I spoke well, or if I acted differently, I would be ostracized. I decided I was going to be as dumb as everybody else. By the time I hit the eighth grade, I achieved my goal: I got *horrible* grades. I knew that if my mother found out, she was going to kick my ass. I would be grounded in the house for the whole summer, so I decided to change my grades. The thing is, our grades came on carbon paper. But since I had made myself into a *dumbass*, I didn't just change the paper that went home. I changed the *whole* paper—the part that went home *and* the part that went to the counselor's office. I took the *brilliant* extra step of changing my grades to all A's, which was sure to be noticed.

My counselor spotted what I had done. "You know you didn't get those grades," she told me. "But you know what? *You could have.* I'll tell you what. When school starts next year, I'm going to put you in the accelerated classes. If you pass, I forget about this. If you fail, I'm going to tell your mother exactly what happened."

That fall, I went to the accelerated class. The other students were people I never even knew went to my school. It was Nerd Central: the Japanese kids, the kids with braces—and me. I bet Obama was in that class. I had to work harder than I ever had in my life to simply pass. I even managed to get all B's and C's. The lesson *should* have been that I could do it. But the lesson *I* got was that being smart takes too much work. I was so exhausted by all that effort that I never went to that school again.

Eventually I transferred to Locke High, the classic urban, inner-city school. It was a school so bad that other schools were scared to play football there. Since Locke was only two miles from my house, I showed up wearing red because I thought they were all Bloods.

They were not.

Sure enough, some Crip kids chased me up to a liquor store on Imperial and Avalon. This was not going to be a case of bullying: This was going to be a case of murder. I ran into the store, terrified, while they waited for me outside. The Korean lady who ran the place wasn't interested in giving me sanctuary. "Get out of my store!" she yelled. "I call police!"

I was like, "Bitch, you *call* the police. I'm not going anywhere."

I squatted down in the Hostess section behind all the Sno-Balls—the pink ones *and* the white ones—and the Honey Buns. All I could smell was that honey icing and my fear. I didn't know what to do, so I just prayed. "God, please help me. These guys are going to kill me. Please, God. Please deliver me."

I looked up and saw my father walking into the store. He walked past me to get some pork rinds and a case of Lucky beer, the kind that had riddles underneath the bottle caps. Well, the lucky one was me and the riddle that I had solved was how to get the hell out of that motherfucking store and back home to safety.

Eventually my dad noticed me scrunched down there. "*Darryl?* What are you doing here?"

I didn't know what to say to him. "I was . . . I was . . . "

"Get your ass out of here and get in the car! What the hell is wrong with you?" I walked past the guys with my dad, and nothing happened to me—except I never went back to Locke High. I knew they'd be waiting for me the next day, and the day after that.

After that I went to San Pedro High—until I got kicked out for fighting. I transferred to Gardenia Adult School—until I got kicked out for fighting some undercover police officers. Now I couldn't go to school *anywhere*, even if I wanted to.

Eventually graduation day came around. All those people I was trying to be as dumb as, all those people I was trying to be with, got their diplomas. And me? All I had to show for myself was a nauseous feeling whenever I smelled Honey Buns.

# # #

That's why I can see it when people feel like they have to act uneducated and play down to the lowest common denominator. I spent *years* trying to do just that. Look at all the professional athletes who speak poor English. They've gotten college educations from some of the greatest learning institutions in the world. Even if they can't make it as an athlete, they've got a $200,000 degree behind them. Are they really going to speak the same way in the job interview as they do when the cameras are on them?

The way they talk speaks to how proud some people are of not knowing. Young black men are *proud* that they don't speak well, *proud* that they don't read. Forced illiteracy used to be the slave master's greatest weapon to keep the slaves uneducated and in check. Now the adage is, "If you want to keep a black man from knowing something, put it in a book." You don't even need to go to college to get an education. If you read a newspaper every day, after three years you'll have the equivalent of a bachelor of arts. Can't afford it? Read it on the computer or even your cell phone.

There's this mentality in the black community where, if you don't think like everybody else, there's something the matter with you. The shit that is ascribed to being black is silly to me. "You're getting your ghetto pass revoked" is the expression. Where do you get a ghetto pass to begin with? Who do you pay your dues to? Do they take EBT? Who tells you when it's been revoked? How can one pass cover a race that's got both Barack Obama and Lil Wayne?

For a long time, I used to think in those terms myself. I hated *The Cosby Show* because I felt as if black people don't live like that. I had this idea of what a black sitcom should be, with the characters having blue-collar jobs, having never gone to college. They definitely weren't doctors and lawyers. But I was wrong and Bill Cosby was right. I was thinking like a pussy-now guy, and Bill Cosby was urging people to think in pussy-later terms. Cosby made it cool to go to college, or to aspire to be a yuppie—something that had previously been the whitest aspiration possible.

I came to realize that it all comes down to this: Why the fuck would anyone need or want a pass to get into the ghetto? It's not like the ghetto has big impenetrable fences keeping people out. They're falling down with holes. *Everybody's* getting through them. Those fences aren't to keep people out; they're to keep people *in*.

The only pass you should want is the one that gets you *out* of the ghetto. When you're in jail and you get a day pass, that's to let you out—not to stay *in*! A hall pass is to leave the fucking classroom. You get a day pass, you can do whatever the fuck you want. You need a pass to go to Six Flags; you don't need one to come *home*. A ghetto pass is permission to *leave*, motherfucker, not *stay*.

I think Tiger Woods is a great example of someone getting a ghetto pass, in my sense of the term. The only reason people are interested in Tiger Woods is because he's a great *black* golfer. If you want to be a popular sports hero, both black and white people have to like you. People have to want to buy your jersey, or your shoes, or your golf clubs. The commercials said this explicitly: "I wanna be like Mike," or, "I am Tiger Woods." Black people didn't care about golf until Tiger Woods came along. He gave us permission and made it okay to play a white dude's sport. They did it, so now it's cool for you to do it.

But my definition of the ghetto pass, unfortunately, is not the prevailing one. Black kids are taught to ignore the future, and getting an education is discouraged. There is another problem with not being educated: *You have no sense of what's out there.* I can talk about any place in the world because I watch the news and read the paper. I can discuss astronomy, though I'm not going up in a spaceship. But an uneducated person is limited to the information provided by his senses. In a very real sense, these kids' world consists entirely of their ghetto neighborhood.

Humans naturally define ourselves by borders. Even though a New Yorker has more in common with a Canadian than a Louisiana redneck, his group is defined by the 45th parallel. It could be Chicago or Brooklyn or Oakland or Rwanda or Haiti. It's the same shit. That whole East Coast–West Coast thing? That's not a joke to those cats. Wherever our mothers rented houses is what we decided was the most valuable land. The rest was enemy territory.

The thinking is completely tribal. Maybe you're not the same religion, or you don't speak the same language, or I'm Hutu and you're Tutsi. If you're from the east side, you're not from the west side. You wear red and not blue. This is my small area, and if you don't fit into it, then your life doesn't mean *anything*.

This arbitrary us-them demarcation is not just a black thing. Everyone has some sports team they love, and they hate the rival team with a passion. It's like a dude who says he can't date some broad because she's a Red Sox fan and he's a Yankee fan. He truly believes that this difference will make a relationship between the two of them impossible. Same thing with someone going to a rival high school. Every group has some other group that they dislike for some silly reason, sometimes for literally *no* reason.

When I grew up, I could give less than a fuck about people

who didn't live in my neighborhood. From my very first memories of it, it was always, "That nigger ain't shit." *My entire world had a four-mile radius.* If you didn't live within that, I didn't care what happened to you. *Nobody* around me did. You couldn't break into somebody's house in our neighborhood, but if you stepped outside the borders it was cool. Cats would brag about how many bodies they had, and you knew it was black people that they had killed. I remember being a kid and watching a dude get shot, and people laughing while he was dying. I said something; I knew it wasn't right.

"Fuck that nigger, man!" was the response.

# # #

It was when I was in junior high that I had an experience that truly showed how deeply entrenched this tribal mentality was. We may have hated going to school during the school year, but we used to hang out there all the time during the summer when the school was officially closed. It was our school, we figured, so we could do whatever the fuck we wanted.

I came by the school one summer day to see what was going on. There was this older cat I knew, high school age, and he called me over. "Hey man," he told me, "we're running a train on this girl."

"Really?" I said.

"Yeah, we gave her some Spanish fly." I was still a virgin at the time so I wasn't really sure what "running a train" entailed. I *did* know what Spanish fly was, because it was typical dumb schoolyard bullshit. Supposedly when you gave it to a broad, it made her hot. You had to be real careful not to give them too much or it'd make them blind.

I followed my friend and he took me out back where his partner had this girl. I don't know how old she was, probably their age, but I didn't recognize her and so I knew she wasn't from my neighborhood.

"Oh, man!" my buddy said. "We doin' it!"

Like I said, I had never had sex before. Yet I still knew what it looked like when someone was upset—and this girl was *not* happy. Whatever was going on, she didn't dig it. The two dudes were acting like it's just a thing, and were about to go at her.

"This is not cool," I said to them. "She's not with this."

I'm not going to pretend that I'm some sort of superhero who bravely came in to save the day. Those two guys were older than me and bigger than me; on some level I was afraid. I didn't step in because I was trying to be an upstanding moral member of my community. I stepped in because on a visceral level it just felt *wrong* to see a female like that.

"Fuck that, man," my buddy said. "She knows she's with it."

I didn't start arguing or explaining because I didn't need to say anything else. I knew they were mad, but I knew they were also ashamed on some level. They *knew* what they were doing wasn't right, and that stopped them from doing anything to me. (Or maybe they *didn't* know, and that would have been sad.)

I grabbed the girl by the hand and gave her her pants and her top. After she got dressed, I walked her out of the school. I asked her where she lived, and she managed to give me her address even though she was crying and shaking. I knew where that address was: enemy territory. She lived in a Blood neighborhood like me, but her people were a different kind of Bloods. It was a bit far, close to a mile, and I walked her the entire way not saying much of anything. What kind of small talk could I do, in that situation? And with a high school girl, from another neighborhood?

All I could fixate on was her smell. I'll never forget the smell. It was a mix of pennies and sweat and fear. To my young mind, it was just *weird*. I didn't know how she got to my school, and I didn't know what happened before I showed up. I had no idea how many dudes had it with her. I guessed that some had, because her hair was so messed up and she just looked like she'd been through *something*.

When we eventually got close to her house, she pulled away from me and started running home. Her brother (I'm guessing it was her brother) saw her, grabbed a butcher knife, and ran at me. I could see it glinting in the sun, and I could hear it whizzing through the air. I wasn't about to stand there and explain myself with a butcher knife coming at me as fast as this dude could run. I ran like hell, and then his boys starting chasing me through the neighborhood, too. I was running, running, running, and they were chasing, chasing, chasing.

Finally, they caught me. Her brother made the obvious assumption, that I had done something to the girl. They held me as her brother came closer and closer. That's when the girl popped up. "It wasn't him!" she screamed. "It wasn't him! He saved me! He saved me! *Stop it!*" Even though she was hysterical, she managed to get out the story of what had happened.

Yet the brother did not lower the knife and shake my hand. He just came closer and said, "Tell me who the fuck it was!"

"Man," I said, "I don't know who it was."

"Motherfucker, you know, dammit."

Obviously I knew who it was. "Man, I don't know who they are, man. I was just coming through school and I saw them."

He wasn't going to let it go. "Tell me who it is. Motherfucker, if you don't tell me who it is, I'm gonna cut you."

Here's what people who didn't grow up like I did need to understand: *I never even considered ratting out the dudes that did it.* I was a kid, being held in places by dudes I didn't know, with a butcher knife being waved in my face and a hysterical broad screaming in the background. The tension and adrenaline could not possibly have been higher. It wasn't like I *considered* telling him the names but decided against it. I didn't consider it any more than I considered growing wings and flying away. It was something that was completely out of the realm of possible behavior for me. *That's what the tribal mentality is like.* It's not about *choosing* your people over another group of people. The mentality *makes* the decision for you, and your thought process doesn't even acknowledge that you *have* a choice. If anything, I shouldn't have been helping this broad from another neighborhood to begin with! If it had been a dude getting beaten up or even killed, for example, I *definitely* wouldn't have helped or even *thought* to help.

So I just closed my eyes and told the brother, "You're gonna have to cut me because I don't know who it is." He let me go. No one thanked me or anything like that. In fact, a couple of people punched me as I left. Months later I saw the brother at the liquor store. He got to his burgundy Impala and he said, "Thanks, man." Then he drove away.

I'm older now, and I see the world a lot clearer than I did when I was a kid. But the effects of my upbringing haven't gone away. I went to Gardena High for a stretch, but Gardena was also a rival neighborhood. When I was asked to appear at the Gardena Jazz Festival a couple of years ago, part of me felt *wrong* about doing it. It was just this subconscious, visceral reaction. I'm a grown dude with three kids, and I *still* have the hang-up. As recently as 2009, I made friends with dudes from Gardena. I play golf with them and hang out, normal stuff. Yet my brother-in-law wouldn't do it. If those Gardena guys were there, he wouldn't be around. "I don't trust those niggas, man."

When I played a gig in Hermosa Beach in 2011, a lot of people in the audience were from a rival neighborhood. As adults, we can't believe that it was like that and that we were ever that way. But the young folks are *still* just like that. The same circumstances that were there when I was a kid are there now, so of course this cycle of hate continues.

When Tookie, the founder of the Crips, was going to get the death penalty in 2005, plenty of people I grew up with were ecstatic. It was more as if we Bloods had won the World Series than that a man was being put to death. But if that was the way you operated growing up and you had never been anywhere else, you'd probably feel the same way. You wouldn't have anything to compare it to.

So now we have black kids who don't think of the future, who are discouraged from being educated, and who see the world as beginning and ending with their neighborhood. They may be ignorant and they may be oriented entirely on the present, but that won't be enough to make them a criminal. Mentally handicapped people are ignorant and oriented on the present; they're the *opposite* of hardened.

So how would you make these kids into criminals? It's kind of like a battered wife. If you tell a woman over decades that she's worthless, stupid, and ugly, she will come to genuinely believe that she is worthless, stupid, and ugly. Conversely, if you tell someone that he's a great singer, he'll *act* like a great singer. He might not *be* a great singer, but he'll go on that *American Idol* audition and make a fool of himself.

Making a kid into a criminal requires the same approach. Treat him like a thug, and he'll start acting like one. When it comes to thug life, there isn't much sunlight between *being* one and *acting* like one. Here's a question that doesn't require much of an education to answer: What group treats young black men like thugs?

## CHAPTER 12

JUST FOLLOWING ORDERS.

—NYPD, ECHOING NUREMBERG

A lot has been written about Rodney King and police brutality. But what is less often discussed is the *effect* an occupying police force has on impressionable young minds. To claim that the police are a factor in encouraging crime sounds ridiculous to most people. It's counterintuitive; after all, the cops are there because the crime was there *first*. But that doesn't mean that the cops didn't *increase* what was there already. It sounds crazy, I know. It would have also sounded crazy if I had said that banning the sale of alcohol would lead to a huge increase in alcoholism.

Then Prohibition happened.

The police-brutality cases when people get killed are horrible and huge tragedies. Those stories make the news and they are terrible; no one argues with that. But it's the day-to-day things that have consequences—especially when you're an ignorant kid. Let me explain a little bit of what that kind of life was like.

In the mid-1970s, Smitty's Liquor Store on Avalon Boulevard was a very special place. It was located dead center in between two neighborhoods. On one side you had us, and on the other side was where another sect of Bloods lived. Because we all had to go to that same liquor store, it ended up being like a safe zone. Smitty's was South Central's version of the UN. We may have had beef with each other, but we never did no dirt to anybody when we were at Smitty's.

One of the kids in my crew was a big strong dude named Curtis. Even though Curtis was only fifteen or sixteen years old, he already had a beard. He was basically like a huge freak of nature. Curtis was Tyson before *Tyson* was Tyson. Curtis was always in and out of California Youth Authority, which is basically jail for kids. The cops *constantly* picked on Curtis. He was tough, but at the same time he couldn't really mess with the police. That made them feel like they were tougher than him because he couldn't fight back from their provocations.

One day at Smitty's, this five-star sheriff started fucking with him and Curtis just shook his head. "Motherfucker," he told the cop, "if you didn't have that badge and that stick I'd beat the shit out of you." This cop was a big dude, too. It wasn't like Curtis was a lock to win. But after a while, enough becomes enough.

The two of them went to the alley behind Smitty's. That cop took off his badge and his belt while his partner kept a lookout. We all stood there and watched as Curtis proceeded to beat all five stars out of that fucking sheriff. We were all very excited to see a cop getting his ass whupped like that. Eventually the sheriff's partner had to pull out his gun and start shooting in the air to break the fight apart. That's how badly Curtis fucked that dude up.

Two weeks later, Curtis was dead. The police had found his body after he had been shot to death. There wasn't any doubt in our minds as to who had done it, either. If it was another Blood or a Crip, word would have definitely gotten out. Hell, they would have been bragging about it. But no one had any beef with Curtis like the police did.

Curtis's fate was a story that was beaten into all of us, often literally, day in and day out. There's no bravery in shooting a minor. There's no justice in punishing an unarmed ass-kicker, with deadly force, in secret. *Of course* there was never any investigation. Curtis's life didn't *matter*. None of our lives did, in the eyes of the police.

# # #

Things like that happened *constantly* when I was growing up. One summer when I was ten, I was walking down the street with my friend. A police car pulled up and called us over. I don't remember what they wanted to know, but neither of us were much help. We were still only in elementary school, and pulling a girl's hair hadn't been declared a felony yet.

The cop made me and my friend put our hands on the hood of the car. I can still feel how hot that metal felt in the California sun. "If you move your hands," the cop told me, "*I will blow your head off*." As the two of us stood there, scared to death, the cop's partner sat in the driver's seat revving the engine. I don't know if that made the hood any hotter, but it sure wasn't helping. We didn't have the information what he wanted or else we would have told him immediately. I would have confessed to sinking the *Titanic* to get my hands off that hood.

Most white ten-year-old boys are taught that the cops are their friends. "If you have a problem, ask your local neighborhood police officer for help!" Well, our local neighborhood police officer *was* our problem. A white kid would *never* have been treated the way I had been by the police. As soon as a white kid's parents found out, that cop would've been fired and almost certainly would've had charges pressed against him. But with me, there was no doubt that the cop would have absolutely no repercussions for his behavior. If anything, his partner would claim that *I* supposedly pulled an imaginary gun on *them*.

So in *our* community, the lesson was obviously a different one. Very early on, my mother taught me and my siblings to answer the cops with "Yes, sir" and "No, sir." The fact that we had to be taught this so young meant that interacting with the police was an inevitability—whereas most white people go their entire childhoods without speaking to a policeman even once. The fact that we had to address them as "sir" wasn't a sign of respect. It was a symbol of fearful deference. We were reverting to talking like black people in old movies. Whenever I saw a cop, I instantly turned into Kingfish.

We *had* to be deferential because the cops were always looking for an excuse to harass us. You don't have to have grown up in South Central to know that if you give the police attitude, things can get really ugly really quick. It's like they were daring us to do something so that they could escalate the aggression. I played the game for as long as I could. I wasn't worried about ending up like Curtis, but I wasn't interested in going to jail, either.

# # #

As an adult, I would still often get pulled over for DWB—Driving While Black. I even knew what neighborhoods to avoid. If you went through Torrance, you were being pulled over as sure as night follows day. To this day, every black person I know will make a detour to avoid going through Torrance. I don't know if it's still like that, but old habits are fucking hard to break. It takes some sort of pressure to change old ways. In my case, what happened was that I became a dad.

One time I took Kyle out for a ride when he was a toddler. Soon enough, the sirens came on and I was pulled over. I stopped the car and got my son out of the car seat. I knew that a search of the vehicle was coming next. It was standard operating procedure, like going through baggage check at an airport. You get pulled over; your skin color gets checked; "black man detected"; your car gets searched. What *also* was standard operating procedure is that black men were commanded to sit on the curb. It was completely emasculating and it was entirely humiliating. Everyone could see you sitting there on the sidewalk like a dog waiting for his master to be done at the grocery store.

Right on cue, the cop gave me my orders. "I'm going to check your car," he said. "You and your son sit on the curb."

"No," I said, holding my boy.

"Sit on the curb," he repeated.

"No, man." (Not "sir.") "I'm not going to have my son remember that his father was sitting on the curb."

"I can put you on the curb!"

"Then he'll remember that somebody *put* me on the curb. He won't remember that I did it willingly."

The lovely officer stared at me with anger, but I stared back with calm. "Just go stand over there," he mumbled under his breath. He searched my car and sent me on my way, and that was the end of it that day.

This treatment we all got wasn't black paranoia. Nor was it coincidental or an accident. This type of behavior was the *plan*. Police

Chief Daryl Gates's stated policy was hiring Southern white boys, especially those fresh home from Vietnam. He believed that they knew how to handle these urban niggers. They would have no illusions that they were dealing with anything other than a population of thugs that had to be repressed for the greater good. It wasn't "to protect and serve." It was lynch law, imported directly from the source. Any complaints by the black community would be received like a criminal bitching that his handcuffs were too tight: "Maybe you shouldn't have made us put those handcuffs on you to begin with." Daryl Gates's LAPD was even touted as a model for other police forces to follow. They sent him to Israel and to other places so he could show them how it's done. The fact that what we were living under was presented as an *ideal* made things even more demoralizing. You can't change things for the better if things are regarded as exemplary. If it ain't broke, don't fix it.

Things *never* would have changed if it wasn't for Rodney King. The thing is, I get why the Rodney King jury acquitted those police officers. White people have been so conditioned to believe that black people are "just like them" that they assume our experiences are the same too. Well, they're *not*. Since our experiences color our perceptions, a black dude and a white dude can watch the same thing happening and come to wildly different explanations for what they're seeing. Their stories might even contradict each other's, even if each dude describes only what he thinks is "obvious." Nowhere are racial attitudes more different than when it comes to the police. It starts from what we see as kids, and that attitude develops as we grow older.

So it's not that hard to get why the Rodney King cops got acquitted, and frankly it's not even that surprising. The trial was held in Simi Valley. If South Central is the wrong side of the tracks, Simi

Valley is the right side. It's one of the top five safest cities in the country. Cops live there, alongside sheriffs and firemen. All these types who work in L.A. County live in Simi Valley. In the same way that my perception of police officers is based on my experiences over the years, the same goes for the people who live in Simi Valley. There, the cops aren't an ominous force out to mess with you at every opportunity. They coach the Little League team. They shop at the same grocery stores. Their wives have you over for dinner.

Because of the jurors' experiences with the cops—not "prejudices," actual personal experiences—they couldn't see what the police officers were doing as malicious. They looked for every reason to justify their long and deeply held beliefs that cops are good. Once you accept the premise that "cops are good," then by definition those cops couldn't be doing what they *appeared* to be doing on that videotape. There was more to the story. There *had* to be. It's like finding out your wife is cheating on you or your kid is a drug addict. You will buy any excuse they throw at you because you don't want to condemn them.

The one good thing to come out of the Rodney King fiasco is that much of what the LAPD formerly did in secrecy was now made public. For the first time, white America saw that there was something to what the black community had been saying for years. So if any white people wonder why we're so loud, it's because you never fucking listen to us! The investigators did their work, and the truth came out. It wasn't that hard to find. The LAPD had been *brazen* in its abuse of power. They found cops who were robbing ordinary citizens. It was discovered that there was a task force that would follow suspects around and assassinate them.

Things were revealed to be so corrupt on a systemic level that the federal government had to step in with a ten-year mandate to make sure things got better. The first President Bush, a conservative Republican from a blue-blood political family, forced Daryl Gates to resign. Bush wouldn't take out *Saddam Hussein* when he had the chance, but this police chief was too much even for him.

Now think about those kids growing up with the kinds of experiences that I had, and think about how they would regard police officers. All those children that are now men, raising their sons and daughters with that kind of distrust. It wasn't just L.A. that was like that. It was the same situation in New York and in D.C. and in New Orleans. We all experienced things that we knew to be true—only to be told that *we* were wrong and the *cops* were right. We were told that we were overreacting or that we had brought matters upon ourselves. It made black people feel that white America *knew* what the cops were doing and was okay with it.

I'm not going to deny that things are better now. People don't get pulled over the way they used to in Los Angeles anymore. You've got to really be trying. At some point, the cops decided that if we didn't like the way they were doing it before, let's see how we'd like it when they did *nothing*. So, yes, that's an improvement. But are these examples of *heroism,* going from abuse to apathy? Let's be serious.

Virtually every white person will publicly swear up and down that you shouldn't judge people negatively by the color of their skin. Then why should you judge people positively by the color of their clothing? Don't get me wrong. I *do* believe in heroes. But the only motherfucker I know who puts on a blue suit and becomes a superior human being is Superman—and not only is he imaginary, that dude's not even from this planet.

Police brutality is something that can be addressed. But the antagonistic relationship between the police and inner-city youth is a bigger problem and a *current* problem. As recently as February 2012, I saw an article that demonstrated that "stop and frisks" are at an all-time high in New York. If the police stopped and frisked you all the time, what possible attitude would you have toward them and society in general, other than hostility and antagonism? It's humiliating.

The relationship between cops and inner-city crime is a chicken-and-egg scenario in which the presence of one leads to the increase of the other. It's the same way with parents punishing their kids. If you punish a boy when he takes a cookie out of the cookie jar, he will resent you. But he'll also understand the lesson. Yet what about a kid who gets punished despite having done *nothing* wrong? If you incorrectly punish a boy over and over for taking cookies when he *hasn't*, eventually that motherfucker is going to start taking all the cookies that he can. If he's paying the *cost*, he might as well enjoy the *benefit*. If he's doing the time, he might as well do the crime. Punishment to kids doesn't have to mean putting them up against the wall and frisking them. It could be as simple as the way they're spoken to and the way they're watched. It's being questioned for no real reason. After a while, fuck it. He might as well go down the wrong road. All the cool kids are doing it anyway.

Now we have black kids who don't think of the future, who are discouraged from being educated, and who see the world as beginning and ending where their neighborhood ends. They start to dabble in crime both due to peer pressure and how the authorities regard them. Eventually, like any ignorant kid, they'll fuck up and get caught. *That's* when the hammer of justice comes into play.

## CHAPTER 13

THE BUSINESS OF AMERICA IS JUSTICE AND SECURING THE BLESSINGS OF LIBERTY.

—GEORGE WILL

O UR legal system is just like our political system: It is designed for the benefit of the wealthy. Yes, there are allowances for people who can't afford things. But no one who is on food stamps is thriving. No one with an overworked public defender is going to be "taken care of," so to speak. In this country, you get what you pay for. And when you can't pay *anything*, you get shit in return. It's no surprise what happens to poor, ignorant inner-city kids when they have dealings with the justice system. Let me first show how things operate from the *other* perspective: the buying of "justice."

In late 1997, I was playing a gig in Westchester County, New

York. At the time, I was bringing my gun with me *everywhere* I went. But at that same time, New York had a law that said that you couldn't carry a gun. We had ourselves a *dilemma*.

I got to JFK airport with my gun in my bag. Back then, Delta had it set up so that you went through the metal detectors before you even walked into the airport. Before I had a chance to declare that I had a gun, the skycap ran my bag through the machine. Naturally, the alarm went off.

I got arrested.

I went directly to central booking. There was a kid in there with me who was sixteen or seventeen years old. Back in the day, he had written on a public desk and gone to jail. I don't know if it was at a school or at a library or whatever. All I knew was that his mother hadn't had the two hundred dollars to pay her son's fine.

That boy had ended up going to Rikers Island. When you're at Rikers and you're a teenager and you're scared out of your mind, you're not thinking about following the law or good behavior. You're thinking about *survival*. Something happened when he was at Rikers—I never found out what—and that kid got sucked into the legal system. By the time I had crossed paths with him, he was in the process of getting two years. I asked the officers if I could take care of his present fines myself, and they told me it had to come from a parental figure. Someone had to go to court and simultaneously declare that they would be responsible for the kid.

Has anyone ever heard of a *white* kid going to jail for writing on a desk? Or even being suspended from class? But for the fact that kid was black, he never would have been arrested. But for the fact that kid was *poor*, he never would have gone to Rikers. I can't imagine what those two years in jail did to him. Can anyone claim that this was *justice*? How long would it take for him working at minimum wage to get that desk repaired and restored to as-new condition? A week, *maybe*?

If you drop out of school, you can redeem yourself. You can get a GED or take adult-education classes later. Once you're in the system, that's it. Criminal records are like the scarlet letter of our day. That ignorant kid making a stupid mistake is marked for *life*. Every other judge in the future will see him as a serial criminal—and the cycle will continue.

But *I* didn't have to go to Rikers. There was a twenty-four-hour court, so instead I went straight in front of a judge. "Mr. Hughley," she said, "haven't you been watching the news?" She had a point. Christian Slater had just gotten in trouble for pretty much the same thing, and some big famous newscaster was also in hot water for trying to bring a gun on a plane.

"Your honor, I didn't know."

"You can't come to New York with a gun!"

She wanted me to stay in New York until the trial, but I said that I had a family and that I had obligations. And I sure did. ABC had just picked up my show *The Hughleys*, and if I didn't get back to Los Angeles, who knows what would have happened.

"We don't know if you're going to come to court," the judge said, "so we're going to have to impose a significant bail before you can be released on your own recognizance."

I felt my mouth go dry. I didn't know what she meant by "significant," but it sure as fuck sounded more expensive than "insignificant."

"That'll be ten thousand dollars," she decided. That meant that I would have to post a one-thousand-dollar bond.

One thousand dollars? That was it? Shit! At that rate, *everybody* could go home with me. I had just played the gig, so I had all cash on me. I was ready to make it rain in the courtroom. The judge charged me with a class D felony. Class D is better than Class A, which is for things like murder, but it still came with mandatory jail time.

I left court and got on a Delta Airlines first-class plane all the way to L.A. When I got into L.A., I was still wondering what was going to happen. This could have killed my new series before it even started, so I wasn't about to leave anything to chance. My business manager knew of a lawyer named Murray Richman. They call him No-worry Murray because he takes on clients and always gets them off. I hired him, just like DMX, Jay-Z, and Ja Rule hired him. That motherfucker knew how to play the game. I paid Murray thirty grand and talked to him on the phone twice. The following week, I returned to New York. We went to court at eight a.m. Murray walked into that court wearing a black-and-white tie that said O.J. WAS FRAMED. This was at a time when people were still pissed about the verdict.

The court was packed when we entered, with many cases to be tried that day. Murray talked to the prosecutor and made a compassionate argument on my behalf. The judge *apologized* and told me that I should have never been arrested. By 8:20, the arrest was expunged from my record. Twenty minutes might be way too generous: It might have been even faster than that.

Now imagine that same situation if I didn't have a good lawyer. I would be going to jail. That's what "mandatory" *means*: You have no option but to go to jail. Any argument I made that it was a misunderstanding or that they ran the bag before I could say anything would have made me a laughingstock.

Now imagine that same situation if I didn't have a good lawyer and it was 2012. I'd probably be declared a terrorist.

After we were finished, I saw the lines of poor browns and

blacks waiting for their chance to have their cases heard. If *their* cases were going to take twenty minutes, the outcomes would have been diametrically the opposite of what mine had been.

"Man, only suckers go to jail," Murray said. "I *told* you that you're not going to jail. All of them on bonds, that don't have the money? *Those* guys are going to jail."

Some people might find his comment offensive. But I don't understand how anyone can be offended at a statement that perfectly captures the *truth* of the situation. It might be wrong, or it might be fucked up, but at the end of the day, Murray was right. *That's how the justice system works*, and I had just fucking *witnessed* it work in exactly that way. Lawyers are just like lobbyists: You throw money at the expensive ones, and they make your problems go away because of their connections. It really is as simple as that. What poor youth has access to a wealthy lawyer? This ain't *Diff'rent Strokes*, this is real life.

# # #

But even though things worked out in my favor, the situation still left me with a very ambivalent feeling. I was walking out the door, but those kids were *fucked*. I know people who get fucked by the legal system *all the time*. I had a friend who was my warm-up. He got into an argument with some dude and said, and I quote, "I'm going to kick your ass. Motherfucker, I'm going to kill you! You don't know who you're fucking with." That exact quote is being said by a dude in some bar in America right now. We've all heard it, and we all roll our eyes at it. It's a stupid, ridiculous thing to say. It's a *cliché*.

My friend got charged with *making terrorist threats* because he publicly threatened to kill someone. This is not some left-wing fear-mongering scenario. This happened to someone I know, and it's obviously happening many times to people I *don't* know. *The anti-terrorist laws are being used for purposes that have nothing to do with terrorism*, even remotely.

My friend called me, scared out of his mind. They had set the bail at $250,000. If he wanted to get out, he would have to put up *$25,000* just for running his big mouth. My wife would have been found guilty of murdering *me* if I tried to put up that money. It was just not going to happen. My friend ended up having to take a public defender to get a plea deal. He didn't do time, but he got convicted. It was a strike on his record—and he's one third of the way to getting "three strikes and you're out," to getting *life* in prison.

But the three-strikes law isn't really a deterrent against crime. It's a deterrent against crime *in California*. In 2007, my twenty-two-year-old nephew was in a store with his white girlfriend, and they were shoplifting. They were putting women's clothes into the baby carriage that *she* was pushing. Guess who got in trouble when they got caught? The girlfriend never got charged with *anything*. She never even went to jail. My nephew got a public defender and pled out, with this counting as a strike.

Very intelligently, he left California. *That's* the thing behind the three-strikes law: "We don't care where you're going, but you're getting the fuck out of here. *We want you to leave.*" Is this a government of laws and not men, where everyone is treated fairly wherever they go in this nation? Shrinking budgets are causing the states to turn on one another, and it's only going to get uglier.

Our justice system is further being used to divide family and friends. People my age remember the horror stories about the Soviet Union and the KGB, how their government had spies among the people so that everyone was always paranoid about who they talked to. It was inhumane and held up as an example of the brutality of communism. Well, at least the KGB *paid* those motherfuckers! Uncle Sam is drafting us into service for *free.*

Right after 9/11, Congress passed a piggyback law for wiretapping. In a society in which people's rights are respected, like the right to privacy and the right to be secure against unreasonable searches and seizures, the police need a warrant to tap into your phone. Fair enough. But then they changed the law. Now if I'm talking to someone who has a wiretap against them, *his warrant can be piggybacked and applied to me.*

As a result, many cats I know went to jail—and not a single one of them had anything remotely to do with the terrorism used as an excuse to pass this law. After a while, I was like, "Man, don't call me. *Ever.*" *Everybody* I know has *somebody* in their family that's shady. You could be talking to them about *anything.* He could be trying to talk you into doing something, and you're point-blank refusing. It doesn't matter. They can't get him, so they want you to tell on him—*to betray your own family member in the name of "building a strong community."* They'll arrest *you* for some minor bullshit to *make* you tell on him.

Case in point: Michael Vick went to jail because a dude who was supposed to be his boy told. Foxy Brown went to jail because the motherfuckers who were supposed to be her people told. The government plans it that way. They usually get to their targets right when the working week ends. On a Friday, they'll arrest a bunch of people. That way, they've got the whole weekend to freak. They'll be told that the first one to get to the DA gets the deal. You'll see motherfuckers racing in there to tell, *racing.* Who can stand up under that pressure? The people who *can* are the hardened criminals we really need to be worried about anyway!

This is not some political issue that I care about in the abstract.

They almost got my kids. My younger daughter, Tyler, was hanging out with these kids over at somebody else's house. She was in high school at the time, and she was doing what high school kids do all over the country: going to a party. Everyone at the party was drinking. Toward the end of the night, these two guys were messing around with these girls on tape. They were simply feeling them up. That's not exactly *classy*, but it's hardly a porno.

While this was happening in California, I was in New York staying at the Hudson Hotel and gigging at Caroline's. My wife, *who never listens to me*, called me, freaking out. "The police are here and they want to arrest Tyler!" LaDonna screamed. "*Don't let them arrest my baby!*"

I didn't know what was going on, and I didn't know what had happened. But I knew what to do in the situation, regardless of what had led up to it. "You tell the police that Tyler is not there," I said.

"They're already in here and they're talking to her!" LaDonna confessed.

I felt like I was living in a fucking horror movie and "the call was coming from the house." "See?" I told my wife. "You never listen to me, and this is what happens." I called my lawyer and my lawyer got on the phone with the police. Then I called back Tyler to try to talk some sense into her and to find out what had happened. She explained what had been going on at the party. It turned out that not only were they trying to get *her*, but e*verybody* who was at the party was getting arrested.

"What the fuck," I asked my daughter, "possessed you to a) ever answer my door anyway, and b) answer the door for the *police*? What would ever possess you to do that? Don't you *ever* answer my door anyway, and *especially* to answer it for the police. That's my goddamn door. Then, when the police ask you a question, don't ever tell them shit. *Ever.*"

Here's another thing about the police. If my neighbor came to my house and asked to borrow a drill or a handsaw or some other tool, I would be glad to lend it to him. Maybe sometime down the road I would need a favor and he could reciprocate. Maybe he'll never get to pay me back, but it sure doesn't hurt to be cordial with people you are living in close proximity to.

But if that neighbor said to me, "I can and will use this power tool against you," I would run into my house as fast as I could, lock the door, and get my gun ready. No one would ever warn you that they mean you harm unless they do, in fact, *mean you harm.* So when the police explicitly tell you that anything you say "can and will be used against you," why the *fuck* would anyone ever give them those weapons? Has any police officer ever recanted and said, "Nah, forget what you just said. It's water under the bridge." Or will they twist the words to make it seem much worse than it is, so that they're perceived as bringing in a stronger case?

Cooperating with the police is like cooperating with a mugger. Yes, you should do it—but only if the consequences of noncompliance are much worse. The cops are not there to protect someone proactively. They *can't.* They can retaliate *after* someone fucks with you. But to protect someone before anything happens? Anyone who has ever had to deal with harassment or stalking or anything like that knows what bullshit "to protect" really is.

As I was trying to knock some sense into my daughter's head, my lawyer was calling the cops. In *minutes,* they left without arresting Tyler. We made a deal with them that she was going to turn herself in that Monday. *All the other dudes at the party went to jail and stayed there for the whole weekend.*

I flew home that Monday to try to clean up the mess. I knew a lieutenant for the LAPD, and he was friends with the person who worked the case. That lieutenant was telling us information—and it wasn't pretty. The first response was that they wanted Tyler to plead guilty, which would have resulted in her being registered as a sex offender. She was fifteen years old, and for being at a party she was going to be publicly marked as a sex offender for the rest of her life.

It's no way *in fuck* that I was going to let that happen.

My lawyer took care of everything. It cost me $65,000 to do it, but it went away. The charges were dropped, nothing ever came up, and they didn't find anything. Thankfully, because Tyler was going to fight it, everybody else's cases got dropped. All those other kids got out without having their lives ruined over nonsense.

A similar thing happened with my oldest daughter, Ryan. She got a DUI, and we had to get her a lawyer and pay for it. She could have lost her license, but ended up getting it suspended for six months instead. Ryan was in England for an exchange program anyway. We wouldn't be seeing her for six months, and by the time she got back, it was done.

# # #

I'm in a fortunate place where I could keep things from spiraling out of control for my kids. I'm *not* letting them get away with what they did. I have the same deal with both my daughters: I'll pay for college, but they have to pay me back the tens of thousands of dollars I spent on lawyers to keep them out of trouble. I'm not going to pay for their stupidity.

Kids don't have the right to be stupid—*but they are.* This idea that kids should have their lives ruined when they make teenage mistakes is completely absurd to me. What most people don't realize is that these kids, these *kids*, are treated in the same manner as professional criminals are treated. That's especially the case when it's teenage black dudes. The legal professionals genuinely believe that they're the thin line keeping these animals from dragging us all down into savage anarchy. The presupposition is: *We've got to teach these people a lesson.*

The authorities have such *pride* in the fact that they're doing "the right thing." But does anyone really *like* a self-righteous person? Are self-righteous people ever really *righteous*? Right-wingers like to make fun of people who shop at Whole Foods (founded by a libertarian!) and listen to NPR, acting as though they're the anointed ones making the world a better place for the uneducated and unenlightened masses. These officers of the law are the exact same phenomenon. Any attempt to treat black youth as people, in their view, is based on a fallacy and therefore doomed to fail. If the leftists think they're sophisticated because they follow politics in foreign countries, the agents of the justice system think they're insightful for a different reason. From *their* perspective, they're the only ones seeing us savages as we really are. That may be a lot of things, but *just* isn't one of them.

Their perspective is understandable. When these judges see kids who look like their own children—or themselves at a young age—they'll feel empathy. They'll think this is a kid making stupid-kid choices. But when they see a young black male—and they see *a lot* of them—they're going to see the boogeyman. How can anyone distinguish in such a short interaction between a kid who needs to be put back on the right track and a criminal dead set on doing harm? The rules of the street demand that you seem tough and fearless, displaying no weakness. In a court setting, that comes across as angry defiance. The consequences are inevitable, and they are tragic.

I felt a taste of that, and that was enough for me. In 2004, I starred in an independent film called *Shackles*. Part of the movie was filmed inside a penitentiary where two dudes from my neighborhood had gotten killed, which made it eerie. As we were shooting one scene, the phone kept ringing and ruining the take.

"Shit," I said. "We gotta do this over."

"Why, what's wrong?" said the director.

"That fucking phone keeps ringing!"

"D.L., there ain't no phone. The offices have been closed for two months."

I rolled my eyes. "Sound got it. I heard the phone. Come on now, quit playing."

But sound *didn't* get it. I listened to the playback and there was no extra noise whatsoever. "They say that happens all the time," the director told me. "People hearing noises or what have you." I'm not saying it's haunted, but I didn't know what the fuck was going on.

Prisons don't convert to movie sets all that easy. Because we were so far out from the city, we had to use the cells for wardrobe. The particular cell we were using as my dressing room had previously been used to keep prisoners under psychiatric observation. It was small and cramped, very minimal, and it only had one tiny window way up high.

When I was in there changing, the fucking door to the cell closed all of a sudden. It's not like it was windy or drafty in there. Even if it was, how much of a draft could one tiny window have on a heavy steel door? Whatever, so the door closed. We'd get the prop master to open it and everything would be okay.

But they couldn't find the prop master.

I knew there was no possibility, *zero*, of me staying locked in that cell for hours, let alone days. I knew that the crew would not give up until I got out. I could see the people through the door, and they were talking to me and keeping me company. In addition, I am not claustrophobic in any way. It's just not a thing with me.

Despite all this, I literally almost went insane. I almost lost my fucking mind. I'm not trying to be dramatic or over the top, but when I say "literally" here, I mean *literally*. I was in there total for only about an hour, knowing the whole time that people were frantically trying to get me out. They could see that I was starting to freak despite my efforts to keep my composure.

This happened when I was a successful grown man in my forties. After I got out, all I could think about was, how could a *child* who is fifteen, sixteen, or even twenty stay in that cell and *not* go insane? There would be *no one* trying to get him out of that cell. Rather, an entire system was set up to make sure he stayed in there. That kid would know that this is what the rest of his life was going to be like.

Prison is like thug boot camp. After you've gone through it, you know you can survive it and handle it. You've got experience living it. Threatening to send you back becomes less and less of a deterrent, if it ever was one to begin with. I know guys that had been going to jail since we were in junior high school. I saw them in junior high, then I saw them again at the end of high school. I saw them a couple of years later, when I was in my twenties. Then I never saw them again. They had three strikes, and they were out. Because they fucked up in junior high, their lives were ruined. They never got to see anything, and they never got to go anywhere. They never got to eat at a cool restaurant or see one tourist spot. It's just *sad*.

But if you were one of these people, how *could* you value a life? If life, to you, only meant what you saw in front of you, then why would it be valued? What the fuck is it worth? *You're* regarded as so worthless that people will just as soon lock you up and throw away the key. You're an unwanted dog in a kennel. How are you expected to look at life as something to be guarded and respected, if that's all you know? If you're looking at life through a keyhole, how are you going to have a balanced view that takes all sides into consideration? You're not even seeing things from *one* side, but a tiny *piece* of one side.

In captivity, any animal only grows to the size of its environment. If you keep a fish in a small tank, it's not going to become the monster you'd find in the Amazon. It's the same way with people. If you have small-minded people in a small community enclosed with a very real border—shit, it's on the map!—to create a small environment, those people will never be able to break through those walls to grow to their full potential.

Because of the focus on the present, because of the disdain for education, because of the lack of perspective and the ignorance that comes from being young, the kids who can escape captivity are few and far between. My manager, who is white, desperately wanted to adopt kids. He went to the adoption agency to find out what his options were. To adopt a white child, the list can take up to five years. A mixed-race child takes three years. But my manager didn't care about the kid's race; he just wanted a child *now*. "How long would it take for a black child?" he asked the lady.

"How long can you wait in this office?" She was joking—but only a little bit. The joke was based on the truth that adopting a black kid could happen a *lot* faster. Animal charities generate sympathy by showing puppies in their ads. "Won't you please help . . . ?" Now try doing that with young black kids who aren't adopted. They wouldn't even run the commercials. Just look at how comical it is:

I made that comment to a friend once and he wrinkled his nose at me. "Are you saying we should be *dogs*?"

"No," I told him. "If we were, we'd be treated better."

# # #

America fell in love with Barbaro the racehorse. They kept him alive after he broke his leg, and he had the whole country crying. He was insured for $20 million. They don't have that kind of insurance on Kobe Bryant! Of course I'd rather be Barbaro than a negro.

California had a referendum that said that animals had to be confined in a humane way. Chickens got bigger cages; veal calves were set free from their pens. But you could still do almost anything to young black men. If you damage the California Tiger Salamander's habitat, the punishment is a $50,000 fine and a year in the federal penitentiary. But you could gun down a young black kid and nothing would happen. There are more black men in prison than in college. More black people are in prison than ever were slaves—but no one's uncomfortable with it. Nobody *ever* feels sorry for black men—including other black men. By any standard, we are the worst off in America. *We need the most help.* Whether it comes to life span, economic mobility and average income, or education level, we are at the bottom. Our lives *are* worth less.

The left regards black criminality as a function of "socioeconomic factors"—but never really wonders what those factors are or how to change them. The right sees it as the outcome of feral animals out of control. But if we can turn a wolf into a poodle, can't we turn a black man into an attorney? It wasn't that long ago that the stereotype of the black male was deferential, studious, and dependable. I'm not saying we should go back to being *servants*, but maybe being valued, productive *employees* would be a great place to land.

Back during the slave era, teaching a slave to read or write was a crime with huge repercussions. The consequent illiteracy that caused was then used as evidence to demonstrate black inferiority. There's a similar situation at work today. *You can't deny people fair access to the law, and then blame them for their subsequent lawlessness.*

There was a very famous political philosopher who addressed this very point. Despite defending dictatorship, Thomas Hobbes is regarded as the first *liberal*. That's because he tried to address why people should obey their monarch in terms of both logic and their rights, rather than the prior "because God says you should." His famous conclusion was that without a government, life is so "nasty, brutish and short" that any ruler is preferable.

Hobbes was right. Human beings *need* a system of justice. When fair use of the formal legal system is denied to them, as it is in the ghetto, they have no choice but to develop their own *informal* system of justice. People start looking out for one another *themselves*. Without some sort of *peaceful* arbitration process, the only response to wrongdoing is making sure that motherfucker thinks twice the next time. Just like in the Wild West, if you can't sue the person or call the cops on him, you've got no choice but to turn to *violence*. It happened all the time. People from a young age enforced the law of the streets upon one another.

When I was about eight years old, I was playing in the street with a couple of friends of mine. This dude who was in his early twenties came out of a nearby house. He went up to me, and I don't know whether he was drunk or high. All I knew was that he was messed up. "I want you to touch my dick," he told me.

I didn't even know what that meant. "*What?* Boys don't do that!"

"C'mon, touch my dick."

I had no idea what the hell he was talking about, but I knew that it was *weird*. I ran away until I bumped into my pal Jerome, who was the same age as the drunk guy. I'd always do errands for him, going to get candy or passing his messages on to other people. "Hey, it's my little homeboy!" Jerome said. "Slow down, man. Why you running?"

Only then did I feel safe. "Some guy just told me to touch his dick."

"He said *what?*"

I told him the whole story of what just had happened. "I didn't know what to do so I ran away."

"Come with me." Jerome brought me to a couple of his friends. "Tell them what you just told me."

Now a whole posse made me lead them to where the dude was. Then they made me repeat what he had said to me. "That motherfucker's lying," the dude said.

"Listen, motherfucker," Jerome told him. "He don't even know what that means. *How the fuck would he even know how to lie about that shit?*"

Right in front of me, they started whupping his ass. The idea that somehow I shouldn't watch what was going on never even entered their heads. It was like a public trial, and I was the audience. They kept beating him and beating him and beating him. *They're not stopping*, I realized. *I think they're going to kill him.* By the time all those dudes were done, he was more dead than he was alive.

This kind of thing happened all the time. My sister got pregnant by a guy, and he wouldn't acknowledge it—so a couple of dudes from my neighborhood beat the fuck out of her boyfriend. Now imagine if your whole community, what you consider your whole *world*, thinks like that. How many places can there be where we *all* see eye to eye?

When you witness violence as the norm, you grow to see it as the solution to your problems. When someone does something wrong, you don't tell. You kick his ass. But maybe the guy whose ass you kicked thought *he* was right. Then he gets his friend and they kick *your* ass. Well, you're not going to let these motherfuckers kick *your* ass. You get your friends and go after them. Now they're outnumbered. To even the odds, someone grabs a knife. Where does this escalation lead to? Logically and inevitably, motherfuckers grab their guns—and they never let them go.

## CHAPTER 14

THE ONLY MISUSE OF GUNS COMES IN ENVIRONMENTS WHERE THERE ARE DRUGS, ALCOHOL, BAD PARENTS, AND UNDISCIPLINED CHILDREN. PERIOD.

—TED NUGENT

I have been around guns my entire life. I will be around guns for the rest of my life. Any attempt to get guns off of the street is an impossibility—and a policy based on the impossible is a failure at best and counterproductive at worst. Guns have been a part of American culture since Washington's troops brought their own pieces to the fray. Black Americans have been here since the very beginning. We've been around guns long before we've been living in the ghetto.

When I was fourteen years old, I came home from school to find my cousins sawing a bunch of wood. "What are you guys doing?" I asked them.

They kept sawing and didn't look up. *Hsss, hsss.* "Just building a room," one eventually said.

"A *room*?"

Hsss, hsss. "Yeah." *Hsss, hsss.* "A room."

"Who's it for?"

Hsss, hsss. "It's for you, motherfucker."

Sure enough, they built this little room for me outside of the main house, and that's where I had to sleep from then on. Maybe my parents felt I was getting into trouble too much, maybe they were sick of my bullshit, maybe they wanted to ostracize me. I was never told what the plan was. I just knew what the *result* was, and that was *spectacular*: I was fourteen and basically had my own studio apartment. They made the space up and it was actually pretty damn cool. It had a carpet, a bed, and electricity. I had a fan for when it was hot, and a heater for when it was cold.

The setup was terrific except for one crucial thing: It didn't have a bathroom. My parents locked the door at nine o'clock at night, and locked me out of the house in the process. I didn't really have a choice in the matter if I had to pee. I just went to the peach tree that we had and pissed on that out of necessity. After a while, I started pissing on those peaches just out of spite. I knew exactly which fruit to aim for, too, since the low-hanging peaches at the bottom were the sweetest. Every Sunday my mother would make peach cobbler, and every Sunday I would never eat it because I knew I had pissed on the fruit. I won't eat peach cobbler to this day.

That sort of solved the bathroom problem. There was a whole other problem that I had to deal with. Sleeping in that room by myself was *horrifying*. I was out there all alone. It doesn't matter how tough you are: When you're fourteen and you're sleeping in complete isolation every night, it gets pretty creepy pretty quickly. They brought in another bed, and my brother Kevin started sleeping in that room with me. I was glad to have his company.

Unlike the main house, my room didn't have a lock on it. It did have a sliding glass door, so every night I would put a stick between the door and the frame so no one could slide it open. The door was at the foot of Kevin's bed. He couldn't see through it when he was asleep, but from my bed I always had a perfect view of the outdoors.

One night there was a full moon, an especially bright one. I could see everything outside, and that's how I watched a big, strange man come up to the glass door. To be fair, I don't know if my imagination made him bigger or if he was just a big man. Whatever the case was, it wasn't a good thing. The man looked to his right, then he looked to his left, and then he tried to open the door. Nobody could hear Kevin or me if there was any trouble, and this most certainly was trouble. There was no way the man could have seen me or anything else inside my room. I knew how dark it was from the outside. My heart was beating very fast. I didn't want anything to happen to me or to my brother. Fortunately, I knew exactly what to do.

I grabbed my gun.

In the silent darkness, I chambered a round. Click *click*. The man heard the sound and he knew exactly what it meant. *Everyone* knows what that sound means. He turned around and walked off just like nothing had ever happened. After a minute, I took out the stick that was holding the sliding door closed and went outside in my boxers to look for the dude. With my little .25 in hand, I felt safe—and I *was* safe. I never found the man, and it's probably a good thing for both of us that I didn't.

Even though I'm not a hunter, I grew up with guns and I always carry them. There is a tendency to put people in categories, and as a progressive I'm expected to be opposed to guns. But all we are is the sum total of our life experiences. Guns, to me, aren't a political issue so much as they are a cultural issue. We live in a gun culture, and I grew up in a gun culture.

The first time I ever saw a gun was in fourth grade. This classmate of mine named Vincent had a cute .25 in a little box. He just showed it to us and nothing really came of it. It was a couple of years after that that I became aware of what that small metal weapon could do. A bunch of us were hanging out at the elementary school that was down the street from my house. It was dark one night, and all the kids were there drinking beer and talking shit.

This cat named Derek—who's a preacher now—picked up this .357 Magnum and shot it three times in the air. *Boom! Boom! Boom!* It was the first time I'd ever heard a gun. The force of that sound was also the first time I'd ever *felt* a gun, because the power of that thing reverberated through the air. The shock waves alone were enough to scare me. I couldn't get my head around what it would feel like if one of those bullets hit you. I went home right after that, jarred.

But I wouldn't have to use my imagination about the power of guns for much longer. Up the block from me lived two brothers who used to get drunk all the time. Then they used to get drunk and *argue* all the time. Eventually, they would get drunk, argue, and shoot guns into the air all the time.

Everyone knows where this story is going.

They were brothers and they loved each other. One day, though, they got too drunk and too argumentative and too trigger-happy.

We didn't see one brother accidentally kill the other brother. We simply saw the effects of him getting shot, and we saw the police and the ambulance come.

Now I had seen guns, I had felt their power, and I had seen their effects when used irresponsibly. It was in seventh grade that I first saw guns being used at their worst. There was a kid named Bradley who was a couple of years older than me. Bradley was this light-skinned dude with a lot of hair, and all the broads loved him. His ambition was to be an Eagle Scout. Bradley would go to scout meetings, and he wore a scout uniform. At the time he was a Life Scout or whatever the level is before you get your Eagle patch. I was obviously never meant to be any kind of scout, so I never really found out. But a ninth grader who is trying to be a scout is obviously on his way to becoming a pretty upstanding citizen.

I was playing ping-pong in my buddy Tommy's garage when this other kid rolled up on a bike. "They shot Bradley," he told us.

I couldn't even believe it. "Bradley is *never* getting in trouble," I blurted. "He's a good dude."

The kid shrugged. "That don't matter. They got him."

We followed the kid to where Bradley was still lying on the street. We got there way before the cops or the ambulance came, of course. We *never* had to worry about them coming to save nobody. I've never seen *that* happen. I saw Bradley there on the ground, struggling to breathe. The blood was everywhere. I would say that it looked "like a crime scene" but for the fact that it actually *was* a crime scene.

I quickly learned what had happened. These cats in my neighborhood always, always, *always* started shit. The previous Saturday had been no exception, and they'd been at a party with some Crips where they once again started shit. Cut to the present. They were standing on a corner and some dudes pulled up—those same Crips. Everybody knew what time it was, so everybody ran. Everyone, that is, except Bradley. He was sitting on his bicycle, thinking he ain't in it, so he didn't flee. Those Crips pulled out a .30 and emptied a clip into him.

I watched Bradley lying there, and then he took this deep, long breath that I had never heard a person take before. It's almost impossible to describe what that breath sounds like to someone who has never seen a person die. Decades later, I read a Stephen King novel and he mentioned that a character "expelled the last of his tidal breath." That was what it like, a pulling in and a last push out just like the tide.

All the various ways that I'd seen cats with guns informed the way that I saw the world. I knew that it was better to have one than to not have one. The cats with them didn't have to worry; the cats without them did. We used to always say that it was "better to be judged by twelve than carried by six." We said that so often it was practically our version of "Have a nice day."

# # #

It was when I was fifteen years old that I finally got a gun of my own. Even though it was only a little .25, I just wasn't scared anymore. Not only wasn't I scared, I wasn't even *cautious*. I felt like I could do what I wanted, and that I could go where I wanted. I felt *powerful*. There was a different feeling with it in my pocket. When confronted with danger, everyone's usual reaction is either fight or flight. Only for me, now there wasn't no flight.

That same year, I was walking home when a car started to pull up alongside me. The driver cut his lights off and slowed down. I knew exactly what that was. The guy in the car was from a different neighborhood and he started talking shit. Before I'd gotten my heater, I would have been running long before he rolled to a stop. Now I was still scared—but I was excited at the same time. I wanted to see what would happen. He got louder, and then I got louder. Quickly I said, "Nigga, I've got a piece. *Fuck* this." I flashed my little .25, and he drove away. After that, I never was the same.

I always had my gun on me from that point on. Gradually, it went from being thought of as a tool of defense to a tool of offense—or even vengeance. When I was nineteen, I was at the Redondo Beach pier with a bunch of people late one night. My neighbor, a big, strong dude, started fucking around and picked me up by my shirt. Then he hung me over the pier, still joking, until he lost his grip and accidentally dropped me in the water.

Being dropped into that water felt like I was being smothered. Those waves were very rough, it was pitch black, and underwater my clothes seemed like they weighed thirty or forty pounds. It felt like somebody was trying to pull me down. It was horrifically frightening. I don't know *how* I lived. I struggled to get out of the water, and I still don't know how long it took. The concept of time was completely out the window. Finally I made it to the shore. I walked straight from the beach past everybody. I went to my car, opened my glove compartment, and got my gun. I went back to where everyone was, but my neighbor wasn't there.

Now, let me explain the difference between a prank and an assault: A prank is when both parties are in on it. I wasn't laughing. I had almost died, and my Jheri curl was ruined. My neighbor knew that it was a wrap. He knew what I was going to do. If he would have still been there, I would have shot him. No ifs, ands, or buts about it.

I drove home, soaking wet and freezing. I pulled into a parking lot where I could see my neighbor's door, and I waited for that motherfucker. It was a couple of days that I did that. Fortunately for him—and for me—I didn't see him. I was literally going to kill him, after he literally almost killed me. By the time I saw him later, I had calmed down and he apologized.

It wasn't like my neighbor would have been *surprised* if I shot him. Everyone in my neighborhood knew the drill. Even after I became a comedian and those days were long behind me, my mentality really never changed.

When I was a grown man and a dad, my brother came over to my house. We had never been close growing up. A large part of that, I think, was because of how much better our mother treated him. It wasn't his fault, but he always reminded me of those times and I didn't like it. Now that we were adults, we decided to make a concerted effort to try to become closer.

I was hanging out with him downstairs, just catching up, while the rest of my family was upstairs doing their own thing. It quickly came out that my brother had just gotten fired from his latest menial job. He had gotten into an argument with his boss, and I have yet to find any boss on any job who enjoys being argued with. My brother was complaining and complaining and complaining about how it was unfair, expecting me to give him sympathy instead of simply telling him the truth.

Well, I did tell him the truth. "It's your fault, man."

If my brother's going to argue with the man who signs his paycheck, *of course* he's going to argue with his sibling. The argument got louder and louder, and it kept escalating and escalating. It got to the point where my brother stood up and delivered a low blow. "Does your wife know," he yelled, "that you been out there fucking these bitches at Birdland West?" There was no question that it was loud enough for LaDonna to hear, and there was no question that it was *meant* to be loud enough for LaDonna to hear.

I stood up, looked him straight in the eye, and said, "Wait here. I'll be right back."

Now let me digress for a second. I know I'm breaking form, I get it, but I really need to make one thing clear. What I have to say is so important that it might save someone's life. It's so important that I'm going to put it in a special fancy box so that whoever sees this will always remember it. I'm such a humanitarian, I'm also putting it in this special fancy box so that even the cheap assholes flipping through this book at the store, wondering what that fool D. L. Hughley has to say, will catch their eye on this page and pause for a second to read it. Here it is:

> **If a motherfucker says "Wait right here" or "I'll be right back," you'd best not be waiting there when he gets back.**

This is a universal truth. Don't sit around, don't wait, don't get your girl, don't get your coat. *Just get the fuck out.* I don't know *how* many parties I went to that were broken up with one of those phrases. People hear that, and people *leave*. That's it!

So I went upstairs to get my gun, and my wife forced herself in my way. LaDonna pleaded with me to stop, because she too knew what it says up in that special fancy box. "Please, don't!" she yelled. "Come on, it's not worth it! You would shoot your own brother?"

My wife and I often have a difference of opinion about the value of certain things. In this case, it most assuredly *would* have been worth it. There was no negotiating with me because I was seeing red. There was nothing she could do to stop me. My brother knew even more than my wife did what it says in that special fancy box. There was not a trace of him by the time I got back downstairs. He had driven off and was long gone.

# # #

There's obviously a profound difference between how I grew up around guns and how most rural Americans grow up with them. Their primary introduction to guns is through hunting, and their dads teach them how to use them responsibly. For me, it was for when you're going to pop a cap in a motherfucker or rob someone. It's just the same thing as how a lot of parents don't want their kids to learn on the street about sex. That's *precisely* how I learned about guns. As a consequence, my relationship with them wasn't as *healthy* as, say, some kid in Omaha's might have been. It was only in 2008 when I *stopped* having a gun with me. That's when I got an apartment in New York, and it would have been illegal to have a gun there. For me, it was a weird and unprecedented experience to be in a big city where I couldn't have a gun.

I'm not some gun nut, of course. I don't like people who *love* guns—that's kind of past the point where I am. I don't get those who go to NRA meetings and feel like the only thing standing between us and a totalitarian government is our firearms. I have a healthy kind of respect and fear for guns and what they can do. There are seven guns for every single human being that lives in America, and I am right on the button with that statistic. I personally have seven guns, three of which are semiautomatic. But let me be real clear: I'm not a hunter. There's personally no sporting element in gun ownership for me whatsoever. I just think guns are necessary, even if I might wish that they weren't.

I wanted to recount all my history with firearms for several reasons. A lot of people see me on TV espousing a strong progressive viewpoint, and they assume that I get my talking points from the DNC or whomever. *Nothing could be further from the truth.* Despite the racial stereotype, I have *not* drunk the progressive Kool-Aid. I consider myself a political progressive for the simple reason that the progressive perspective hews much, much closer to how I see the world. But the gun issue is really one where I don't agree with many people on the left.

I don't understand the position that guns are inherently "bad." They obviously can be a very bad thing sometimes, and I think that there could probably be more restrictions, but I don't think they should be ever taken away. Sometimes you need a *bad* thing to counter a *worse* thing. Our entering World War II was a horrible thing with a gigantic cost, financial and otherwise—but it sure as fuck was superior to the alternative. For me, a gun feels like a strong friend that you need to trust and one that you have to have.

This idea that if only guns were outlawed then everything's going to be fine is not a very realistic one. It parallels the dumb Republican idea that somehow we're going to get rid of all the illegal immigrants. If guns were banned *tomorrow*, and if illegal immigration ceased *tomorrow*, how would we deal with the millions that were already here in this country? It doesn't make sense even theoretically. Any perspective predicated on eradicating one or the other is doomed to fail. It's just like Prohibition. It might be a nice idea as a vague concept, but implementation is literally impossible—and any attempt would bring exorbitant costs, financial and otherwise.

As someone who is on the road every week, I've seen how diverse America really is. The relationship of Americans to guns is no different. In big cities like New York, the more reasonable and the more urbane people are, the less that they like guns. But in other places it's simply as much a part of life as shopping at Walmart, hating blacks, and loving Jesus. Guns are a symbol of American independence. I did a gig in Boise and learned that they passed a law in 2001 that says you could carry your rifle in your truck at school, in case you were coming home and you wanted to go hunting. In Arizona, you're allowed to have concealed weapons at a *bar.* I went to a strip club in Florida, and they had one of those signs listing all the things you couldn't do. At the end of the long list, it specifically said, NO GUNS IN THIS ESTABLISHMENT. If some people have to think twice about whether they're going to bring a gun to see a stripper, can their mentality reasonably be changed? They equate safety with guns, just like I do. A cop might not get there in time. But a gun can be relied upon. It doesn't think or make choices for itself. It does as it's told, every time. That's the definition of reliable.

The other perspective, the idea that the police department is that thing that makes you safe, I don't find very reasonable—to say the least. When I see a cop, I see *trouble,* not salvation. In order for gun control to work, *everything* would have to work. The police would have to get there immediately, they'd have to be courteous, and they'd have to be effective. And while we're at it, I'd like a palace on the moon.

The same way that many "Christians" *applaud* the idea of a poor, retarded man being given the death penalty, Americans are really talking out of both sides of their mouth when it comes to guns. There is no greater arbiter of American values than Walmart. It is the center of the middle American community and represents our hopes, dreams, and aspirations, God help us. You can buy guns at Walmart, but you can't buy a rap album that mentions guns in the lyrics. I like Jay-Z's hooks, but I've never seen him stretch out a room. I've never witnessed one of his songs slaughter six people at a political rally. It's not like Biggie's rhymes took out Tupac; they didn't turn up the volume to take the dude out. Battling on wax doesn't kill anybody.

# # #

Gun violence is another example of American hypocrisy. Growing up, people used to do drive-by shootings *all the time.* I probably saw more drive-bys than I saw ice cream trucks. If I heard jingling, I didn't know if Mister Softee was rolling down the block or if someone got a cap popped into him at the laundry and dropped all his quarters. Yet the first time this country got nationally aware of it was when this little Asian girl got killed in Westwood. *Then* the media was in an uproar about how drive-bys were a problem. Well, gun violence was always a problem for *us*—and that's why it's always had to be a *solution* for us as well.

The question that no one dares broach is this: If guns are as prevalent among young people in our inner cities as they are in our rural areas, why is so much of the gun violence found in the *former*—and so little in the *latter*? I'm sick of hearing that bullshit line, "Guns don't kill people; people do." Those people wouldn't be *trying* to kill anybody if they didn't have a gun. They certainly wouldn't be successful if they were throwing rocks. It's a vapid cliché that doesn't get to the root of the issue. The real question is, "*Why* do people kill other people with guns?" The answer is what I've been talking about all this time: Black life, especially young black male life, is valued less in this country. It's especially valued less by *other* young black males.

Many people in the black community rail against the death penalty. They are pissed off that the only people that the justice system sees as fit to execute are poor, brown, and retarded. But it's unjust in the opposite sense too: How many people have been given the death penalty for *killing* black people? The deck is stacked on both ends.

I have to disagree with my fellow progressives on this issue. The death penalty *is* a deterrent in one very specific sense. I don't believe that any criminal thinks, "I'm gonna get the death penalty if I do this," and thereby refrains from committing a crime. That's a long-time-preference approach. But the motherfucker who gets the death penalty? *He'll* never do it again. Death is the ultimate deterrent. The death penalty is really about *vengeance*, and sometimes vengeance *is* necessary for the most heinous of crimes.

Yet our community's focus on the injustice of the death penalty misses the point. There were forty-six people executed in the United States in 2010. That year there were also 6,043 white murder victims as well as 6,470 *black* murder victims. Over 90 percent of *those* were murdered by other black people. You ain't gotta go to Detroit. You don't see hordes of white people hacking hordes of other white people to death in Rwanda or the Sudan. *Black people kill black people all over the world.* It's like Tupac said: "The same crime element that white people are scared of, black people are scared of. While they waiting for legislation to pass, we next door to the killer. All them killers they let out, they're in that building. Just because we black, we get along with the killers? What is that?" And those words weren't just true; in his case, they were tragically prophetic.

People get more angry about a cop killing someone instead of when another black kid does it. If we stopped killing ourselves, eventually people would get the message. "You know what? They value their lives, so we better stop fucking around." Blacks killing each other is not even shocking. It's the norm—but it's swept under the rug. If you know, you have to *do* something about it. If you know, there's an *expectation*. But if you *don't*, then it doesn't matter—and we live in a world right now where you can tailor-make your reality. You can live on the Internet and have a pseudo-life there. Because of technology, you can hear only what you want to hear and see what you want to see. If I want to hear this kind of news, I watch one channel; if I want to hear another kind of news, I watch another channel. If I don't want to listen to the news at all, I can listen to music on my iPod. Uncomfortable truths become ignorable trivia.

I can't *completely* explain the phenomenon of why black people place such a small value on the lives of other black people. I can certainly talk about the *result* of that mentality. It's men being hacked to death by other men with machetes. It's men fathering children with women and never seeing those kids. It's men being as abusive as they can be, or selling dope to somebody who looks like them, or shooting in a neighborhood where people are going to school and kids are outside playing. Judges, cops, and prosecutors might put us in jail. But the thugs and killers of *our* community are putting us in the ground.

That's how young, poor children are turned into killers before they're fully grown: They are taught that they have no future, and see no life beyond their neighborhood. They are treated like criminals and branded as such. They see violence as the means of solving disputes and arm themselves to be safe. They're trained to appear tough so no one would ever guess that they are suffering. They have no regard for their own lives, so obviously the lives of others are meaningless as well.

If you start walking on this road when you're a kid, how the hell are you supposed to go to college or make something of yourself? When you're old enough to get it, it's already too late. So what's the answer? Lock them all up? Crime is a symptom of a community in crisis. If everyone in a town developed cancer, the people would get chemo—but they'd also desperately try to figure out *why* they're getting sick. I've done my best to address the *causes*. Now let me address the *solutions*.

## CHAPTER 15

THE BAD NEWS FOR DAD IS THAT DESPITE COMMON PERCEPTION, THERE'S NOTHING OBJECTIVELY ESSENTIAL ABOUT HIS CONTRIBUTION.

—PAMELA PAUL, AUTHOR OF
PARENTING, INC.

THE mechanism through which children are changed from dumb-asses into contributing members of society is *education*. It's a public good, meaning that it benefits everyone. Everyone wins by getting educated, and everyone wins by being in an educated community. But the assault on public education has been going on for decades. I would peg the tipping point to a specific year: 1978.

That's when a man named Howard Jarvis changed California forever.

At the time, wealthy Californians were pissed. The court had ruled that tax money should be apportioned for educational purposes on a fair, equitable basis. It wasn't right that kids in rich neighborhoods should have great educations while poor kids were sucked into a system that was educational in name only. So property-tax dollars were taken from rich communities and used to subsidize schools in poor communities.

That was why Howard Jarvis and men like him put Proposition 13 on the ballot in 1978. Proposition 13 tied property taxes to a one-time assessment of a person's home. It strictly limited how much those taxes could increase annually, even if the value of a property doubled or tripled. If property-tax dollars could no longer be used on behalf of rich children, then they weren't going to be used on behalf of *anybody*. Proposition 13 passed—and budget cuts came with it, virtually overnight.

As a schoolboy at the time, I didn't know a lot about politics. But I immediately learned how Proposition 13 affected my life. I couldn't go to school in the district that we were technically in because my house was in an unincorporated area of Los Angeles, like we were Palestinians or something. The high school I ended up being sent to, Gardena High, was seven miles away. It wasn't a big deal for me and the other kids who lived by me. We had buses; we had bus passes; we could get on the bus; we could get to school.

Then Proposition 13 kicked in.

I remember perfectly that it was January, and my mother told me that I had to find a way to get to school. I didn't have a car. None of us did—and none of us were going to be walking for miles, literally, every day to school. It was an hour-and-a-half walk up and an hour-and-a-half walk back, and that walk back was in the dark. I had to go through Crip neighborhoods, from the Pay Back to the Shot Gun through to the Fives, to my neighborhood. It was just like *The Warriors*. Everybody in every neighborhood knew which way I had to walk. Sure enough, one night some cats I was into it with beat me unconscious on Rosecrans and Vermont. After a while, *fuck* that.

It was so hard to get to school that I used every reason I could to avoid going. *Of course* it's an excuse and *of course* it's something that I wouldn't do now. But if I knew what the fuck I was doing then, then I wouldn't have needed to be going to school to begin with. Kids are uninformed by definition.

At the same time that they took our bus passes away, they took the after-school programs away too. Avalon Gardens Elementary was much closer to my house, and it used to stay open. They had games for people to play, and they had job-fair programs. I would think Howard Jarvis would have rather had kids occupied with wholesome activities than growing up on the streets. Isn't it better for these young black children to hang out and play Yahtzee at school than be on the corner chilling out with the Bloods? But that's a long-term kind of thinking, and our nation is really very selfish and very short-sighted. So what happened right after that? Reagan came into office, and there was a huge rash of drive-by shootings. What did they *expect* would happen? If it's true that black people have poor habits, it's because white people stopped investing in what we need to develop good ones.

This kind of thinking is what I see behind the charter school movement. The charter schools are explicitly based on the idea of putting budgets before education. The biggest argument charter school advocates make is that they are cheaper. They also claim their schools are just as good as public schools—but that's like an afterthought to them. Public education is a function of government. The government is fine with a present-day loss so long as the long-term payoff is there. It's why President Obama and so many others refer to education as an "investment." The payoff is not immediately there. But a charter school turns education into a *commodity*. All they want is to get their cash *now*, and the way they get their cash is to make sure the kids do well on a certain test. *Teaching children to take a test is not the same as educating them.* It's preparing them for a year-end exam. What happens to the kids in twenty years is not the charter school's problem. Their responsibility is done—and the government is stuck with the bill should the kids have problems as adults.

The most successful American company is Walmart. Do we really want our kids raised on the Walmart model? The private sector cares very little about *results*. Walmart stocks aisle after aisle of cheap, unhealthy food. They don't pressure the food companies to develop cheap, *healthy* food for the benefit of their customers. All they care about is their money, which is (arguably) fine enough in that context—but is calamitous when it comes to educating our kids.

I am not saying the public school system is doing great. It's doing *horribly*. So let me compare the public school system with another government program that seemed hopeless: the Iraq war. In 2007, everyone except for the completely delusional neocons knew that the war in Iraq was a complete shit show with very little hope of improving. President Bush, John McCain, and all those types got together and started analyzing the situation with one simple premise: Failure was not an option. At the same time, they didn't want to admit that *success* was not a *possibility*. But the way things were going, that shit couldn't stand. It was embarrassing for America, it was humiliating, and it made all the time, effort, and lives expended up to that point seem not only wasted but downright counterproductive.

Those military minds and politicians worked up a plan. They threw manpower at the problem and they threw money at the problem. The war was wildly unpopular politically, but they weren't ready to "cut and run." They used the very term "cut and run" as a slur against those who thought otherwise. To some extent, things improved. At the very least, they improved enough that President Obama was later comfortable bringing the troops home.

So if the educational system is failing American youth in general and black American youth in particular, where the fuck is the resolve to do something? Where are the committees meeting to find a way out of this mess? There are none. That's because *they consider it easier to bring democracy to Iraq than a diploma to a nigger.* The former scenario is very strenuous, and it will take a lot of financial resources, time, and simple sweat. But the latter option, to them, is an *impossibility.* They literally believe that it's not possible for black people to be educated—even though *dogs* are capable of receiving successful job training. If the slave masters thought of us as subhumans to be owned and sold, is this new perspective supposed to be *progress*?

I don't think it was a coincidence that Howard Jarvis came along when he did. That selfish mentality speaks to a larger problem facing America and how our country had changed. People forget that the 1970s were called the "me decade" because of how the nation turned away from 1960s idealism. It's easy to get it confused, because Reagan's '80s made the '70s seem like a big, happy time.

I'm not delusional enough to claim that the public school system cares about results either. But with public schools, it's a different situation. When a charter school fails, you yank your kid out and to hell with everyone else. But when a public school is in trouble, that's an opportunity for the community to get involved and to improve things for *everyone*. The public school system made this country what it is. It's the mentality surrounding the importance of education that has changed. The people who had been the shepherds of our system changed. That made the goals change, and that made what we believed to be important change.

It used to be that people cared about what they would leave their children. Now that's just what they say so they *sound* like they give a fuck when they *don't*. My kids and everybody else's kids are just a Tea Party slogan to attack government spending—"We can't let our children inherit this debt!"—even though they inherited a national debt from *their* parents. There used to be a time when men made sacrifices so that people could feel better, so that the country could work. There were more people who cared about what their country did. Today our government threatens to shut down more than Microsoft Windows does. I know soul-food restaurants that don't shut down this much.

I am not under the delusion that education is going to make a comeback in this country. Far from it. Children don't vote, so they can't exert political pressure directly. I can see problems. I can offer solutions. But at the end of the day, I face the world the way it *is* and not the way I *want* it to be. I was very fortunate to have this reality-based perspective beaten into me at a very young age. I had what so many American children lack in this day and age: a father.

# # #

Our next-door neighbor growing up was a pedophile named Mr. Moke. He was a big, fat dude with a big, fat wife. I can't be sure she knew what was going on in her house, but everyone else in the neighborhood sure did. Mr. Moke would pay kids to come over. A while after they entered, I'd watch them come out. They'd look kind of fucked up, but now they would have money.

My father told my siblings and me that we could never even so much as *look* over there. If a ball landed in Mr. Moke's yard, it was lost to us forever. We just had to let that ball go as if we had never had it to begin with. There was never to be any contact with Mr. Moke, *ever.*

One night when I was about twelve years old, there was a really bad earthquake. The next morning, my brother Kevin and I were in the backyard picking greens for my mother. Big, fat Mr. Moke waddled over to the fence and leaned over it. "I heard all that moving around," he told us. "I thought you and your brother had got at each other." In case that vernacular is too "urban," let me make it really clear: What he meant is that he thought Kevin and I were *fucking* each other.

At the time I didn't really understand what the hell he was talking about—but my father did. That motherfucker heard every word Mr. Moke said through the kitchen window. He put down his breakfast, walked out through the screen door to our backyard, hopped the fence into Mr. Moke's backyard, and proceeded to beat the fuck out of that man. Then my father hopped the fence back and finished his scrambled eggs and Polish sausage.

Mr. Moke was just some random pervert, and I had a father to protect me. In this regard, I was very fortunate. But many children didn't have such luck, and the consequences to them were horrible. In this country, we have to have our heroes. We have institutions that we're taught to trust implicitly and not even question. For many women, it's churches. For men, it's the cathedral of athleticism.

It's no coincidence that those very institutions were the exact ones behind systematic child abuse. When I rail against hypocrisy, it's not just because I have a difference of opinion with someone or because I simply find it of comedic interest. I rail against it because hypocrisy in *thought* leads to harm in *action*. Despite all the smiles on television, America is a predatory country. It has *always* been based on predation and exploitation, whether of slaves or immigrants or whomever we can squeeze at any given time. I don't just mean corporations. It really pervades all aspects of our culture.

Coach Jerry Sandusky had a charity for underprivileged kids. And very often, those kids that Coach Sandusky came into contact with didn't have fathers in their lives. He didn't have to go online and lure them to a park with promises of candy bars and toys. Their very own mothers sent them to the slaughter. Even when those boys told their moms what was going on—and I'm sure *some* of them did—they just couldn't believe it. That kind of thing happened in this country all the time, and only now are we finding out about it.

When I was growing up, we were told that if we wanted to stay out of trouble, then we should go to church and play sports. Those "wholesome" institutions supposedly exist for the betterment and protection of the people. Yet between Catholic priests, Bishop Eddie Long, and Penn State, I'd rather be on the streets. My odds are *better* with the dope boys and the pimps. When *they* try to fuck me, it's just for money.

We *despise* poor and underprivileged people in this country. We see them as prey, and we fuck them at every turn—be that literally or figuratively. There's this American idea that we're a meritocracy, that people reach the top through the virtues of hard work and perseverance. But the flipside to that thinking is that the poor and underprivileged must be flawed, lazy, stupid, or whatever other terrible adjective you would like to use. They didn't work hard enough in some kind of way but had every opportunity. Newt Gingrich explicitly says this all the time, and virtually no one blinks. He has claimed that poor kids have bad work habits because they don't see anybody go to work unless it's doing something illegal. Is there any doubt which "poor" kids he was referring to? Let me make perfectly clear what no one else will: "Poor" in this scenario usually means *black*.

Gingrich knows he's full of it, and so do the people who think like him. He's not a stupid man. All it takes is five seconds of thought to imagine being a child in these types of households. I have four female cousins. Between the four of them, they have fifty children. *Fifty.* These are all never-married single mothers, who have these kids and get county checks. No one doubts what the children will inevitably grow up to be. But is it really the children's *fault*? Can anyone doubt that their lives would be better if there was a stable male influence in the home? Nothing good ever comes of the nuclear family being destroyed. The black community used to be just that: a community. Money used to circulate in the black community twenty times. You used to go to a black barber to get your hair done, then go to a black doctor for a check-up, and then buy your groceries at the black supermarket. Then we decided that we should be integrated, which of course we should have the right to do. But now money circulates just once. Is that still a community?

# # #

If education started to go south in the late '70s, things started falling apart for *my* community with the advent of the War on Poverty. America hasn't won a war in so long that we have to stop pretending like we know how to fight one. We got some good licks in, but we haven't been successful in anything we've called a war in the last sixty years. Right around the Korean War is when the best we could hope for was a draw. Whether it's the War on Poverty, the War on Drugs, or the War on Terror, we always know how to start but we never know how to finish. We've got a plan on getting in; we never have one on getting out. Look at the Gulf War, the only major success of that entire period. America had gotten so soft that we had to bring in an *old lady* to win it for us. Margaret Thatcher had to bitchslap President Bush, *a former war hero*, and tell him, "This is no time to go wobbly!" That's British for "Nigga, get it together!"

I think the War on Poverty was a good idea *in theory*. The idea was: We're going to give you money if you don't have a man around. If you took government assistance at that time, you couldn't have a man in the house. But when the government is the father, he's a jealous father. As a consequence, black men left their households. They were allowed or even *encouraged* to abdicate. Many black men got to say that they didn't have to be around—and if you trace the rise of drug use and teen pregnancy in the black community, it started around that time.

Before the late '60s, black men had large families and worked menial jobs—but they were stable and there was nowhere else to go. They were ostracized if they didn't take care of their family. A man would do anything he had to. Mothers stayed with the kids. They didn't have housekeepers.

I remember when I was growing up, people used to tease you if you didn't have a father. Now they tease you if you *do*. The majority of black children are raised in single-parent homes. We're a community of *men* being raised by *women*. Not only do these boys not know what a man is like, their *children* don't know. My mother used to make all of us—me, my father, my siblings—leave our shoes outside because they smelled so bad. But when I woke up from a nightmare and smelled my father's feet, I wasn't afraid. He made me feel safe, even the mere scent of him. I can't imagine what it must be like to be a little kid and to have to be the man of the house. It must be *terrifying*—and I've already discussed what road that kid will probably end up on.

All my childhood sports heroes had fathers: Kareem Abdul-Jabbar, Magic Johnson, Michael Jordan, Muhammad Ali. They'd talk about their coaches as if they were their fathers—even if they *did* have actual fathers. Michael Jordan had a great father, and he *still* talks about his coach in that way. Now look at LeBron James and Allen Iverson. They're guessing at being a man. LeBron James left Cleveland because he tried to win the championship and he couldn't do it. But he should have stuck it out in miserable Cleveland until he got that championship. My father would have said that you have to play it out until you win. LeBron's coach was a puppet who deferred to him, and he lost his star player because that's *not* what a coach should be about. Fathers and coaches are really the same thing: They both tell you to sit down and shut the fuck up.

I learned lessons from my dad every day, and they're not the same kinds of lessons a mom would teach. He once told me that you don't want to be a thoroughbred; you want to be a mule. "Thoroughbreds don't last. Everyone is always going to need a mule. You can be tough or smart or strong—but if you can outwork everyone, you're set." Is *any* mom going to say that? Or is she going to tell you that you're the best and that everybody loves you? People grow up genuinely believing that everyone loves them. In other words, *they grow up completely delusional.* And with our culture edifying whatever you already believe, people will never have to question their delusions. How the fuck is that going to *help* this country, let alone *save* it?

I can tell the difference between how I was raised and some of these children today. I can see it in Obama. He thinks everyone is going to like him and is disappointed when they don't. He is baffled when people don't like him. He honestly feels in his heart of hearts that if you just got to know him, you'd like him.

Now look at the Jacksons and their dad. They wanted to be stars, so their dad told them that they were going to have to practice. "You want me to buy a guitar? You want me to spend this money? You'd better work to be a goddamn star." Whereas a typical mom will be like, "He's tired! He's trying! Let that boy rest." Michael Jackson became a freak when he *stopped* listening to Joe Jackson.

You can always tell the difference with a man who was raised by his father, whether he liked him or not. He didn't even have to be a particularly good father, either. He just had to be there.

The question becomes: Can the nuclear family be rebuilt? Men are getting married less and less—and though this is a huge social problem, I really can't blame them. Our women have forgotten how to land a man and how to keep him. So, ladies, let me take a page out of Steve Harvey's book. Let D.L. teach you what you have to do.

## CHAPTER 16

MEN CAN'T HANDLE ME BECAUSE I'M A STRONG, INDEPENDENT WOMAN.

—EVERY FOREVER-ALONE FEMALE, EVER

MY fellow King of Comedy Steve Harvey has made a great name for himself dispensing romantic advice to women, especially black women. I think what's he's done is terrific, and I salute and applaud him. As a consequence of his success, I often get asked if I have similar advice to give to the ladies. To be honest, I don't think it's all that complicated. Women are naturally very beautiful to me—and the key word there is *naturally*.

Black women claim that they view themselves as beautiful, but they do everything possible to *escape* looking like black women. LaDonna looks much better when her hair is in its natural state than when she's got a weave in it or when she has it all straightened out. Many of the attributes that society calls beautiful stem from black women: plump lips, darker skin, a thick butt. Those are all things that *white* women desire. They get collagen shots, they darken their skin, they get booty pops. At the same exact time, in the shops on the other side of town the sisters are getting weaves and contacts. It's almost like they're switching places.

Women's beauty techniques have become so artificial that it's downright scary. Some sisters get these blue contacts, and it looks like old people who are going blind from cataracts. Where's the sex appeal in that? I even saw a girl who didn't get her blue contact flush, and it was sliding down her eye. *She looked like a Siberian husky.* If she had a fur coat on, I'd be mushing her through the snow to the Palins' house. No one wants to screw a girl who is halfway turned into a motherfucking wolf—and that's all that beauty really comes down to. When I, or any straight man, see a beautiful woman, the thought is, *I want to fuck her.* It's not whether I think she's *nice* or whether I want to hang out with her. Those are all elements of it, to be sure, but in the end the question is: Do I want to fuck her?

There's a move in our culture to equate beauty with accomplishment, and that's just nonsense. A comedian isn't funny *because* he's handsome, and he isn't handsome *because* he's funny. Some of us just happen to be blessed with both qualities. A woman isn't beautiful *because* she's done great things. That doesn't make any sense. It's a completely false notion that's being pushed on men by women. How can you dictate what someone finds *attractive*, or even argue about it? How is that even possible? A woman is beautiful if she causes motion in a man's drawers, period.

I was at a party one time with a really tall Sudanese model named

Alek Wek. She was so dark that she looked like a walking eclipse. Everyone kept telling me how beautiful she was and I just didn't see it, literally. She could be called elegant, or graceful, or lithe, or invisible at night. Those qualities she had. Between her height, her complexion, and her actual features, she looked just like Manute Bol. In fact, I dare people to put pictures of the two of them side by side. It's like one of those puzzles that'll keep anyone occupied for hours, where you have two identical drawings with minor differences that you have to find and circle.

I've even seen articles that called Caster Semenya beautiful. She's a female runner from South Africa who broke world records and is incredibly athletic. That's great, and no one is denying her accomplishments. Bravo! But Caster is *incredibly* athletic. That broad is so fast and so *ugly* that the rest of the runners were saying that that bitch has *got to be* a man. The running organization eventually had to run tests on her to establish her genetic identity. The early reports said that she was a hermaphrodite who had testicles that hadn't fully descended. She supposedly had three times the normal amount of testosterone for a female; strong enough for a man, but made like a woman. That's a tagline for a *deodorant*, not a beauty queen. Beauties don't have secrets like testicles all up inside them, and hormone levels so high that they develop a manface. Yes, she is a great athlete, but no, I do not want to fuck her! I don't even know if I *could* fuck her if I wanted to. That's as far from attractive and beautiful as you can get.

# # #

But beauty is only part of it. The fact of the matter is, *LaDonna is the only black woman I could ever marry.* I like her friends, but I can't really be around them that much. They are very, very loud. I don't just mean one or two of them; I mean *all* of them. It gets really bad when they all gather together in this women's group that they have. They read books, and they pray, and they cry. Sometimes the group meets at our house, and my dumb ass always manages to walk in when one of them is telling some heartrending story: " . . . and then my husband . . . left me . . . when I was pregnant!"

"Jesus is giving you strength!"

"I know, girl!"

My timing is perfect. I always open that door right when the tears are streaming at their peak, and all eyes turn to me.

"Hey, D.L.! Come join us!" they plead.

"Uh . . . *no.*"

If I was married to one of those women, I just know that I'd have to choke the hell out of her. "Who put the quarter in you?" I want to ask them. "Shut up!"

Women read all these books about how to make men like them and what it means when he doesn't call. Forty-five percent of black women will never marry, which either means 45 percent of black women talk too much or 55 percent of black men are deaf. All women just need to know one thing: If you want to make a man like you, then you should try shutting the fuck up once in a while. If a man hasn't called, that means he doesn't feel like talking or he doesn't feel like talking to *you.*

Black women have convinced themselves that black men *can't* handle them. "He goes to white women because he doesn't want a strong woman," they claim. Like I said before, everything in nature seeks the path of least resistance. As part of nature, men are the same way. No one wants to make things more difficult for themselves than necessary. That doesn't make any sense. Every animal experiences some attraction—and every animal also runs away from loud noises. When an elephant trumpets, everyone gets the fuck out of the way.

The truth is, it's not a question of black men fearing a strong woman. It's about black men fearing a constant headache. Strength does not equal volume! Jesus was a strong man with a strong message, but he didn't use a bullhorn when he gave the Sermon on the Mount. His words are in red in the Bible, not in boldface and all-capital letters. If a woman is hunting for a man, she should pretend that she's hunting for a deer. She should refrain from making any sudden movements, make sure that she smells nice, and *above all* not make any loud noises. It's as simple as this: Hush for love. Women only have to do *one* thing: *Be quiet.*

Men, on the other hand, need to do *three* and *only* three things. Or at least that's the way it was when I was a kid. It was like the three commandments of being a man:

1. Take care of your family.
2. Be home before the sun comes up. (Not sundown, sun*rise*.)
3. Let no bullshit from outside come into your house.

That was *it*. That was all you had to do.

When I was a little boy, I decided that I was going to play a prank on my father one day. We had a van with seats in the back that you couldn't really see into from the driver's seat. I knew he was going somewhere so I hid in those seats. We drove and drove and drove and after a while I popped up like a jack-in-the-box: "Ta-daa!"

My father immediately pulled over, mad as a motherfucker. I don't know where he had been planning on going, but he turned the van around and we went back home. He couldn't have me knowing his plans for that day, and I *still* haven't found out. But if

I discovered that my father had a woman on the side, I wouldn't be upset. I wouldn't care at all. Yet if my *mom* had done that to my dad, it would be a problem. Obviously, there's a double standard.

The reason I'm fine with having a double standard is that I don't think monogamy is a particularly natural state. Sex is as animalistic as people can get, and we can learn a lot from nature. One of the things I learned is, *There are very few animals that are monogamous.* I think it's pretty much ducks and horses. Otherwise it's always one male and several females, and there's nothing wrong with that whatsoever.

Women's obsession with monogamy is ridiculous. Look at the Tiger Woods debacle. Tiger Woods is a *billionaire.* If you're a billionaire, you should be able to have all the sex you want. Marrying a millionaire wasn't enough for his wife. She had to have a billionaire. So why should one woman be enough for Tiger? His *name* is Tiger. It's not Horse or Duck. Tigers have harems. They do that stuff a lot, and they do it naturally.

But nowadays, it's a lot harder for a man to be discreet. With Facebook, Twitter, and Skype, everybody could know your business all the time. Not too long ago, LaDonna called me when I was in New York and she was back home in Los Angeles. It was one a.m. her time—which meant it was four in the morning in Manhattan. What was the crisis that couldn't wait until morning? No, there hadn't been a fire. No, our kids weren't in any kind of trouble. The emergency stemmed from the fact that my wife had gotten on my e-mail. LaDonna saw that some girl was flirting with me—and she also saw that I had *never* responded. "Who is this woman?" she demanded. "*Why aren't you saying anything?*"

She wasn't mad because I flirted back. She was mad because I didn't even respond! What am I supposed to do in these situations?

The best thing for me to do is to not take the woman up on it. I'm not going to *admonish* her. If I'm a guest in someone's home and I'm served food I don't like, I'm not going to eat it—but I'm not going to make a scene about it, either, and ruin a relationship. In fact, I'm still going to take that woman's calls if she needs to speak to me about business. At the same time, I'm not going to put myself in a situation where the two of us are alone. I'm in a business where people flirt all the time. That's just the nature of the industry, and it always will be.

That sure makes a lot of sense to me. But not to LaDonna. "If that was me . . . !" she snapped.

Well, it ain't you! I don't understand why women always go for that line. Men and women are very different. A man ain't just a woman plus a dick. Women seek monogamy while failing to understand that men don't want or need it. It's like how we pee standing up. We're just wired differently. Monogamy is so unnatural that they had to do research and involve giant multinational corporations to facilitate it. Viagra wasn't invented for new sex, but for sex with who you're with already. The problem wasn't that your dick couldn't get hard for *new* pussy. They had to make a pill for when you have the same pussy over and over again.

Carlito's Way said it best: "You don't get reformed, you just run out of wind." It's not that men don't *want* women when they get older. We just don't want all the *bullshit* that comes with it. You don't feel like driving, or you don't want to talk. You're tired, or logistically it don't fit in. It's not like men ever become poster children for monogamy. We just get *exhausted*. We stop arguing with women not because we *agree* with them. We stop arguing because we want to go to sleep!

I might be tongue-in-cheek with some of my advice on how to

keep a man, but the issue of absent fathers is really at the crux of many of our social problems. The housing crisis we have in this country is a crisis of broken homes. It's a nation where fathers are absent, and no one is passing on the reality check that only a dad can provide. But I'm no hypocrite. I put my money where my mouth is and try to be the best father I can for my kids.

Unfortunately, sometimes I wish that they'd try to be the best kids they can be for *me*.

## CHAPTER 17

IT SEEMS THAT FOR SUCCESS IN SCIENCE OR ART, A DASH OF AUTISM IS ESSENTIAL.

—HANS ASPERGER

BEING a dad to daughters is very different from being a dad to sons. The dangers are different, and the way they listen to you is different. I'm sure every father feels the same way that I do about his daughters: I love them, but I don't like them. Who *likes* women? I told my two daughters that if a man could have a face only a mother could love, a woman could have a personality only a father could love. They don't help. They won't even open doors. My daughters wait until I open the door for them before they get in the car. They're always telling *me* what to do! It's *horrible*. They will get together and know that they are annoying the fuck out of me. Then

they'll say, "But you have to take care of us until we get married."
They really believe that.

My daughters don't ever leave me alone. They bother me *all the
fucking time*. I can't even sleep, because one of them will call in the
night asking me dumb shit. "Daddy, there's a mouse here! What
am I supposed to do? I'm horrified!" "Here" would be New York
or D.C. when I'm in Los Angeles. What could I possibly do to help?

My younger daughter, Tyler, is *certain* that she's loved, even
though I like her the least. She is so confident that I like her the *most*
that she's convinced everyone else. It's not true! I can tell it to her
face. Here I am, putting it in writing. She simply will not fucking
accept it. "Oh, Daddy. *Whatever.* You got *them* fooled. That's some
bullshit." Her sister and my wife are so convinced that Tyler has me
wrapped around her little finger that when they want something,
they have *her* ask me for it.

My eldest daughter, Ryan, went to Smith and now lives in
D.C. working for Senator Boxer. Ryan is smart, worldly, and
progressive—and she talks *a lot*. Ryan is into politics because she's
just like me—only, being a woman, she's scared all the time. She's
the most fragile of my three kids, but from outward appearances
you would never know it. She's the one who *always* needs some kind
of affirmation. She needs to hold my hand and to hear how much I
love her. Incessantly. *Constantly.*

Both Tyler and Ryan like to come to New York and visit with
me whenever they can. I have what amounts to "dates" with them.
We spend time together and then go out to dinner. I listen to them
talk about their dreams and problems. It's really kind of a weird ex-
ercise for me. Generally, the only reason I'll listen to a woman is if
I'm getting something out of it. If I let their mother talk that much,
there'd better be a blowjob about to happen. But nothing's in it for

me when I spend time with my daughters—except for the fact that they feel better about themselves, so they'll make better decisions. I always think of it as kind of a hustle on their part, because the girls get to go to a great restaurant and no dude is annoying them about some bullshit. I'm an ideal date, and they're not expected to put out.

While we're in New York, we also go shopping or out to some cool events. Even their mother tells them to wait until their father gets to New York, because she knows there's going to be some fly shit. They don't have to spend their money; they can spend Dad's money. They're *users*, both of them! Of course I love them anyway—but not *because* of that. I can actually do without the using. I would, in fact, love them *more* if they *didn't* drag me down all the time.

One weekend around the time of the Obamacare debate, Ryan came to New York to stay with me. When I met up with her, instantly I knew something was wrong. She didn't say much after we had dinner, but I didn't prod her, either. At the end of the night we came back to my apartment and I went to bed. Ryan changed into her pajamas and lay down next to me to talk. I thought it was the weirdest shit ever, because she was twenty-two years old. But I didn't say anything about it. When she left the next day, I put her in her car and told her to call me when she got home safe.

I found out later that she had posted as her Facebook status: "Sometimes you need to lay next to your father, put your head on his chest, and know that everything is going to be okay." I never would have thought that about her. I thought this little broad just wanted to go to dinner and scam me out of a free meal. What happened was, she'd been answering phones for Senator Boxer that week. Everyone knows how answering the phones works, whether it's at the Senate or the cable company. You cuss out the dude that picks up at Delta airlines. You never get to yell at Mr. Delta himself. All those Tea Partiers had saved their venom for my daughter and said the meanest shit they could think of. "You're a nigger bitch that I hope dies of cancer."

Now imagine being a woman in this world who is that scared, who faces that much animus, but who *doesn't* have a chest to lay her head on. Imagine not having a relationship where she's the most important thing. She might think she could approximate that with some dude—but the dude just wants some ass. For a lot of women, that's where they are. They have no point of reference for how it's supposed to be, to be in a relationship predicated on love. The first and most resonant love for a woman is her father's love. Yet over 70 percent of black girls are growing up in households where the father ain't around. Increasing numbers of young white women are having the same problem.

When I was growing up, most women had a relationship with their father. If it wasn't their father, there were a lot of positive male role models around. These women had self-esteem, went to a church where everyone watched out for one another, and had many people that they looked up to. They believed that they were valuable. It meant that getting pussy was hard. Having sex with them was almost impossible. No matter what game you spat, the response was the same: "You want me to put that *where*? Sir, I know you've got a job to do and I respect you. But I'm not comfortable. You can call my father."

The way women view relationships and how they feel about themselves, then and now, is all based on how the first man in their lives interacted with them. The way I see it, my gig as a dad is for my daughters to have as few dicks as possible. That's the *overriding* goal. The more a woman has a relationship with a male role model, the more it reinforces to her that she's valuable—and the less inclined she is to give that shit up to just anybody. She becomes that much more selective about her partners.

But so few women have relationships with positive male role models now that they're always looking for a way to have it happen. They want someone to be that male role model who loves them and gives them some kind of attention. No matter how old they get, they're still looking for their real father.

I don't want to be like Laurence Fishburne and wake up one day to find out my daughter has been making a porno. Sometimes I have to suck it up and do things I would not normally do. My daughters will occasionally get mad at me and not call. If this were anyone else in the world, my response would be, "Fuck you! I'm not calling you either." That would *especially* be the case if it was just some random girl, like I'm going to let a *woman* do that to me. But I always end up being the one to call my daughters first, because I know that I *have* to stay close to them. I've got to swallow my pride and call so they know that no matter what they do, somebody loves them. It's *infuriating*, but I do it.

It turns out that Ryan recently got an apartment. "It's in a rough neighborhood," she announced, "so I know that you would want me to have an alarm system." Now why the hell would anyone *choose* to move somewhere where you need an alarm? She thought that she was going to live wherever she wanted, and I was the motherfucker who was going to take care of it and make it safe for her. It annoyed the hell out of me.

I told her, "Sometimes you want to be my child, when it suits your purposes, and sometimes you want to be a woman. *Pick one.* You can't ask for my money but not my advice. You can live your life and I'll just kind of observe it, and it'll be cool. But if you want the accoutrements of being my daughter, you have to be my daughter all the time. So which is it going to be?"

"I want to be your daughter."

Well, I did say that she was smart.

# # #

Now, as hard as it is for me sometimes to bite my tongue and play the father role to my daughters, raising my son was that much harder. Every dad sees himself in his son. But when Kyle was born, it brought back some really bad memories of when I was a kid.

We all have moments that, at the time, seem like any other day—but that haunt you for the rest of your life. I've had my share of misgivings just like everyone else. But one of those events is so shameful to me that I've never mentioned it to anyone or even said out loud. Next door to my elementary school was another school called Benjamin Banneker. Both of them are still there. Benjamin Banneker is a school for retarded kids—and those of us from Avalon Gardens Elementary used to give those kids *hell*. We were *horrible* to them. We just didn't know that we couldn't and that we shouldn't. Of course I know that *now*, but I wish that I had known that *then*.

The worst day—although there are plenty to choose from, believe me—was when a bunch of my friends started messing around with a paraplegic boy. Push came to shove, literally, and they knocked him out of his wheelchair. He looked at me, looked me straight in the eyes, and said, "Help me."

I didn't even pretend that I couldn't hear him. "No," I told him. I knew that if I helped him, then my so-called buddies would turn on me next.

That incident and those like it took on a new significance when my son was born. Very early on, I knew something about him just wasn't right. My wife, on the other hand, was a separate story. Most women have blinders on when it comes to their children having flaws. With LaDonna, that tendency was exacerbated to the nth degree. For a long while she was in denial, and for an even longer time she was extremely protective of Kyle. But as time went on, even my wife couldn't deny the signs.

When Kyle would talk, he would keep on talking and talking until he ran out of breath. Not even women talk that much, and he was just a little boy. He never knew how close to stand to another person. He was always in their space and couldn't seem to grasp that it was rude. Every time there was a loud noise, like an ambulance going by, he would get upset and cover his ears. *Every time.* He would always sit and fiddle with his hands. I didn't even register that as symptomatic until my mother pointed out that I used to do it myself. I'd just called it playing with my hands. I had no idea what it was, or even that it *was* something. But now I realized that other kids didn't do that.

By the time Kyle was old enough to go to school, the officials told us that they wanted to evaluate him. Now LaDonna didn't really have a choice but to face that things were off with Kyle. She knew that there was *something* that we had to do so that he could have a life. *Whatever* was wrong, I just didn't want the school to have control over that kind of information. I had seen what they did with young black boys who were considered to have something the matter with them. Nothing good ever came of it. I knew they would either give Kyle some medication or put him in some special-needs class. Neither of those options was palatable to me.

If I paid for the test, however, then there wouldn't be any notes in his official school chart. My son's educational choices would be made by me and my wife, not by some stranger who didn't know him. We took him to UCLA and paid to have him evaluated ourselves, so that we could finally find out what the issue was.

The specialist looked our son over, ran some tests, and finally gave us his diagnosis: Kyle had a form of autism known as Asperger's syndrome. It's a very complicated condition, but effectively it meant his brain was wired a little differently. He would always be a bit *off.* They even had a term for his playing with his hands. It was called "stimming," because he was "stim"-ulating his psyche with physical activity. At the time, autism was regarded as existing on a spectrum. At one extreme were kids who had virtually no communicative skills whatsoever. At the other extreme were kids like Kyle, who could get by. The specialist told us what kind of resources were available and what kind of exercises we could do. But no matter what we did, Kyle would never be "normal." His brain was simply wired a different way. When all was said and done, I just didn't know if he would ever be all right.

I kept a careful eye on him growing up, and LaDonna *completely* monitored his every move. I'd see him in the schoolyard by himself, stimming, and it made me realize that it was my genes that did this. It made me think of the Bible, and how the sins of the father are visited on the son.

As Kyle got older, more and more of his condition became more and more evident. Instead of talking until he was out of breath, he became much quieter and shier. He wasn't able to be a good liar, either. An autistic person will tell a woman, "Yes, those jeans do make you look fat," and then be genuinely clueless as to why she starts crying. Kyle didn't really have the *capacity* to lie, which makes it horrible to be a black man.

At the same time, I couldn't really joke with him because everything I said he could only take literally. A friend of mine took his autistic nephew to an event one evening, and his nephew was very worried that the celebrity wouldn't show up. "She's here," my friend insisted. Sure enough, the celebrity was there and the event went off without a hitch. At the end of the event, my friend turned to his nephew. "See?" he said. "I told you she's here."

"Yes, you did," the nephew replied matter-of-factly (it's *always* matter-of-factly with them). "Why do you bring that up now?" That's what it's like talking to someone who is *literally* completely literal-minded.

Where LaDonna's instinct was always to step in and to protect Kyle, I hoped to raise him to the point where he wouldn't *need* our protection. I couldn't always be there to look over his shoulder, and one day I wouldn't be there at all. When Kyle was on the set of *The Hughleys* as a teenager, some other boy started an argument with him. Soon it escalated into shoving, and then they were fighting. By the time it was over, Kyle had whupped that boy's ass. Though I didn't say so in front of everybody else, it made me very, very proud that he could stand up for himself.

When he was going to turn sixteen, it was time for Kyle to learn how to drive—just as for every other boy his age. I didn't want to be impatient with his driving, so I figured I'd pay a professional driving instructor. He had to go through two different courses and take his driver's license test four times. It was like JFK Jr. trying to pass the fucking bar exam. And just like JFK Jr., eventually he got it right. For his sixteenth birthday, I bought him a brand-new red Mustang.

Yet Kyle wouldn't drive his new car, and he always asked his mother or me to take him places. He was too scared. I finally just said, "You either go where you want to go—or you don't. But we're not taking you anymore." That's how he started driving, and another ordinary milestone was passed.

Chauffeuring Kyle around had gone on for *years*. Part of the reason was that my wife and I consciously fight very hard to make sure that our family remains close. I invited my father-in-law to come live with us, for example, and he's been living in my home for fifteen years. These feelings run in both directions. Kyle *adores* his mother and his sisters, and nothing upsets me more than when he doesn't get along with his sisters.

Occasionally, like a typical female, his sister Tyler would be impatient with him when they were growing up. Kyle would be talking, telling her something in that specific cadence that all people with autism have, and she'd snap at him. "Hurry up with the story!" It was almost crippling to me, it really was, because I couldn't be defending him against a *girl*.

Eventually I couldn't take it anymore and I sat Tyler down. "I can provide the shelter and safety," I told her. "But when you and your brother argue like that, or are indifferent to each other like that, it hurts me so bad it's almost palpable. It's almost causing me physical pain. The only reason I've ever worked this hard was to have my children be close. That's the one thing I always wanted, because I never was close to *my* siblings." To some extent, that message did get through with her.

# # #

Okay, that's enough with the cornball family-values shit. Let me talk about pussy.

There's a tendency among parents of kids like Kyle to think of their children as precious angels that God has sent to them. I didn't look at my son like that, for one simple reason: *Angels don't fuck.* To sweep the sexuality of autistic children under the rug is to deny a central part of regular human experience. Dehumanizing these children is supposedly a very bad, horrible thing and precisely what many of their parents are fighting against. I wanted my autistic boy to grow up to be an autistic *man*.

Like a lot of dads, I sat my son down and gave him some advice about getting laid. I was under no misconception that Kyle would be a pussy-later dude instead of a pussy-now type. But I just wanted to make sure he wouldn't end up being a pussy-*never* motherfucker. Autistic people are very blunt. It's hard to flirt when everything you say—and everything you *hear*—is taken literally. That could be disastrous.

I knew from experience that any time I had given him advice, I had to be overly simple. I thought for a while about how best to help him out. It dawned on me that Kyle was actually in the best situation possible when it came to speaking with women. "You don't talk that much anyway," I told him, "so pretend like you're interested. Don't say much; just listen. Then, when *she* says something, repeat the same thing she just said but in a question. If she tells you that she likes her job, you say, 'So, you like your job a lot?' "

Eventually my advice paid off. Kyle came home one day and told me that he had gotten some for the first time. He was with an older woman who was just trying to be friendly. I told LaDonna, and to her great credit, she didn't freak out in any way. LaDonna even said that I needed to call that woman and say thank you. I know people could look at it all kinds of ways, but I certainly took it as a very loving thing to do. It's a loving act to give somebody your body, knowing that it's going to be their first time, and to shepherd a dude through an incredibly awkward time.

When it came time for Kyle to go to college, my wife and I had a big argument. She wanted him to go away to school. Part of her being protective is pretending like he's just like everybody else. Well, he's *not*. "He's not going away to school," I told her. "A dude goes crazy when he gets a certain amount of freedom at that age. Until he can prove that he can interact with people, and come home, and do all the regular things—have a social life, get laid, and not go crazy—he's staying here. To have that freedom with no kind of structure or guidance is putting him in a situation where he is more prone to fail than to succeed."

I understood that most black men gotta get the fuck out when they reach a certain age. But I wanted Kyle to stay until he was *ready* to go. He ended up staying home and got his college degree. He got a job. He went out on road trips, by himself. Every father wants his son to grow up to be an athlete, a scholar, and a ladies' man. I got a wonderful human being, one who has already accomplished more than many of the people that I grew up with have. *I* didn't go to college. I don't know Krav Maga, the fancy Israeli kung fu—but my son does.

Throughout all the things that he's gone through—and that we as his parents have gone though—Kyle has always been somewhat protected. People might have thought he's weird, but they invariably liked him. As a result, he never really got the brunt of the nasty things that people can say. That will come now, when people don't know him, when he's not in school among friends or at home among family.

My daughter Ryan wrote a paper last year that perfectly laid out my perspective. She wrote about how LaDonna would try to stop the kids from touching the hot stove, while I would stand there while they did it. In other words, I wasn't going to let them hurt themselves—but I *was* going to let them get burned a little. Now that Kyle is twenty-three, I *want* him to get bloodied a little bit. I don't mean some heinous injury where he would get irreparable damage. I don't want my son to lose a limb or get a skull fracture. But I do want him to be prepared for a world that is often unkind. My wife has even come around to my perspective a little bit. She moves out of the way when I deal with Kyle. She knows there's only so much she can do right now.

# # #

This is why the recent anti-bullying movement is something I do not agree with. I'm really in a position to speak on this issue. If there's *anyone* who would be a victim of bullying, it's autistic kids like my son. I am not defending bullying in the sense that I think it should be encouraged. I'm simply saying something that is often impossible for people in this country to understand, let alone agree with: *Sometimes horrible things have positive consequences.*

Bullies are kind of like Los Angeles smog: It's there and it can hurt you, so you just have to watch yourself. Sometimes the threat is really high and they give you warnings, so you've got to be even *more* careful. But just like Los Angeles smog, bullies are a fact of life. They are always, always, *always* going to be there. The mentality now is to purge us of bullies, and I don't know if there's any way that you can do that.

I wouldn't be the man I am today if it wasn't for a bully.

When I was in fourth or fifth grade, this dude named Clifford used to take my lunch money from me all the time. Every day, he came to me and told me the same thing: "Give me your quarter or I'm gonna whup your ass." He was bigger than me and he was stronger than me, so every day I gave him that twenty-five cents.

At that time, the kids had a rule for dealing with bullies. You either fought the dude that was messing with you or you fought your father when you got home—and you had to do that in front of the neighborhood. A lot of us fought bullies because we didn't want to fight our old man.

The next time Clifford asked me for my lunch money, I refused. "Nah," I told him. "You're going to actually have to kick my ass." Then and there, we fought—and Clifford did, in fact, kick my ass. He gave me a bloody nose—but I didn't give him my quarter.

Getting my ass kicked every day was not going to be a better situation. When I told my father what had happened, his advice was very simple. "Darryl," he said, "you fight that bully until you win." I knew that sticks and stones can break a bully's bones just as easily as they can break anyone else's. Clifford could say whatever he wanted, but if he put his hands on me I'd have to pick up a stick and knock the hell out of him. I decided that I was going to listen to my dad and fight Clifford until I won.

Every time I saw Clifford, I would start fighting him. If he was coming out of the school bathroom and I happened to be in the hall, I would run at him. If he was coming out of the liquor store with groceries for his parents, I started a fight. If we were at the playground, I started a fight. Unfortunately, there never happened to be any sticks or stones for me to use, so it was an uphill battle for me. But I knew if I was meaner than Clifford, I could win. I also couldn't become bigger and stronger, so I just became faster.

By about the seventh or eighth fight, it started to get inconvenient for Clifford to deal with me. The last two times Clifford and I fought, I ended up winning. And the *second* time I won, I won in front of *everybody*. Clifford and I eventually even became friends. I learned as much from the bloody noses that Clifford gave me as I ever did from any book.

Now, let me be clear: Bullies are horrible. I'm not denying that. But people are saying that horrible things are avoidable when they're not. There will always be *something* horrible out there. There will always be cold weather, there will always be traffic, and there will always be STDs. Has denying the inevitability of horrible things made us better? Has it made us have fewer enemies in the world? Are people getting along better—or are they better at pretending that they're getting along?

A lot of what people are calling "bullying" is just people being insulting. Bullying means someone putting their hands on you, not just calling you a name. Nowadays students can get "bullied" on their phone or on their e-mail. How are you getting "bullied" on your computer? Turn it off! How can you get "bullied" on Facebook? Unfriend the motherfucker! Cyberbullying is not when someone sends a nasty e-mail and the screen chirps, "You've got hate mail!" Cyberbullying is when someone beats your ass with a computer.

If you're not sure if you're being bullied, refer to this chart:

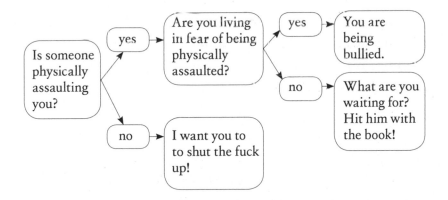

Bullies, *real* bullies, do serve a purpose. They teach you what's socially acceptable, that there are certain things that you can and can't do in society lest you suffer unwanted consequences. And if you *did* those certain things again, then you had to fight to defend your position. That's life! People may not like it, but sometimes you have to stand up for yourself against someone bigger than you. Having had to fight for my food as a kid means I'm prepared to fight for my values as an adult.

It's the bullies who prepare you for dealing with adversity. If you've never been emotionally or verbally abused, how will you be prepared for marriage? How are you going to be ready for a relationship, *any* type of relationship? I'm talking about life, I'm talking about a job, I'm talking about traveling and interacting with people. It's not always going to be smiling and nodding. There's a lot of stuff I wish wouldn't happen—but it *does*. Everybody ain't always going to like you—but nobody can take your lunch away unless you let them.

It's not just the bullies that are being taken away. It's anything that's an affront to our kids' self-esteem. Kids *shouldn't* have self-esteem in the same way that grown-ups do! If they were smart, they wouldn't need school. If they were tough, they wouldn't need their parents protecting them. If they knew shit, they could get a job. But of course kids are *none* of these things. Even the sting of a dodgeball is something that children these days don't have to handle. But if you tell a kid he can't handle getting hit by a ball, then guess what? He won't be able to handle getting hit by a ball!

Little boys are being charged with sexual harassment for kissing little girls on the cheek. I'm not so old that I don't remember that kids at an early age are the *same size*. In fact, the girls hit puberty *first* and they get taller *first*. Is that little girl going to be cry "sexual harassment" every time she is denigrated at work? That may be *legal*, but it sure as shit won't be the way for her to break the glass ceiling.

Our kids' food has all sorts of warning labels on it. It feels like any day now, someone will come out and ask for the surgeon general to slap a sticker on a can of Dr. Pepper. We have allergies to gluten and shellfish and dairy and God knows what else. Meanwhile, the children of the rest of the world are allergic to *hunger*.

How is this focus on protecting our children's delicate sensibilities going to play out in the future? "Don't ask, don't tell" is now a thing of the past. The boys and girls of today, gay and straight, are going to become the men and women of tomorrow, gay and straight. What happens if we're at war, a war on our shores like in a Pearl Harbor situation? *Everyone* is going to be fighting then. How are kids who fear a *rubber ball* being flung at them going to handle *bullets* intended to kill them? Will kisses lead to our surrender, or gluten grenades? It sounds absurd, but that's only because we're *preaching* absurdity.

If only Uncle Sam could see us now. We'd tell him that rolling up his sleeves is a sign of aggression. We'd ask him not to point, because that singles people out and makes them nervous. We wouldn't care what *he* wants, because what our kids *like* to hear has become more important than what they *need* to hear. I bet Uncle Sam would look at how fat, soft, and ignorant we've become—and how loud, obnoxious, and delusional. Then he'd shake his head, bitch-slap us with his striped hat, and tell us, "*I want you to shut the fuck up.*"

## CHAPTER 18

HE DIED KNOWING THAT YOU LOVED HIM.

—A COWARD

NO matter where I go and no matter what I do, someone will always come along and ask me about Bernie Mac. There are people who don't care for Steve's books or who think Cedric ain't that entertaining. As for me, I obviously have my share of haters. But I've never met anybody who didn't like Bernie Mac. He managed to be loved and in your face at the same time. I've never seen anybody else who could do that.

The first time I ever played with Bernie was a daytime gig at the Music Hall in Detroit. Comedy was so hot then that we could do a show at 2:00 p.m., 4:00 p.m., 6:00 p.m., and 9:00 p.m. Even on a Sunday, we could do that many shows and fill two thousand seats at each set. It was *crazy*. We were just kids and neither of us knew anything, and we both thought this was the most spectacular thing that had ever happened.

Soon after we met, we went on a Schlitz malt liquor tour where we hit different cities on Tuesday, Wednesday, and Thursday. It was me, Bernie, and whatever new comic was in the city we happened to be in that night. One thing about Bernie was that he wore these colors that no one else would ever wear or ever think of wearing. He was a really dark dude, and he was so *proud* to be wearing gators with a lime-green or pink suit. Me and my team would always be waiting around to see him get off the elevator, just to see what he was going to have on. I didn't get how he even had the vocabulary to describe some of those colors to the tailors. Who was even making these fabrics? It was chartreuse and fuchsia and vermillion, the kind of words they use to trip up spelling-bee contestants.

Every night after our show, we stopped at the roughest liquor store so Bernie could get pork skins, a little thing of hot sauce, and MGD. *Every fucking night.* And every fucking night, we would talk and talk and talk. Bernie always had a mantra about how he would walk alone, and it started to shape the way I would later look at things comedically.

At the time, I don't think that I really knew how to express myself as an individual. I just knew how to be *funny*. Bernie taught me about being a man and speaking the truth as I saw it. He really started to guide me as a performer. After a couple of tours, Bernie decided that he was going to go out on his own. It wasn't that he didn't love me and I didn't love him; it was that he wanted to do his own thing. We went our separate ways, but we stayed close. Then in March of 1990, I was performing at the Apollo. I was waiting backstage for Sinbad to introduce me. "Whatever you do," Sinbad said, "don't tell them you're from L.A."

"Fuck that," I replied. "You tell them that I'm from L.A."

As night follows day, he told the crowd that I was from L.A.—and they practically booed me off the stage. I remember that night so well because it happened to be the night that Robin Harris died. "Well," somebody said to me, "now Bernie's going to get his shot." At the time, I had no idea what that meant. But they must have been referring to the fact that Robin and Bernie had so many similarities. It was kind of a natural evolution between the two, and I think Bernie took things somewhere that even Robin wouldn't have been able to. I'm not talking from a talent perspective, but just from a personality perspective.

I don't remember who had said that to me, but that person was wrong. Bernie didn't really get a shot after Robin died. It took ten years after Robin passed for *The Kings of Comedy* film to come along. Bernie and I got even closer in the interim, and now Steve and Cedric were in the mix as well.

# # #

When I joined the Kings of Comedy tour in 1997, they had already done one leg with just the other three guys. The idea of a movie was not something on our minds at all. Besides, I had gotten my TV series and was doing pretty well for myself. The guy who started the whole tour, Walter Latham, had a very effective and very old-school marketing strategy for us. He went to black radio stations, black newspapers, beauty shops, barber shops, and black message boards. It was a very similar approach to the way Tyler Perry made his name soon after. Walter invited a very specific group, and the people whom he invited came—and they came in droves. It immediately became really big, and we started playing arenas without having to do any mainstream press at all.

After a while, it was just on fire. When we were playing Chicago's United Center, we came close to selling it out in just a couple of days. Then they put up a second show, and by the time it was all said and done we ended up playing the United Center four times. We played Houston four times; we played D.C. multiple times.

The crowds that came were virtually all black, and they were all very *proud*. They'd get dressed in their best and they'd spend their money gladly. It was really one of the few and first times when black art was being created for a black audience. It wasn't like the Harlem Renaissance, a brief period when the white intelligentsia realized these colored people had something to say (which is why Langston Hughes wryly referred to the period as "when Harlem was in vogue"). It wasn't like Motown, which crossed color barriers and brought the youth of our nation together through music. Us four comics knew something was happening. We didn't really discuss it in depth; it was so above and beyond that we really didn't need to.

We didn't set out to say, "We're going to make this so that only we get it." But that kind of happened as a consequence of our backgrounds. Steve and Cedric were on the WB, and I was on ABC. On our series, we had to tell jokes that we were sure that *everybody* got. We had to *speak* a certain way on network television. When Bernie and I had been on a tour previously, we drew a lot of white people—and a lot of those white people said they couldn't understand him or that I talked too fast. Crowds had complained that Steve shouted, or that Ced played music they didn't get.

Now we had *none* of those concerns. We could write for people that looked like us, purely from one side of the room. It was a narrow, small perspective that was *universal* to those eighteen thousand people in the crowd. It was *liberating*. We were the writers, directors, producers, and editors of our own individual segments. Obviously many people mainly came to see Bernie or whoever their favorite of us was. But the show flowed and everybody had a great time. In the end the four of us would come out and take a bow, and they would just *erupt*.

I remember talking to Bernie at one point, and I said this must have been what the Negro leagues were like. The few white people who came did so in groups, but it was never an ominous environment for them. They were welcomed just like everybody else. It was a time for laughter, not for animus. I'm not an overly spiritual cat, no doubt about it, but on that tour there was a spirit that seemed light and whimsical. Things seemed *human* and *approachable*. I just wanted to hold that spirit forever—at the same time knowing full well that it would never happen.

We made our way across the U.S., getting off of planes like we were rock stars. Wherever we played, everybody had their own nice dressing room. We had a caterer there with a white chef's coat on, asking us when we wanted to eat. Whatever we wanted, we got. We'd have steak, shrimp, and lobster. We had the best food, wine, liquor, and great cigars. Tailors would come to the shows and we all got tailor-made suits. We always stayed at the Ritz-Carlton hotels. After a while, the Ritz-Carlton people would know what I wanted. I didn't have to say anything. No matter what city I found myself in, I had warm peanut butter cookies, milk, and a drawn bath waiting for me. The whole experience was just fucking amazing. I couldn't believe it.

As much love as we gave those crowds, that's how much love they gave us back. If anything, it was magnified a thousandfold. Sometimes, when I stood next to the speakers onstage, the noise vibrated inside my head. But when I made a Chicago audience laugh one night, the pitch was so loud that it went through my skull and hurt my teeth. A few minutes later, it happened again. I was scared to tell my last joke. I thought that if I did it again, they were going to fucking blow my head off. Part of me honestly worried that the crowd would laugh me to death.

I don't think *any* four kings, whether *actual* royalty or self-proclaimed like us, ever shared such a sense of respect for one another. None of us ever went over on time, and nobody stole anybody's jokes. The audience was responding to seeing four men who had an affinity not only for the craft, not only for the crowd, but for each other. There was no sense of competition or sizing each other up. No one ever argued about their turn. I defy anyone to take a tour across this country with four black artists for three years and not have one fight break out. It *never* happened, and I think that was just part of the bonus.

The closest we ever came to an altercation was during a leg in Texas. I was sleeping in my hotel room, and I was very high. Suddenly, I heard the door open. "Hey, who's there?" I yelled out.

"My bad," the intruder yelled back.

"Partner, you're in the wrong room."

"I *said*, 'My bad,' *partner*!"

"Man," I said, "you better get the fuck out of my room!"

"Who the fuck you talking to?"

I grabbed my pistol, threw on a robe, walked out of the room. There was Bernie Mac, standing there with *his* pistol drawn. "Nigga!" I yelled, as we both burst out laughing. But that was *it*.

After every show, we four would have to sign merchandise. It would take hours, literally *hours*, because people would buy booklets, pictures, T-shirts, cups, hats, whatever. If they bought it, we had to sign it. We would take pictures with them with big smiles on our faces. It was crazy, but it was *spectacular*. After the show was done, we would take a private jet and go to the next thing.

At the same time, we were still getting close to *zero* media attention except from black sources. The thing is, *not a single fuck was given*. We were the best comics in the country; what did we care if CBS said so or not? Why would we possibly care what they thought of us? We didn't need them. I suppose if we wanted to sell movies and we wanted to do television shows, then we'd need that mainstream validation. But for us, those things weren't even thought about. It wasn't even something I was really aware of.

During the tour, I stopped in Charlotte to shoot an HBO special called *Going Home*. But unbeknownst to me, a movie was exactly what was on Walter's mind. Some people from MTV had come out when we were playing Madison Square Garden, and Walter brokered a deal with them to do a film. I was touring with the material that was in my special, but if we were going to do a movie, I'd need an all-new set. It takes a *very* long time to write a lot of material, and I had shot my wad with HBO. This was no joking matter. It was *murder*. I had to write a fresh thirty minutes in a few short months for a movie that *Spike Lee* had now signed on to direct.

The movie, in its own way, did capture a part of that tour's spirit forever. I think *The Original Kings of Comedy* took on a life of its own after the theatrical release. That's when people *besides* black people went out and bought the tape or the DVD so they could watch it in the privacy of their own homes. I don't know how many people have seen it that way. We were like FUBU's campaign of being "for us, by us." We were the first and might have been the only time some viewers went out of their way to experience black culture, something made without regard for any other audience whatsoever.

The reason that movie resonates so much, and has spawned so

many knockoffs, is that it's authentic and it's organic. It's kind of like how Jewish people eat Chinese food at Christmastime. That got started because the Chinese restaurants were the only fucking places that were open. Yet after time, it became a tradition born out of a shared experience and out of a shared necessity. It took on a life of its own. There was a need; the need was met; the need became celebrated.

Obviously, it was the most transcendent kind of experience for myself, as I'm sure it was for Steve, Ced, and Bernie—and as I'm sure it would be for *any* comedian. Yet there's a *before* and there's an *after.* You understand what those moments feel like *now.* It girds you up to know that if you've been there, then you can get there again. The whole process profoundly changed me. The idea of just trying to be funny without it having some level of import had been repulsive to me, and it *still* is. I thought comedy in general—and hoped my comedy in particular—had the power to change people's minds. So to have the power to make arenas erupt with laughter made me feel as if my conviction was coming to some sort of fruition.

# # #

I have a tattoo that says, THERE'S NOTHING FUNNY ABOUT A CLOWN IN THE DARK. I never wanted to be that. I was always trying to find a way to say the things that I felt were important, needed to be said, and had some relevance. I used to want to make people laugh so hard that they changed their perspective. That was my constant mindset, and I would always be agonizing after the show. It was me in the back, drinking and talking shit, lamenting what I had done and what I hadn't done, and what jokes I should or shouldn't tell.

Bernie and I would just hang out in the dressing room for hours, talking and smoking cigars. When I told him what was going through my mind, he just shook his head at me. "Man," he said, "you need to give yourself a break. This shit ain't that important. Just be who you are. Some people will get it, some people won't, and that'll be it." Spike Lee said the same thing, that I was too hard on myself. And neither man is exactly a softie.

Like most comics, I see the world from a slightly different angle. I thought pointing shit out would lead to . . . *something.* But it *doesn't.* When a commentator says that America is a lazy country, the backlash is violent and it is immediate. Yet we *are* a lazy country. We don't get fat from being *active.* Our school systems don't fucking fall apart from being *active.* We are so fragile as a society that the truth angers us because the comments strike a nerve.

It's like how fat people get mad if you call them fat. But they *are* fat. Dumb people get mad if you call them dumb. But they *are* dumb. In both those instances a person can do something about it *if* he accepts the reality of the situation. From an outsider's perspective, never forcing people to question their reality is the greatest disservice ever. If somebody's breath is bad and you don't tell them, their breath is always fucking bad. If they got a booger in their nose and you don't tell them, they're going to keep a booger in their nose. That's the way it goes.

I used to think that it was comedy that could force people to change their reality, and I learned over my career that it couldn't. I remember trying to do episodes of *The Hughleys* and jokes on tour that I thought were important. But most people just kind of want to laugh. They don't want to think or they don't want to care. If they *do* want to think, they only want to think what *they* want to think. If they *do* want to care, they only want to care about what *they* want to care about. Comedy might not be able to change minds—but it can certainly expose truths and knock down fallacies. Once I make a joke about something, whether onstage, on TV, or in this book, whoever hears me can't claim ignorance. They can't say they didn't know better. They might still feel the same way, but now their actions are informed. They have to face the truth behind their deeds, or at least the truth as I see it.

The idea that comedy can change minds has long since been dead with me. It's been many years since we deaded that one. Yet during *The Kings of Comedy*, that's really what I believed, and in some ways that's really what was moving me. So when I watch the DVD and see myself with that twinkle in my eye, that conviction that all these jokes were going to make a big difference, it's like seeing a kid who still believes in Santa Claus. On the one hand, you know he's an ignorant dumbass who's going to have to learn the truth eventually. On the other hand, damned if his silly earnestness doesn't make you smile just a little bit.

# # #

Sometimes it's easy for me to forget that it's good to be earnest, and that cynicism isn't always the way. When we were shooting *The Kings of Comedy*, Bernie joked that a dude who looked like him and was as dark as him would never get a TV show. America would not watch someone like that on their screens. Bernie really believed that was the case. People would say that they couldn't understand him, that he bugged his eyes and he talked too fast.

Fortunately, cynical Bernie was proven wrong. He *did* get a show. He also got a lot of movies, like *Bad Santa* and *Ocean's Eleven* and *Twelve*. Things were happening for him career-wise. But things ended up happening for him health-wise, too—and those weren't the good types of things.

Bernie was always a big and strong dude. I heard he was sick, but it didn't really register with my image of him. It was in 2005, when he came on to do my show *Weekends at the D.L.*, that I first noticed something was wrong. He was on oxygen and would take air during the commercial breaks. It seemed real weird to me. I almost couldn't believe what I was seeing. I just never associated Bernie with any sort of weakness or vulnerability, and he never looked like anything was wrong. Partly that's because Bernie didn't have another gear. He didn't know how to be anything else. He was consistent; he seemed perpetual.

In 2008, Bernie was hired to host an Obama fundraiser. He told a joke that he had told many times over many years. "My little nephew," Bernie said, "came to me and asked, 'Uncle, what's the difference between a hypothetical question and a realistic question?' I said, 'Go upstairs and ask your mother if she'd make love to the mailman for fifty thousand dollars.' The boy came back and said his mom told him that she would. So I said, 'Go ask your sister if she'd make love to the mailman for fifty thousand dollars.' The boy came back and said that she would, too. 'Then *hypothetically* we have a hundred thousand dollars, but *realistically* we are living with a couple of sluts.' "

Everyone was being so protective of Obama that there was a mini-backlash over that joke. When CNN stuck a mike in my face and asked me about it, I just laughed it off. "That's the Mac man," I told them.

A while later I heard that Bernie's health was deteriorating. *He's going to understand that I'm doing what I gotta do*, I thought, *just like he's doing what he gotta do.* I was in the middle of a run in Las Vegas at the time. After the run, I promised myself that I would go visit him and see how he was doing.

At about four or five o'clock in the morning, I got a call telling me that Bernie had died. This was the second time I had heard that; rumors of his death had circulated a few months earlier. In the back of my mind I hoped that this was another bit of false gossip—but some part of me knew that it wasn't. I turned on the news and saw them walk up to Steve for some comment. That's when I knew it was true.

I was out of it all day, and then I went back home to Los Angeles. It just seemed surreal to me that Bernie was gone. I packed for his funeral—and I packed for my upcoming gig in Tempe, Arizona. That's how fucked up comedy is. I had to find time in my schedule for the funeral of one of my dearest friends.

I flew to Tempe and played the gig on that Friday night, knowing that Bernie's funeral was the next day. People weren't there to see me mourn; they had paid to laugh, and the show must go on. I got up early the next morning and got on the plane to go pay my respects. Everyone was there at the funeral: Steve, Ced, Chris Rock, all of the many people who knew Bernie and loved Bernie. We all said our good-byes, and we all had our moment. Then we all got on separate planes, flying across America so we could go out and tell jokes.

Things didn't feel weird to me until the third show that I was doing the next night. I was onstage and I just started crying. What struck me at that moment, what was so hard, was that I knew Bernie was sick and at the very least I could have gone to see him. I just thought that he would get better. In my mind, I'd visit and we would catch back up where we'd left off and everything would be cool. But that's not what happened, and that's not what would ever happen.

After the show, somebody said to me, "Well, Bernie knew how much you loved him. He knew you loved him like one of his family."

But that's what cowards say when they haven't done the right thing. That's something you say to let yourself off the hook. How could you *know* that somebody knew you loved them? I took some comfort in the fact that Bernie knew the stand-up life. If it had been me, he would have gone on to play his shows, too. That's how comedy is. It's the most selfish thing in the world. I got it, and Bernie got it, but it's very hard for someone who *isn't* a comic to get what the life is like.

# # #

I remember being a kid and not knowing what I would do—but knowing that *something* was out there. I knew that if I stayed alive and stayed *clear*, something would come along. Given my circumstances, the odds were very, very heavily against me. But I was so sure that something was out there for me that I never even questioned it. I didn't need to ask myself when. I was never one of them dudes, wondering why my chance hadn't come along. I just *knew*.

The minute I picked up a microphone, I got it. It's like when you've been in the dark for a long time. You're in your apartment, and then you walk outside and the sun is so bright it hurts your eyes. Getting onstage *literally* felt just like that. It had been dark—it had been dark *all my life*—and all of a sudden the world was so bright, it hurt my eyes. All of a sudden, my words and my point of view started to take me places I could never have imagined. All of a sudden, I was being paid to say what I think. By now I've being doing this for a couple of decades. I've been doing this in all kinds of incarnations, in all kinds of places. Whether it's a movie or a TV show, a commercial, or even this book, my skill set is my skill set. It's like a meal at Taco Bell: It's the same ingredients, just folded a different way. What's the difference between a nacho and an Enchirito? It's the same shit. That's what my skill set is like, regardless of context.

No matter how tired I am, no matter what I've been through, no matter what I have to do, there is something comforting about walking onstage. It's like your mother making you some hot chocolate when you're sitting down in front of the fireplace. It's that comforting to me. It's like Max Smart's cone of silence. It doesn't matter what else is going on around me. When I'm onstage, everything slows down and everything is clear.

But at the same time, it's like a high. You have to keep chasing it, and you can never get enough. You can get into this rut where for months, *months* at a time, everything is gray. Everything tastes the same, everything looks the same, everything smells the same. It's how the ancient Greeks looked at hell, where you're just a shadow of a living thing.

I'm not the only person to go through this. I was having a conversation with a very famous comic one time. We were just hanging out and talking. Out of nowhere, he asked me, "Have you ever not felt something for so long that you're not sure if you can anymore?"

It was exactly what I was going through at the time. *Exactly.* It's like those deprivation chambers where they cut off all your senses. It was during one of these gray periods that I saw this random girl wearing a red sweater in Dallas. I was shocked because, finally, I noticed *color.* I don't know why or what happened, but she broke through out of all the gray. I went up to her and I thanked her.

She laughed. "What are you thanking me for?"

"Just, *thank you.*"

No matter how gray you feel—or rather, don't feel—you still have to go back home. None of your family knows what it's like to be in that gray period. Everybody is loud and moving around. You can't hear yourself. Now it's almost like you have to come down.

I never had the luxury of coming home and *relaxing.* I had to be a husband, a father, a friend, and a disciplinarian in the seventy-two hours I was back—and then go hit the road again. I knew that I couldn't be tired when I landed. I had to hit the ground running, kind of like being a father on speed. I knew that they were going to want to go to dinner. I knew that everybody was going to want to tell me everything at one time. I knew I was going to have to hug them and love them as hard as I could in those three days. If they had to be disciplined, it would always make me feel bad. Here's this guy they hardly see, and all of a sudden he comes home and he's shouting at somebody. It was always a balancing act, being a dad.

The cycle rarely changes. I get home on Monday; I unpack on Tuesday; I go to dinner, play golf in L.A., I lay up in the bed, and talk to my wife a while. On Wednesday, I'm already planning in my head what to pack, the set I'll do. Then I'll go to meetings or whatever I have to do. I'll meet with the cats I write with. On Thursday night, I'll go. For years, this was the approach. For *years*.

Because I'm away so much, a lot of my relationship with my family has been lived remotely. I remember when my oldest daughter, Ryan, was going off to college. They put together a slide show of memories before she left. I didn't remember one picture. *Not even one*. I remembered the *time* of the pictures. I remembered her in that period of her life. But not one resonant picture did I remember, not one time when she was doing something in the slide show.

Much of my life is spent alone. I've got a nice apartment in New York City. I dig it, and it's fun. But no one else lives there. When I'm on the road, it's even more downtime. I read a ton, I smoke weed, and I think. I can't remember the last time I walked to the grocery store. I went to see *The Hangover Part II* with my daughters when they were visiting me, but I can't remember the time previous to that when I went to the movies. I've only ever been to one play. *One fucking play.* The high of performing is so intense that everything else bores me in minutes.

I spent so much time by myself that I grew to hate the sound of my voice. When I'm doing shows every night, I hear it *a lot.* It got so bad that I would change the voice in my head when I read a book. Instead of hearing the book as read by D. L. Hughley, I started reading it like James Earl Jones. He's always the voice I use because it's the most distinctive and I don't have to think about it. I was so sick of hearing myself think, and I started to be such horrible company for myself, that motherfucking *Darth Vader* was an improvement.

Domestically, I've flown almost four million miles on American, two million miles on Delta, and one million miles on United. I can tell people something about every airport. *Every single one.* I know about the secret entrance between the Westin and the Detroit airport. I know that Pittsburgh has the best airport mall in the United States, and Minneapolis is second.

Concierges got nothing on me. I know what restaurants to go to in what cities, what time, and where to get what when. You want the best lobster in the country? Go to Gibson's in Chicago; that's on Rush Street. This is not knowledge I have sought to acquire. It's just information I've picked up along the way.

I'm not saying these things in an effort to get sympathy. Don't cry for me, Argentina. I am the last person anyone should feel sorry for. I might *literally* be the last person anyone should feel sorry for. If they lined up everybody and asked who has it worse, I would be very close to the end of that line.

All of these things are worth it just to be onstage. There's nothing like it. I'm the one who feels bad for people who don't get to experience it. Once me and LaDonna were arguing and she said, "You get to do something you love, and that's not everybody's reality!" It was the first time it registered that this wasn't the way most people live their lives. It's a terrible thing, that not everyone gets to do what they love.

I am very fortunate in that there aren't a lot of people who get to do what I do. You have to work very, very hard for a very, very long time to be able to be a professional comedian—but it never becomes *easy*. Being a professional comedian is like being a championship weight lifter. For everyone else, lifting that weight is impossible. But that doesn't mean it's easy for the weight lifter to lift that weight. It just means it's *possible* for him to lift that weight. It's still an extremely challenging thing that he is pulling off.

Because of what I do and what I love to do, I miss out on a lot. I miss children being born; I miss birthdays and weddings; I miss funerals. And I missed out on saying good-bye to Bernie, and I will never have that chance again. I wish I had told Bernie just one more time how much I loved him and how much he meant to me. I wish I had told him what admiration and respect I had for him. Bernie Mac was the quintessential guy. He reminded me of a dude with a lazy eye: At first he seems off. But before you know it, because of the power of his personality, everybody tries to line up to *his* vision. I don't get to spend as much time with my loved ones because of being on the road—and even in my case that's not much of an excuse.

If you love somebody, you have an obligation to tell them. So close this book—it's done anyway—pick up your phone, and dial someone you love but haven't spoken to in a while. When they answer, *I want you to speak the fuck up.*

ACKNOWLEDGMENTS

I'd like to thank my wife, LaDonna, who knew there was a book in me before I was ever sure that I could read one. To my children, Ryan, Tyler, and Kyle, who have made my life richer than it ever could have been. My mother and father, Audrey and Charles, who did the best they could with what they had. My sisters, Rhonda and Denise, and my brother, Kevin, who taught me how to share when I didn't want to. My mother- and father-in-law, Annie and Ken Murphy, who gave me the love of my life. To Sonya Vaughn, who is the best right-hand man a woman can be. To the Oates family, I love you madly. To Tommy Curry, my cat from the time we was four—to be continued. To the Iveys, the Tarvers, the Russells, the Allens, the Muirs, the Macks, my first extended families. To Gary Hughley, Alvin Morris, Red Williams, Robert Hewitt, Craig Frazier, and Gary Monroe, the oldest road manager in the world, for protecting my vision and keeping the flame alive. To Willie Vonner, who taught me if you ain't scared to get an ass-whupping, you ain't scared to give one. To Mr. Boston, teacher, teacher. To Ron Wolf, don't get drunk on the numbers. To my agents, Chris Smith, Brent Galinsky, Andy Cohen, and William Rodriquez, who helped keep a roof over my head and a chicken in the pot. To Yvette Shearer, my publicist, for explaining the unexplainable. To Michael Rotenberg and Dave Beckey, my managers for twenty years of passionate war. To Richard Abate, my new warrior. To my lawyers, Andy Gawlker and Jim Jackoway; the best 5% I ever spent. To Kim Ibrahim and Rolanda Flowers for doing their best to protect me from myself. To Mark Landesman and Susie Steingruber, my new old guardians. To Myles Mapp, my firestarter. To Alexis Martin, alleycat. To chocolate chip cookies, who kept my sugar high and my spirits, too. To Bill Maher, who taught me more than he could know. To Caroline's and the Improvs, who didn't let the protestors scare them. To Aaron Sorkin and Tommy Schlamme, I know we're geniuses now. To John Webb, the big brother I never had. To Neal Clark, Newark's finest. To Greg Montgomery, my friend and protector. To Robert Greenblatt and David Janollari, the most thorough people I've ever worked with. To Nick Gold for keeping me in the air at a reasonable price. To Malik S., Ali Sadiq, Brian Ricci, Clint Coley, Tim Murray, and Steve Wilson, I look forward to reading all your books someday. To the 135ives, who taught me brotherhood, strength, and war. To Walter Latham, Steve Harvey, and Cedric the Entertainer for helping me make history. To Dr. Mark Lavin, who keeps this machine humming along. To Dr. Mason Somers, the counselor of counselors. To Riley, Maxine, Paris, and Joy, my dogs that are still here. To Lexus, Malik, and Sweetie, my dogs that ain't. To CNN, *ya tu sabes*. To HBO, for my three comedy specials. To Cloteal for making me flyer than a mug. To Trayvon Martin and all the Trayvon Martins that will never be. To Bernie Mac, who taught me to believe I ain't scared of you motherfuckers. To Michael Malice, if an eagle has his wings and a knight his armor, I have my you.

To me, I'm not going to insult your intelligence by saying that if I can do it, you can too. But if I can, just maybe . . .

To God, people will say, "How come he didn't put God first?" But You know I always have.

—D. L. Hughley

I wouldn't be where I am today without Harvey Pekar. Huge thanks also to everyone in Hughesboro, to Michael Fazio for making the call, and to D.L. for being the classiest person I have ever met. Finally, I want to thank Ezequeel, whose story remains untold.

—Michael Malice